16.95 CB

LEARNING ACROSS CULTURES

Edited by Gary Althen

NAFSA: ASSOCIATION OF INTERNATIONAL EDUCATORS

NAFSA: Association of International Educators is a nonprofit membership association that provides training, information, and other education services to professionals in the field of international education exchange. Its seventy-two hundred members—from every state in the United States and more than fifty countries—make it the largest professional membership association in the world concerned with the advancement of effective international educational exchange. Members represent primarily colleges and universities but also elementary and secondary schools, public and private educational associations, exchange organizations, national and international corporations and foundations, and community organizations. Through its publications, workshops, institutional consultations, and conferences, the Association serves as a source of professional training, a reference for standards of performance, and an advocate for the most effective operation of international educational exchange.

Library of Congress Cataloging-in-Publication Data

Learning across cultures / edited by Gary Althen. — Rev. ed.
     p.   cm.
Includes bibliographical references.
ISBN 0-912207-67-1
1. Multicultural education—United States
LC1099.3.L43   1994
370.19'6'0973—dc20   93-48936
                                            CIP

This and all NAFSA publications can be ordered by calling our toll-free number 1.800.836.4994

Contents

Acknowledgments

David Hoopes and Joe Mestenhauser are the spiritual godfathers of this publication. Neither had anything directly to do with it, but both have devoted much of their professional careers to making information and ideas from the field of intercultural communication available to practitioners in international educational exchange. Hoopes was among the early conceptualizers of the intercultural communication field, and Mestenhauser was the moving force behind the first edition of *Learning Across Cultures*.

Peggy Pusch, in her role as a member of NAFSA's publications committee, helped to develop the concept of this revised edition and to identify authors. And she herself contributed a chapter.

All the authors in this volume graciously agreed to contribute, despite heavy demands on their time and energy. Robert Kohls was kind enough to read and make helpful comments on Chapter 3.

I owe a considerable debt to several people who work in my office. The director, Stephen Arum, unfailingly supports us all in our "professional development" efforts. The competence and dedication of the other members of the foreign student advising staff — John Rogers, Lisa Dings, and Maggie Brooke — made it possible for me to undertake the extracurricular task of editing this volume.

Three other people in my office helped with this book. Our remarkably patient and competent receptionist, Julie Blair, makes life easier than it would be otherwise for all of us. Kimberly Meyer's expertise with computers made all the authors' drafts, which came to me on disks with assorted formats, easily accessible for editing. And Jean Larson's skill in word processing, along with her patience, contributed inestimably.

v

Introduction to the Revised Edition

The first edition of *Learning Across Cultures* sold out, as did several reprints. When it finally fell out of print, and NAFSA continued to receive requests for it, NAFSA staff asked several "intercultural experts" among its members whether the book should be reprinted yet again.

"No," they agreed. Too much had changed since the original publication appeared. Books and articles by Dean Barnlund, Stephen Bochner, Richard Brislin, Adrian Furnham, William Gudykunst, Geert Hofstede, Young Y. Kim, L. Robert Kohls, Craig Storti, Stella Ting-Toomey, by several of the contributors to this revised edition, and by many other scholars and practitioners had brought about a more refined understanding of the complexities of relationships among culturally different peoples. While many of the ideas in the first edition remained pertinent, many others had been improved through research, thinking, and writing.

But the need persisted for a single source that could make this contemporary material in intercultural communication accessible to international educational exchange practitioners, who, even before the last decade's burst in publications on the topic, could not keep up.

This revised edition is intended to help meet that need. The chapters collected here are written by practitioners or by scholars who, in most cases, have a background in practice. People who work in any capacity with students or scholars coming from or going to other countries can find information and suggestions in these pages that will help them refine their understanding of the issues that arise in intercultural situations, and perhaps help them devise more effective approaches for dealing with those issues.

Gary Althen
Iowa City
June 1993

1

Intercultural Communication: A Unifying Concept For International Education

Judith N. Martin

Scholars in intercultural communication have been applying their theories and concepts to the field of international educational exchange since the 1940s, when the Foreign Service Institute employed Edward T. Hall and other scholars to design cross-cultural education for their employees working abroad. As Wendy Leeds-Hurwitz (1990) describes this undertaking, these scholars recognized the limitations of previous language-based preparation and, in an innovative move, extended linguistic methods to the study of interaction of individuals from different cultures, thereby founding the field of intercultural communication.

The field has matured since Hall's days at the Foreign Service Institute, and intercultural communication scholars and international educational exchange practitioners still have much in common. Both fields have an eclectic knowledge base, drawing from a variety of disciplines, including anthropology, linguistics, psychology, sociology, and education. Professionals in both fields are interested in the application of knowledge. For example, scholars and practitioners in both intercultural communication and international education are interested in understanding how cultural differences influence communication in a variety of contexts, particularly during the educational sojourn, the focus of this chapter.

This chapter offers some ideas from the field of intercultural communication that are particularly relevant to the international educational exchange professional. The first part of the chapter presents recent trends in intercultural communication and illustrates how these trends relate to international educational exchange. The second part of the chapter outlines a theoretical framework and relevant research findings for understanding the role of communication in the international educational sojourn.

Recent Trends in Intercultural Communication

The primary focus of the study of intercultural communication is on the intersection of culture and communication, the study of communication between persons from different cultural backgrounds. Communication can be defined as the attribution of meaning to behavior or the negotiation of meaning in interaction. Culture can be understood as patterns of learned perception, behavior, attitudes, and beliefs shared by a group of individuals. (See Gary Althen's description of culture and model of culture in Chapter 3.) Memberships in these groups may be involuntary (for example, family, biological sex, age, racial groups) or voluntary (professional, religious, national groupings), and these memberships provide individuals with a set of cultural expectations, largely unconscious, for communication contexts.

Recent trends in intercultural communication research and theory have touched on the very foundations of the field—on the definitions of culture, on conceptualizations of the process of intercultural interaction, and on the relevance of existing theory to practice.

An Expansion of the Definition of Culture. Culture is no longer conceptualized as applying only to national or ethnic/racial groupings, but is expanded to include gender, age, sexual orientation, and other groupings as well. In fact, Marshall Singer (1987) argues that individuals' perceptions and behavior are influenced more by their membership in involuntary groups (race, age, gender) than by membership in voluntary groups (national citizenship). For example, the interaction between an international student and an adviser may be influenced as much by differences in gender and age as by national differences.

The Recognition of the Importance of Potential Power Differences in Communication Contexts. Early communication research focused primarily on cultural differences in values, nonverbal and verbal behaviors, and other cultural patterns. Recently, communication scholars have recognized that intercultural interaction is also influenced by the power differences among different groups stemming from historical and political factors (Folb 1991; Singer 1987). One useful perspective on this issue comes from Communication Accommodation Theory (CAT). The underlying assumption of CAT is that whenever individuals interact, their communication styles tend either to converge (become more similar) or diverge (become more different), depending on a variety of variables, including power differences and perceived threat. Interactions where speakers converge in their verbal and nonverbal behavior (e.g., similar speech rate, tone, loudness) are generally believed to reflect more positive feelings and more effective communication. In contrast, divergent speaking is perceived as less positive and less effective and more likely to occur where there are cultural differences (Gallois et al. 1988).

For example, in an interaction between two European international students where there are few power differences and little threat in the situation, the two students may converge in their style (same speech rate, tone, loudness). However, in a heated discussion between a foreign student and a disciplinary board, where the situation is threatening and power differences are evident, the communication styles may be more divergent, emphasize cultural differences rather than similarities, and be less likely to result in effective communication.

Walter and Cookie Stephan's (1985, 1992) theory of intergroup anxiety also emphasizes historical and political influences on intercultural interaction. In several studies they have found that individuals from cultural groups with a history of oppression report more anxiety in intercultural interaction than those with less experience with oppression.

These recent research findings may help explain some intercultural interactions in the educational exchange context. For example, African students in the United States may experience more difficulties in communication with white Americans than do Western European students in the United States. These difficult interactions are based not just on lack of cultural knowledge on the part of white Americans, but on a historical pattern of racism and oppression toward individuals of African heritage.

These historical power differentials may mean that foreign students and domestic minority students will find some concerns in common, but they may also find their experiences on campus to be quite different with respect to issues of power and discrimination. As Janet and Milton Bennett describe in Chapter 7, the international education professional may also be called on to help resolve these differences and conflicts.

A Move from an Assimilation Model to a More Pluralistic Model of Cultural Adaptation. Previous intercultural communication research often identified the goal of international sojourners as assimilating or adapting to a monolithic United States culture. Given the recent demographic and immigration trends within the United States, this emphasis on sojourner assimilation has been replaced by an emphasis on understanding how multiple cultural groups can coexist within the United States (and other countries as well) while retaining their own cultural characteristics. As Arthur Schlesinger (1991) has noted, the focus of the U.S. national motto "E Pluribus Unum" has shifted from the "unum" to the "pluribus."

For international education professionals, this trend may mean encouraging international students to recognize and understand the variety of distinct cultural patterns among racial and ethnic groups within the United States. It may also mean helping international students to retain more of their own cultural identity while adapting to this variety of cultural patterns.

For example, a Malaysian student at an urban university in the northeastern United States will experience and have to adapt to different cultural and communication patterns from a Malaysian student at a rural southern university or a church-related college in the Midwest.

This trend also has implications for interactions between domestic and international cultural groups. As Janet and Milton Bennett suggest in Chapter 7, there are similarities and differences in international and domestic diversity and the international education professional needs to be aware of them. The Bennetts also argue persuasively that many of the concepts and applications of international interaction are useful in understanding and working with issues of domestic diversity.

A Renewed Interest in Wedding Theory and Practice. While the study of intercultural communication originated with the Foreign Service Institute's response to practical concerns of overseas workers in the 1940s and 1950s, the 1970s and 1980s saw scholars focusing mostly on theory development as they struggled to achieve academic credibility for this new social science discipline. With credibility somewhat achieved, there currently seems to be a return to more practical concerns and finding ways to make theory applicable to everyday challenges of intercultural interaction. For example, Geert Hofstede's recent books, *Culture's Consequences* and *Culture and Organizations*, explore the influence of cultural values on the everyday workings of organizations, and Richard Brislin's *Applied Cross-Cultural Psychology* applies theory and research findings to a variety of intercultural communication contexts.

A very recent move within the communication field applies European Critical Theory to the study of intercultural interactions and integrates several of the recent trends identified above (Grossberg 1992). One of the fundamental assumptions of this perspective is that all research—from decisions about what is studied to what and whose work gets published—is political, value-laden, and occurs within a context of power hierarchy. A further assumption is that researchers need to recognize and identify the role of power in research (for example, considering situations in which the researcher and research subjects are from different social strata) and the implications of these differences for research findings. Finally, there is a strong belief that research should include a social agenda—that findings should be accessible and applicable to practitioners.

While the majority of the work in European Critical Theory has been conducted by mass media scholars, some intercultural communication scholars are currently applying a critical eye to their research and noting that much of it has been conducted by European Americans who describe the communication patterns of other cultural groups from a distance and from a privileged position, and that some research seems irrelevant to practitioners' needs. These concerns are reflected in calls for more culturally diverse research teams, more recognition of the role of power in intercultural communication, incorporation of multiple research methodologies (both quantitative and qualitative), and more interest in applying research findings to a wider range of intercultural interactions (Gudykunst and Nishida 1989; Martin 1993).

Intercultural Communication in the Intercultural Sojourn: A Framework

As noted above, the study of intercultural communication has focused on understanding how patterns of cultural differences influence the communication process in various contexts. One such context is the intercultural sojourn. Young Yun Kim (1988), a communication scholar, has provided a theoretical framework for understanding contact during the international sojourn and the role of communication in successful cultural adaptation. Taking a general systems approach, she suggests that the individual sojourner, as a system, experiences stress in the unfamiliar host culture and decreases this stress through communication with host culture members. This reduction of stress and concomitant adaptation result in personal and intellectual growth. Kim conceptualizes the sojourn as a continued cycle of stress, adaptation, and growth.

There are four components to this model:
- The sojourner's adaptive predisposition
- The environmental receptivity
- The communication of the sojourner with the host members
- The specific outcomes of adaptation, including an enhanced sense of intercultural identity, psychological health, and functional fitness.

The first two components (individual and environmental factors) influence the third, (the sojourner's ability to have successful communication with host members), which in turn influences the fourth, the sojourner's eventual adaptation. While Kim's theory/model is focused on long-term adaptation of adult immigrants, it can, with some modification, be applied to the shorter term international educational sojourn and can provide an organizing framework for understanding the potential role of international educators in facilitating cross-cultural adaptation and learning. In the following sections the adaptation outcomes are discussed first, then the individual and environmental factors and finally the crux of the process—the role of communication in the sojourn.

In presenting Kim's model, I have interpreted and modified it somewhat. While I have tried to remain true to her general ideas, I have altered wording to achieve more clarity, and I have tried to make the model applicable to the international sojourner experience instead of the immigrant experience about which Kim was originally writing. Readers are urged to refer to her original work.

Adaptation Outcomes. According to Kim, successful adaptation has three dimensions: psychological health, functional fitness, and intercultural identity. Most scholars have focused on one or at most two of these dimensions.

Psychological Health. The first dimension of adaptation in Kim's model relates to the traditional definition of cultural adaptation and is discussed extensively in Chapters 2 and 5. It has to do with the subjective sense of adjustment and internal equilibrium, of feeling comfortable and mentally healthy in the foreign environment. The majority of research studies (U-curve, W-curve, and so on) have focused on this dimension, and international educational exchange counseling and advising have often centered on assisting students to feel more comfortable and mentally healthy.

Increased Functional Fitness. The functional fitness dimension refers to the ability to carry out one's daily life with ease, to feel that one "belongs" in a particular environment. This is related to the social learning/skills approach proposed by Adrian Furnham and Stephen Bochner (1986) and described by Thomas and Harrell in Chapter 5.

Intercultural Identity. Kim describes the intercultural identity dimension this way:

> In spite of, or rather because of, the adversarial nature of the cross-cultural adaptation process, [sojourners] grow beyond the psychological parameters of the original culture. Their increased cognitive complexity allows them to differentiate between the new and the old milieu, which in turn helps them to develop a broader perspective in dealing with the new culture and the ability to overcome cultural parochialism . . . .
> The intercultural identity can be observed . . . as an inclusive viewpoint that represents more than one cultural perspective—either the home culture or the host culture, but at the same time, transcends both groups. (1988, 144)

This dimension emphasizes that cultural adaptation is more than just psychological health and/or the ability to function in a foreign culture, that there can be a concomitant psychic growth in the sojourner's sense of cultural identity. This dimension also integrates several concepts in previous literature, including Peter Adler's (1982) "multicultural [hu]man," Milton Bennett's (1986) developmental stage of "constructive marginality," and the "integration stage" in Berry and Kim's (1988) model.

Kim's comprehensive conceptualization of cultural adaptation is useful in that it captures holistically the experience (goals) of an overseas educational sojourn. Counselors and advisors can help in all three dimensions. For example, Kay Thomas and Teresa Harrell suggest that counselors can identify where a student client stands with respect to identity issues—Integration, Assimilation, Separation and Marginalization—and then assist the student in functional fitness and psychological health issues. In addition, this conceptualization can be easily adapted to characterize the more pluralistic notion of domestic intercultural interaction. As Janet and Milton Bennett discuss in Chapter 7, individuals' psychological health and cultural identity are important outcomes in domestic interaction, as well as in the international sojourn.

Now that the adaptive outcomes—the goals of the overseas educational sojourner—are described, we can ask what factors promote these outcomes, and we can consider the process by which these occur. Two factors that influence these outcomes are the sojourner's adaptive predisposition and environmental receptivity.

Adaptive Predisposition of the Sojourner. According to Kim's theory, an adaptive predisposition will facilitate communication in the host country and ultimately promote adaptation and growth. This predisposition relates to three aspects of the sojourner: his or her cultural background (specifically, the degree of similarity of home and host culture), personality attributes, and the sojourner's preparedness for change.

Cultural Background/Similarity. Like Kim, Adrian Furnham and Stephen Bochner (1982) have hypothesized that the degree of cultural similarity between the international student's background and the host culture and society (in terms of political, linguistic, economic, and other factors) influences the ease of communication and adaptation. Most studies support the notion that foreign students adapt more readily if they are proficient in the local language and have religious, political, and economic backgrounds that fit well with those of the hosts. For example, Austin Church's (1982) literature review concludes that in the United States, students from European countries experience less difficulty than those from Asian and South Asian countries. Torbiörn, in Chapter 2, cites studies on this same point.

However, a more recent study of United States study-abroad students (Martin and Rohrlich 1991) found that those students who studied in England expected to encounter few cultural differences and little problem adapting. However, on returning, they reported more unmet expectations and more difficulties in cultural adaptation than those who studied in Spain, Germany, and Italy. This finding suggests that it is not just the degree of cultural difference between the host and home culture that influences how sojourns are experienced, but also the sojourner's own expectations.

Personality Attributes and Personal Characteristics. Personality attributes include characteristics such as open-mindedness and personal flexibility. The influence of personality characteristics on adaptation will, in some measure, be dependent on the particular host country. Personality attributes such as extraversion and assertiveness may facilitate communication and adaptation in the United States, but may inhibit adaptation in societies where assertiveness is less valued.

15

Age and gender are also personal characteristics that influence so-journer communication and adaptation. Here, the research seems divided. Some indicates that younger sojourners acquire foreign language proficiency more quickly than older individuals and therefore may experience less culture shock (Kim 1988). However, other research finds no relationship between age and cultural adaptation (Uehara 1986) or an inverse relationship, with younger sojourners (because they have not yet completely formed a cultural identity) more susceptible to culture shock (Gullahorn and Gullahorn 1963). Concerning gender, a number of studies suggest that, in general, female sojourners report more cultural adaptation difficulties than males (Rohrlich and Martin 1991). However, as Kim and others note, these findings must be interpreted with caution because in early studies gender was often confounded with other variables. For example, female sojourners tended to be spouses and to have less education, so they had a different sojourn experience from males.

Preparedness for Change. The final adaptive characteristic, preparedness for change, relates to formal educational experience or predeparture training—where international education practitioners may facilitate the adaptation process. As Margaret Pusch points out in Chapter 6, international educators may design and/or conduct training at different points in the sojourn, from predeparture orientation to on-return. (See also Grove 1989.) Kim discusses this preparedness training as the setting of realistic expectations, the importance of which Torbiörn's chapter also stresses. According to Pusch, the content of training (the setting of these expectations) often comes from research and theory in intercultural communication, and includes information about cultural differences in communication styles and expectations about appropriate behavior in various communication contexts.

Host Environment Characteristics. Kim identifies two environmental conditions that influence communication patterns and adaptation during the intercultural sojourn: receptivity toward sojourners and conformity pressure. Theoretically, the more receptive the environment and the more conformity pressure that is exerted, the more opportunities there will be for sojourner-host communication and the more likely the sojourner is to adapt successfully.

Conformity Pressure. Societies vary in conformity pressure, in the degree of permissiveness or tolerance for sojourner deviation from the norm. Kim suggests that societies such as the United States that are generally more democratic, pluralistic, and heterogeneous tend to have a higher tolerance for cultural diversity. Societies that are relatively controlled, totalitarian, and homogeneous tend to demand greater conformity from sojourners. Certainly there are regional as well as national variations in this respect.

Receptivity Toward Sojourners. The receptivity dimension refers to the degree to which the host society offers openness, acceptance, and the potential for interaction and communication. The more receptive the environment, the more potential for host-sojourner communication and the more likely adaptation is to be successful. In the United States, university students, faculty, and staff may generally be receptive to international students, while the surrounding community may be less so. Other cultural groups may be much less receptive to foreigners. International students in Arab countries or other countries where there are strict gender-specific rules for socializing, or where foreigners are viewed as more suspect, report much less receptivity and more difficulty in communicating with hosts (Kauffmann, Martin, and Weaver 1992). William Gudykunst (1983) provides a taxonomy of host-foreigner relationships based on the receptivity of the host environment and the intentions of the sojourner, ranging from receptive, short term (tourist) to hostile, long term (unwanted refugees).

A related area of research on the "contact hypothesis" has investigated very specific conditions that promote intercultural tolerance, and the connection between intercultural contact and attitude change (Allport 1958; Amir 1969). This research is particularly useful for international educators who have the opportunity to structure campus opportunities for intercultural interaction or to design study-abroad programs. Walter Stephan (1985, 643) summarized this research and identified conditions that foster successful intercultural contact. The more of these conditions that are met in any contact situation, the more likely the contact will result in positive attitudes:

- Cooperation within groups should be maximized and competition minimized.
- Members of both groups should be of equal status both within and outside the contact situation.
- There should be similarity of group members on non-status dimensions (attitudes, belief, values).
- Difference in competence should be avoided.
- Strong normative and institutional support for the contact should be provided.
- The contact should be voluntary.
- The intergroup contact should have the potential to extend beyond the immediate situation.
- Nonsuperficial contact (for example, mutual disclosure of information) should be encouraged.

Nancy Mark's description (Chapter 8) of strategies for internationalizing student life at Michigan State University provides a good illustration of the implementation of this research. The programs she describes provide opportunities for nonsuperficial, enduring, equal-status, voluntary contact among students from different cultural groups. In addition, she describes the extent to which there is also strong institutional support for this contact. Her case study stands in contrast to much of the intercultural contact on campuses, which is often between individuals of unequal status (for example, between professors or teaching assistants and students), competitive (for example, class situations where students are competing for grades), and/or superficial (international food fairs, "Ethnic Night," and so on).

Richard Brislin, in *Cross-Cultural Encounters*, cautions that there are other factors to consider in intercultural contact and that, many times, these factors are beyond the practitioner's control. These factors may include attitudes individuals bring to the contact situation, the existence of a history of oppression and racism between groups, and people's language competence. In general, it can be observed that contact among members of different nationality groups in the United States (for example, between foreign students and host nationals) often meets more of these conditions than does contact between or among various domestic groups (Gudykunst 1977).

The Role of Communication in Cultural Adaptation. Given the sojourner characteristics and environmental conditions discussed above that seem to facilitate intercultural communication and cultural adaptation, what is the process by which adaptation occurs and what is the role of communication (and of international educators) in that process? The third component in Kim's model, as I have modified it for purposes of this chapter, is communication in the host country. It comprises four dimensions: communication competence, communication with host members, communication with sojourner's cultural group, and communication with friends and family at home. (Kim's model had two dimensions related to mass communication that I have dropped; in their place I have added the dimension on communication with friends and family.)

Communication Competence. According to Kim's model, an important variable affecting adaptation is the sojourner's communication competence, or capacity for successful sojourner-host communication. Researchers have struggled to understand what constitutes effective intercultural and intracultural communication. Those who work in international contexts think we can identify it when we see it, but describing it and training others to be effective are much more challenging tasks.

Early researchers thought that intercultural competence was an innate, broad-based ability—"universal communicators" were born, not made. More recent discussions have centered on whether it is a capacity (as Kim describes) or the demonstration of that capacity (that is, we are communicatively competent to the extent that others believe we are), as Brian Spitzberg and William Cupach (1984) have proposed. In any case, most scholars agree that communicative competence involves an interaction of three major dimensions: affective (attitudes, including motivation), cognitive (knowledge), and behaviors (skills).

First, the *affective* or *attitudinal dimension*. Perhaps the most important aspect of sojourner attitude is *motivation*. Theorists and practitioners alike have often ignored this aspect of competence, assuming that if individuals merely understand cultural differences and adapt to others who are different, they are effective. Now, researchers and practitioners realize that if individuals (or groups) are not motivated to interact, there is little chance that their communication will be effective. This lack of motivation may explain some of the social isolation and lack of interaction between foreign students and host nationals. In Chapter 3, Gary Althen offers suggestions for ways in which international educators can understand resistance to intercultural interaction.

Other requisite attitudes in Kim's model are the attitudinal orientation toward oneself and the host environment (withholding judgment, accepting and affirming cultural differences), aesthetic/emotional appreciation (capacity for fulfilling aesthetic needs in the host culture).

The second component of communication competence involves the *cognitive knowledge of the host communication system*. Intercultural communication researchers have identified cultural differences in verbal communication style and, as Althen (1992) suggests, these communication differences reflect more fundamental cultural patterns, such as value differences (Kluckhohn and Strodtbeck 1961; Hofstede 1991), differences in high and low context meanings (Hall 1991), or differences in thought patterns (Stewart and Bennett 1992).

William Gudykunst and Stella Ting-Toomey (1988), two eminent intercultural communication scholars, identify four dimensions of verbal communication style differences applicable to the sojourner communication:

1. Directness/Indirectness. The directness/indirectness dimension refers to the extent to which one's true intentions and feelings are communicated. A direct communication style, typical of many cultural groups within the United States (particularly European-Americans), is characterized by an emphasis on honesty, "telling it like it is," not "beating around the bush." An indirect style is characterized by expression that can mask actual intentions and feelings. Gary Althen (Chapter 3) and others (for example, Condon 1980, 1985) have described the dilemmas of intercultural interactions where a foreign student using an indirect style comes in conflict with university staff who expect a direct and "honest" form of communication.

2. Elaborated/Exact/Succinct. Gudykunst and Ting-Toomey's second dimension of verbal communication style refers to the quantity of talk that is valued and the extent to which metaphorical language is used in everyday speech. The Elaborated style is "wordy, metaphorical, incorporating religious or other metaphors in everyday speech." Students from the Middle East often use this style. An Exact style characterizes the speech of many cultural groups within the United States, who are guided by the maxim "Say

only as much as needs to be said to get the information across," using limited metaphorical language. The exchanges between United States government officials' "exact" style ("we're going to find the 'cancer' and cut it out") and Iraqi officials' elaborated style ("the holy war, the mother of all battles") during the Persian Gulf War were vivid illustrations of these contrasting styles.

The Succinct style emphasizes understatement and is more tolerant of silence in conversation. It is associated with high-context cultures. For example, students from Japan and Thailand often perceive Americans as too talkative, needing to verbalize everything (Althen 1992).

3. Personal/Contextual Style. The Personal style is individual-oriented, contains linguistic devices to enhance the sense of "I" identity, and places the burden for making things clear on the speaker. This style describes the communication of most European Americans. In contrast, the Contextual style emphasizes the reciprocal roles of the interactants, rather than of the individual, and the status relationships between them. This style has been identified with Japanese, Korean, and Indian-English speakers. Okabe (1983, 15) notes the difference between European American and Japanese speakers:

> [European] Americans shun the formal codes of conduct, titles, honorifics, and ritualistic manners in the interaction with others. They instead prefer a first-name basis and direct address. They also strive to equalize the language style between the sexes. In sharp contrast, the Japanese are likely to assume that formality is essential in their human relations. They are apt to feel uncomfortable in some informal situations. The value of formality in the language style and in the protocol allows for a smooth and predictable interaction for the Japanese.

4. Instrumental/Affective. The Instrumental style of communication is more sender-oriented and goal-oriented and reflects an emphasis on persuasion, Gudykunst and Ting-Toomey say. That is, anyone can be persuaded of anything if the speaker is persuasive enough.

In contrast, the Affective style is receiver-oriented and places the burden of understanding on the sender. Sheila Ramsey (1984, 142) describes the affective Japanese style:

> [T]hey value catching on quickly to another's meaning before the other must completely express the thought verbally, or logically. *Haragei* (*hara*-belly, and *gei*-sensitivity or subtleness) is referred to as the Japanese way of communication.

Japanese students have told me they find it very difficult to write in the English compositional style, because it seems insulting to readers to make thoughts so explicit on paper and not leave it to readers to intuit and reach their own conclusions.

While these four dimensions have been proposed to describe national variations in speaking patterns, they can also be used, as Milton and Janet Bennett point out in Chapter 7, to describe speaking variations (and often to identify the root of misunderstandings) among domestic groups within the United States.

Another cognitive dimension of communication competence is *knowledge of host nonverbal behavior*. Research on nonverbal communication has focused on the question of the degree to which aspects of nonverbal behavior are universal, and the degree to which they are culturally specific. Results of the long-term, cross-cultural and biological research of Ekman and Friesen (1987) suggest a degree of universality in facial expression. It seems that the primary emotions (anger, fear, happiness, sadness) are expressed in the same way in many cultural groups, although what triggers particular emotions and the contextual rules governing the expression may vary. For example, an American and a Japanese may both express sadness by the same facial expression; however, what triggers the sadness and what other behaviors accompany the facial expression may vary.

There is more cultural variability in other nonverbal behaviors, such as proxemics (personal space). The major work here is still Hall's dichotomy of contact and noncontact cultures explained in his 1966 book, *The Hidden Dimension*. He suggested that national groups can be placed on a continuum from more physical contact (stand closer together, talk louder, more eye contact, more touching, more sharing of breath) to less physical contact (stand farther apart, talk less loudly, less eye contact, less touching, less sharing of breath). Many scholars have categorized countries and world regions as contact (Latin America, Southern Europe) or noncontact (England, United States, Northern Europe, Japan).

While these distinctions have been useful in understanding intercultural contact, recent research suggests that many other factors influence nonverbal behavior, including gender, age, and racial/ethnic differences, and that there may be a great deal of variation within national boundaries (Dolphin 1992).

It should be noted that communication scholars have recently emphasized the great unevenness in our knowledge of communication patterns of various cultural groups. For example, there is a rich and comprehensive body of knowledge concerning communication patterns of some cultures (for example, Japanese, Chinese, Mexican), while other world regions (Mideast) and whole continents (Africa) have been virtually ignored in communication investigations (Shuter 1990; Martin 1993).

As Carol Archer points out in Chapter 4, the contemporary language educator is really helping sojourners become not just linguistically competent, but also communicatively competent. Foreign-language teachers, foreign-student advisers, and other international educational exchange practitioners who work directly with people from other cultures need to be interculturally competent, embodying many of the characteristics and skills identified above, and they need to be familiar with the cultural adaptation process, cultural differences in communication style, and the more covert aspects of cultural differences discussed above and elsewhere in this book.

The third component of communicative effectiveness is *behavioral skills*—what people *do* in communication situations that leads others to identify them as more or less effective. These are more culture and situation specific. While communication scholars have identified many of the requisite behaviors for some cultural groups (we know what behaviors European Americans expect in many task and social situations), there are many other groups for whom we have less clear ideas about what constitutes effective behavior (Althen 1992; Martin and Hammer 1989). Yet another challenge for communication researchers is to understand the *dynamics* of intercultural interaction, how two individuals successfully, mutually, accommodate to each other's communication style.

One line of communication research takes a completely different approach, suggesting that we should not focus on effective/ineffective communication, but should instead define *all* intercultural communication as problematic and then focus on what people in different cultural groups do to improve communication when things are not going well in an interaction (Hecht, Larkey, and Johnson 1992; Hecht, Ribeau and Alberts 1989).

Communication with Hosts. Kim suggests that the sojourner's adaptive learning takes place in the context of social communication. By participating in communication, sojourners receive input from the new environment that potentially provides them with the basis for adaptive transformation. The information they receive from hosts provides them with feedback about their communication, as well as information about the host country. Through this process, they reduce stress, become more psychologically healthy and functionally fit, and develop an increased sense of intercultural identity. The process seems cyclical—the more the sojourners adapt, the more communicatively competent they become, the more they engage in communication with hosts, and so on.

Otto Klineberg and Frank Hull's (1979) landmark study of international students' experiences in many countries documented this reciprocal relationship between contact and adaptation—that increased contact leads to better psychological adjustment, which leads to increased and more satisfactory contact, and so on.

Interestingly enough, it is often those sojourners who communicate the most with host culture members who experience the most difficult adaptation but also the most satisfying intercultural experience (Kealey 1989; Rohrlich and Martin 1991). It makes sense that sojourners who have more interaction with the host culture may experience greater difficulty at first because of the stress of learning new cultural behaviors. But these interactions then provide the support and the culture-learning that ultimately lead to better adaptation.

As noted earlier, while not addressed in Kim's model, the differentials in power and historical oppression need to be incorporated into our characterization of sojourner-host communication.

Communication with Sojourner's Cultural Group. It may seem that students abroad should minimize interaction with members of their own nationality/ethnic group, and from the assimilationist perspective that long prevailed among exchange practitioners, interaction with co-nationals was discouraged. However, it now seems that the opposite may be more advisable, particularly at the beginning of the sojourn. Kim (1988) reviews several recent studies demonstrating the importance of the contact with members of one's own cultural group during the adaptation process and points out that this contact serves many functions. It provides emotional and social support (Adelman 1988); culture "brokering" links between the sojourner and the host culture; and important information about the host culture. Kim also suggests that over time this contact may help preserve cultural identity. As Torbiörn notes in Chapter 2, international students should be encouraged to interact with both host culture members and people from their home culture, because both kinds of interaction support subjective adjustment. Craig Storti (1990) believes that sojourners too easily spend their time with others like themselves, and warns of the adverse consequences of becoming "encapsulated by the expatriate community."

Given the critical role communication plays in adaptation, it is useful to reiterate ways in which education professionals can facilitate student sojourners' participation in communication in the host culture. First, they can help develop students' communicative competence, whether as language educators (see Chapter 4) or in developing training programs that inform sojourners about the host culture and host communication rules (see Chapter 6). Secondly, they can promote opportunities for positive communication with hosts—in designing and implementing one-time training activities (see Chapter 7) or more long-term programs (for example, host-sojourner "buddy" systems, conversational partners, host family experiences) (see Chapter 8). Finally, educational professionals may intervene at the individual level in counseling and advising where difficulties in communication with hosts may be present (see Chapter 5).

Communication with Friends and Family at Home. Contact with friends and family at home during various stages of the sojourn also facilitates long-term adaptation. Foreign students who are most successful at reentry are those who have kept in touch with the changes that have occurred at home.

In a recent study of AFS students' reentry, those students who stayed in touch, whose friends and/or family came to visit, or who maintained consistent contact by correspondence, reported the most satisfying reentry relationships (Martin 1985, 1986). This contact allows those at home to experience something of the students' sojourn experience and also helps the students' understanding of changes that may have occurred back home while they were overseas.

Specifically, this ongoing communication between the student and friends and families at home leads to more realistic expectations on the part of both the student and those at home and ultimately to more successful reentry. (Compare Torbiörn's description, in Chapter 2, of reentry adjustment as matching expectations.) Also, communication with those in the home culture during the reentry phase is important because it is through communication that expectations are matched and the sojourner makes the cultural transition. Also, building or expanding professional networks at home seems to facilitate the transition from student to professional for returning international students (see Martin, in press; Pusch and Lowenthal 1988).

Conclusion

According to Kim's theory, the four components described above (adaptation outcomes, adaptive predisposition of the sojourner, environmental receptivity and sojourner-host communication) are linked together in a series of 28 predictive and testable theorems. Those relevant to the framework presented in this chapter are given here.

The greater the development of the sojourner's communication competence:
- The greater the participation in interpersonal communication with hosts
- The greater the functional fitness
- The greater the intercultural identity
- The greater the psychological health.

The greater the participation in interpersonal communication with hosts:
- The greater the functional fitness
- The greater the intercultural identity
- The greater the psychological health.

The greater the participation in communication with the sojourner's own cultural group:
- The greater the initial short-term development of communication competence
- The lesser the subsequent long-term development of communication competence

- The lesser the subsequent long-term development of interpersonal communication with hosts.

The greater the adaptive potential in predisposition:
- The greater the development of communication competence
- The greater the participation in interpersonal communication with hosts.

The greater the receptivity of the host environment:
- The greater the development of communication competence
- The greater the participation in interpersonal communication with hosts.

The greater the conformity pressure of the host environment:
- The greater the development of communication competence
- The greater the participation in interpersonal communication with hosts.

While some of these theorems have been tested, most notably with studies affirming the relationship between communication with members of the host culture and the adaptive outcomes (psychological health and functional fitness), the entire framework provides a good summary of the theory, a rich compendium of research opportunities for intercultural scholars, and a starting point for international educators who want to conceptualize their roles in facilitating the communication and adaptation of international student sojourners and to develop programs, services, and activities with that adaptation in mind.

References

Adelman, Mara B. 1988. "Cross-Cultural Adjustment: A Theoretical Perspective on Social Support." *International Journal of Intercultural Relations* 12: 183-204.

Adler, Peter. 1982. "Reflections on Cultural and Multicultural Man." In *Intercultural Communication: A Reader.* Ed. L. A. Samovar and R. E. Porter. Belmont, CA: Wadsworth.

Althen, Gary. 1992. "The Americans Have to Say Everything." *Communication Quarterly* 40: 413-421.

Allport, Gordon W. 1958. *The Nature of Prejudice.* New York: Doubleday/Anchor.

Amir, Yehudi. 1969. "Contact Hypothesis in Ethnic Relations." *Psychological Bulletin* 71: 319-342.

Barnlund, Dean C. 1989. *Communication Styles of Japanese and Americans.* Belmont, CA: Wadsworth.

Bennett, Milton. 1986. "A Developmental Approach to Training Intercultural Sensitivity." *International Journal of Intercultural Relations* 10: 387-428.

Berry, John, and U. Kim. 1988. "Acculturation and Mental Health." In *Health and Cross-Cultural Psychology.* Ed. P. Dasen, John Berry, and Norman Sartorius. London: Sage.

Brislin, Richard W. 1981. *Cross-Cultural Encounters: Face-to-Face Interaction.* New York: Pergamon.

_____.1990. *Applied Cross-Cultural Psychology.* Newbury Park, CA: Sage.

Church, Austin. 1982. "Sojourner Adjustment." *Psychological Bulletin* 91: 540-572.

Condon, John C. 1985. *Good Neighbors: Communicating with the Mexicans.* Yarmouth, ME: Intercultural Press.

_____, John C. 1980. *With Respect to the Japanese: A Guide for Americans.* Yarmouth, ME: Intercultural Press.

Dolphin, Carol Z. 1991. "Variables in the Use of Personal Space in Intercultural Transactions." In *Intercultural Communication: A Reader.* Sixth ed. Ed. Larry A. Samovar and Richard E. Porter, 320-31. Belmont, CA: Wadsworth

Ekman, Paul, and Wallace V. Friesen. 1987. "Universal and Cultural Differences in the Judgements of Facial Expressions of Emotion." *Journal of Personality and Social Psychology* 53: 712-717.

Folb, Edith A. 1991. "Who's Got Room at the Top? Issues of Dominance." In *Intercultural Communication: A Reader.* Sixth ed. Ed. Samovar and Porter, 119-127. Belmont, CA: Wadsworth.

Furnham, Adrian, and Stephen Bochner. 1982. "Social Difficulty in a Foreign Culture." In *Cultures in Contact.* Ed. Stephen Bochner. Elmsford, NY: Pergamon.

_____. 1986 *Culture Shock: Psychological Reactions to Unfamiliar Environments.* New York: Methuen.

Gallois, Cynthia, Arlene Franklyn-Stokes, Howard Giles, and Nicholas Coupland. 1988. "Communication Accommodation in Intercultural Encounters." In *Theories in Intercultural Communication*. Ed. Young Y. Kim and William B. Gudykunst, 157-185. Beverly Hills, CA: Sage.

Grossberg, Lawrence. 1992. Ed. *Cultural Studies*. New York: Routledge.

Grove, Cornelius. 1989. *Orientation Handbook for Youth Exchange Programs*. Yarmouth, ME: Intercultural Press.

Gudykunst, William B. 1977. "Intercultural Contact and Attitude Change." In *International and Intercultural Communication Annual*, vol. 4. Ed. Nemi Jain. Falls Church, VA: Speech Communication Association.

_____. 1983. "Toward a Typology of Stranger-Host Relationships." *International Journal of Intercultural Relations* 7: 401-415.

Gudykunst, William B., and Tsukasa Nishida. 1989. "Theoretical Perspectives for Studying Intercultural Communication." In *Handbook of International and Intercultural Communication*. Ed. M. F. Asante and W. B. Gudykunst, 17-46. Newbury Park, CA: Sage.

Gudykunst, William B., and Stella Ting-Toomey. 1988. *Culture and Interpersonal Communication*. Newbury Park, CA: Sage.

Gullahorn, J. T., and J. E. Gullahorn. 1963. "An Extension of the U-Curve Hypothesis." *Journal of Social Issues* 19, 3: 33-47.

Hall, Edward T. 1966. *The Hidden Dimension*. New York: Doubleday.

_____. 1991. "Context and Meaning." In *Handbook of International and Intercultural Communication*. Ed. Samovar and Porter, 46-55. Belmont, CA: Wadsworth.

Hecht, Michael L., Linda K. Larkey, and Jill Johnson. 1992. "African American and European American Perceptions of Problematic Issues in Interethnic Communication Effectiveness." *Human Communication Research* 19: 209-236.

Hecht, Michael L., Sidney Ribeau, and Jess Alberts. 1989. "An Afro-American Perspective on Interethnic Communication." *Communication Monographs* 56: 385-410.

Hofstede, Geert. 1984. *Culture's Consequences: International Differences in Work-Related Values*. Newbury Park, CA: Sage.

_____. 1991 *Cultures and Organizations: Software of the Mind*. London: McGraw-Hill.

_____. 1992. *Cultures and Organizations*. New York: McGraw-Hill.

Kauffmann, Norman, Judith N. Martin, and Henry Weaver. 1992. *Students Abroad, Strangers at Home*. Yarmouth, ME: Intercultural Press.

Kealey, Daniel J. 1989. "A Study of Cross-Cultural Effectiveness: Theoretical Issues, Practical Applications." *International Journal of Intercultural Relations* 13: 387-428.

Kim, Young Y. 1988. *Communication and Cross-Cultural Adaptation*. Philadelphia: Multilingual Matters.

Klineberg, Otto, and William F. Hull. 1979. *At a Foreign University: An International Study of Adaptation and Coping*. New York: Praeger.

Kluckhohn, Florence Rockwood, and Fred L. Strodtbeck. 1961. *Variations in Value Orientations*. New York: Row, Peterson.

Leeds-Hurwitz, Wendy. 1990. "Notes in the History of Intercultural Communication: The Foreign Service Institute and the Mandate for Intercultural Training." *Quarterly Journal of Speech* 76: 262–81.

Martin, Judith N. 1985. "The Impact of a Homestay Abroad on Relationships at Home." *Occasional Papers in Cultural Learning,* no. 6. New York: AFS International/Intercultural Programs.

———. 1986. "Patterns of Communication in Three Types of Reentry Relationships: An Exploratory Study." *Western Journal of Speech Communication* 50: 183-199.

———. 1993. "Intercultural Communication Competence: A Review." In *Intercultural Communication Competence,* vol. 1 of *International and Intercultural Communication Annual.* Ed. Richard L. Wiseman and Jolene Koester, 7. Newbury Park, CA: Sage.

———. Forthcoming. "The Intercultural Reentry of Student Sojourners: Recent Contributions to Theory, Research, and Training." In *Education for the Intercultural Experience.* Ed. R. Michael Paige. Yarmouth, ME: Intercultural Press.

Martin, Judith N., and Mitchell R. Hammer. 1989. "Behavioral Categories of Intercultural Communication Competence: Everyday Communicators' Perceptions." *International Journal of Intercultural Relations* 13: 303-332.

Martin, Judith N., and Beulah Rohrlich. 1991. "Testing a Model of Sojourner Expectations." Paper presented at the annual meeting of the Speech Communication Association, Atlanta.

Okabe, R. 1983. "Cultural Assumptions of East and West: Japan and the United States." In *Intercultural Communication Theory.* Ed. William B. Gudykunst. Newbury Park, CA: Sage.

Pusch, Margaret D., and Nessa Lowenthal. 1988. *Helping Them Home.* Washington, DC: NAFSA

Ramsey, Sheila. 1984. "Double Vision: Nonverbal Behavior in East and West." In *Nonverbal Behavior: Perspectives, Application, and Intercultural Insights.* Ed. A. Wolfgang Lewiston. New York: Hogrefe.

Rohrlich, Beulah, and Judith N. Martin. 1991. "Host Country and Reentry Adjustment of Student Sojourners." *International Journal of Intercultural Relations* 15: 163-182.

Schlesinger, Arthur. 1991. *The Disuniting of America: Reflections on a Multicultural Society.* Knoxville, TN: Whittle Communications.

Shuter, R. 1990. "The Centrality of Culture." *Southern Journal of Communication* 55: 237-249.

Singer, Marshall. 1987. *Intercultural Communication: A Perceptual Approach.* Englewood Cliffs, NJ: Prentice-Hall.

Spitzberg, Brian H., and William R. Cupach. 1984. *Interpersonal Communication Competence.* Beverly Hills, CA: Sage.

Stephan, Walter G. 1985. "Intergroup Relations." In *Handbook of Social Psychology.* Third ed., vol. 2. Ed. G. Lindzey and E. Aaronson, 643. New York: Random House.

Stephan, Cookie W., and Walter G. Stephan. 1992. "Antecedents of Intergroup Anxiety in Asian-Americans and Hispanic Americans." *International Journal of Intercultural Relations* 13: 203-216.

Stephan, Walter G., and Cookie W. Stephan. 1985. "Intergroup Anxiety." *Journal of Social Issues* 41: 157-176.

Stewart, Edward C., and Milton J. Bennett. 1991. *American Cultural Patterns: A Cross-Cultural Perspective.* Yarmouth, ME: Intercultural Press.

Storti, Craig. 1990. *The Art of Crossing Cultures.* Yarmouth, ME: Intercultural Press.

Uehara, Asako. 1986. "The Nature of American Student Reentry Adjustment and Perceptions of the Sojourn Experience." *International Journal of Intercultural Relations* 10: 415-438.

2

Dynamics of
Cross-Cultural Adaptation

Ingemar Torbiörn

The focus of this chapter is generally upon adaptation, and specifically upon the dynamics that are associated with transitions to an unfamiliar culture and back to one's own. As the volume of intercultural exchange grows, so does the volume of research on implications of exchange. Thus, individual adaptation to living abroad is only one of several interesting fields of research. Attempts to grasp the current state of knowledge on this issue quite often bring confusion that is nourished by the mix of concepts, perspectives, and levels of interpretation encountered in the literature. Although this may be a characteristic feature of a young field of research, a comprehensive treatment of dynamics of adaptation requires that the constructs and perspectives used be specified in several respects.

Delimiting a Concept of Adjustment

Cross-cultural adaptation can be regarded from various points of view, for example, sociological or medical. This chapter deals with a *psychological* perspective upon reactions of a *generalized* individual facing an unfamiliar culture. The latter notion means that, although reactions are typical, not every single individual can be expected to react in the same way.

In addition, the concept of adaptation or adjustment needs to be specific as to who judges whether a person is adapted, the individual or someone else. Adjustment in the latter "objective" sense could, but does not necessarily, mean the same as in the former, subjective sense. Thus a person might feel well adjusted but still not be judged so by some member of the host culture, such as an employer. Conversely, the person might feel bad but be seen as well-adjusted by someone else. This chapter deals with the *subjective* sense of adjustment, that is, the individual's own reactions and feelings about his or her situation generally.

Psychological adjustment upon transition between cultures is also taken to involve mechanisms that are not specific to cross-cultural encounters, but generally apply to *total situations* where accustomed ways of relating to the environment no longer apply in a great number of respects, thus requiring the individual to develop new behaviors. This is generally the case when one moves from one environment to another, but also when environmental conditions change drastically in the eyes of an individual, for example upon retirement or unemployment, or when the individual undergoes a drastic change due to illness or some such development, and therefore must relate to the environment in essentially new ways.

At a *cognitive level,* the same basic psychological mechanisms should be used in such total situations, provided that the transition from "old" to "new" is fairly sudden and not gradual, and that the new situation will last for a long enough time to require reorientation by the individual. (Today, the transport to a new culture takes place in a matter of hours, but the stay there may last for years.)

It follows from what has been said above that the concept of adjustment, as used here, refers to what is *normal* or expected rather than to abnormal states or reactions. It follows also that being well- or not well-adjusted does not here refer to some personality trait but to the description of a *state* as subjectively perceived by an individual.

It also follows that the adjustment concept requires a distinction between state and *process.* When referring to a state, this state should be explained within the frame of a process. When referring to a process, this should be seen as a sequence of states and explained in terms of rules or mechanisms that bring about transition between states, thereby making them "stages."

Scope of Cross-Cultural Adaptation

According to the above delimitations, adjustment, as discussed here, deals with extended stays in a culture unfamiliar to the individual, and not with short business or vacation trips abroad. Further, adjustment is discussed as pertaining to all facets of an individual's relation to a host culture, not just to professional or private aspects but to the total life setting. This also implies consideration not just of the social interaction with members of the host culture, but of everything in the new environment that is of *psychological relevance* to the individual, even strictly mundane aspects such as sounds, smells, dust, insects, climate, and so on. Thus everything in the new environment may play a part in adjustment, regardless of how much it differs from what the individual is accustomed to in the home culture, as long as it is psychologically relevant.

This also implies that adjustment to a new cultural setting, as discussed here, is not primarily a matter of personal or cultural identity, but rather about reactions to *everyday life* in the new environment. Even so, it may touch on deeper psychological layers, especially as time in the new culture passes.

Adaptation and Strains

Much research on cross-cultural adjustment deals with strains and problems that are associated with transition. Identifying such strains and their causes is the topic of many studies. This applies to the search for possible correlations between international migration and various criteria of "mental health." No unequivocal evidence of such a relation exists (Furnham and Bochner 1989). Other studies focus on stress, psychosomatic disorders, or alienation (Barna 1983; Weaver 1986). This research brings understanding of the character of strains and of its possible consequences.

To the extent that research interprets various symptoms as associated only with cross-cultural transition, and does not specify how the strains are mediated through the psychology of transition, the knowledge might be of limited use in preparations for moving to a new culture. The focus of attention would be one-sided, upon problematic aspects of intercultural exchange, and measures taken would touch on symptoms rather than causes. Much research today is of this kind, that is, descriptive rather than interpretive, giving typologies of phases or styles of adaptation, or purely anecdotal evidence. To the sojourner, this kind of information can bring insights about the general character of certain phenomena and make clear that one's experiences are shared by others in corresponding situations. For the researcher, the task of explaining strains in cross-cultural adaptation requires going beyond the symptom level and providing explanations of strains in a wider context.

Further, such contexts should, in order to provide useful information, not merely label the transition *per se* as the cause of strains. Explanations referring to the fact that moving to an unfamiliar culture is an important *life event* do not help much, since cross-cultural transitions are normal and sometimes necessary in modern life. Nor do explanations that attribute strains to *marginality* help very much. The marginality concept, originally launched by Park (1926), denotes that an individual is, or feels him or herself to be, neither a member of his or her own primary culture, nor of the culture that forms the person's current surrounding. As applied to cross-cultural adaptation, the concept of marginality most often describes the situation or position held by an individual (cf. Berry 1990). Thus, it may seem relevant primarily as a sociological construct. In a psychological sense, however, marginality could be taken to describe a state where an individual lacks access to, faith in, or mastery of a set of norms to guide behaviors and interpretations. Such a state puts strain on anyone, although it does not necessarily result from transition into a new culture, as will be explained below. According to the position taken here, such a transition only marks the starting point of a psychological process at a cognitive level, a process that may well contain a phase characterized by psychological marginality.

The Process of Adjustment: Culture Shock or U?

Adjustment to an unfamiliar cultural setting typically follows a characteristic time pattern. After a first period of fascination, moods deteriorate and give way to a period of confusion, negative feelings about host culture conditions, and sometimes depressive symptoms and psychosomatic complaints. This state is usually termed *culture shock* and appears after a few months stay in the new environment. After another few months, feelings get more positive, satisfaction increases, and towards the end of the first year subjective adjustment is at about the same level as in the initial phase. The process of adjustment relative to feelings about the host culture described here in terms of symptoms, has the shape of a U. Regarding feelings about the home culture, adjustment proceeds according to an inverted U. Thus, for a period, the individual typically upgrades conditions back home, feels homesick, and prefers to be with fellow-countrymen staying in the host culture (cf. Torbiörn 1982).

Figure 2-1 illustrates these adjustment patterns for a generalized or typical person, seen as some kind of a statistical average. Around an average like this there usually is some variance. This means that the type and degree of symptoms and reactions varies across individuals, although the underlying psychological processes at a cognitive level may be largely the same. To some individuals, adjustment may bring no noticeable strain; to others strains may even make them leave the host culture and return home.

Through the years various explanations of the U-curve have been proposed. Some of these attribute the pattern to changing environmental de-

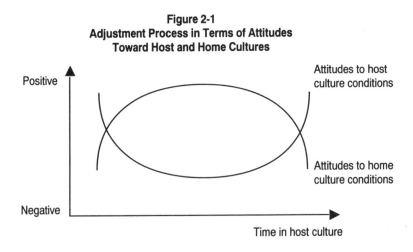

Figure 2-1
Adjustment Process in Terms of Attitudes
Toward Host and Home Cultures

mands upon sojourners. Thus Lysgaard (1955) studied Scandinavian students in the United States and suggested that the trough of the U, coming after about six months, coincided with the most demanding period of studies during a one-year stay. The U pattern was, however, also reported for other travellers on longer stays. Guthrie (1975) denoted symptoms of culture shock as "culture fatigue," and proposed that it should be due to withdrawal of social support on the part of host-culture members, after an initial "honeymoon" where sojourners were seen and helped as newcomers. Storti (1989) suggests a concept of "country shock" to account for some aspects of what is popularly called "culture shock."

Some explanations deny the generality of a U-pattern (cf. Brislin 1981). Thus, Eide (1970) suggested the shape of a converted S, representing a normal learning curve with a "plateau." Such an explanation, however, possibly confounds objective and subjective adjustment. Learning curves normally describe what is being learned in objective terms. In subjective terms, however, such a process should correspond to a person's experience of making progress in learning, that is, it should correspond to the *slope* of an objective learning curve. This slope has a U shape. Such an explanation fits well with what will be suggested in this chapter.

Although the U pattern has been established in many studies, it seems reasonable to question its generality. Most studies so far have been cross-sectional, comparing, at a certain point in time, people with different length of stays in their host cultures. Few studies are longitudinal. Also, generality should be questioned on the ground that the U merely reflects symptoms. These could well differ between persons, even though the underlying cognitive processes are basically the same.

In any case, the notion of culture shock to describe the U or its symptoms overly dramatizes and highlights strains upon cross-cultural transitions. The concept as originally coined by Oberg (1960) could possibly be used as a metaphor that is adequate insofar as reactions appear with some delay upon entrance into an unfamiliar culture, and insofar as they appear rather suddenly. Not to deny the severity of strains involved in experiences of transition, it seems ill advised if ideas, expectations, and measures of persons and organizations disregard the fact that strains are normally not so dramatic. According to the position taken here, the strains reflect a normal and temporary restructuring of views and behavioral schemes that is desirable and to some extent necessary for good adjustment later on.

Dynamics of Adjustment

The perspective applied here holds that cognitive reorientation is what causes various symptoms during the process of adaptation. The concept of cultural norms is central to the reasoning. *Norms* govern people's interpretations and behaviors, denoting what is appropriate, suitable, normal, and so on. Norms are stored in a person's frame of reference in the form of *cognitions*, or views, thoughts, and ideas. As such, they apply to a variety of situations. Norms may be quite specific to a certain individual, or they may be shared by people in a specific group, such as a family or the employees of a company. Norms that are shared by all or most of the members of a society define the *culture* of this society. Any single member of the society thus carries its culture as a set of cultural norms, internalized as cognitions in the frame of reference. Although it includes norms that are strictly individual as well as norms that are specific to groups, the frame of reference will from here on be regarded as a set of cultural norms.

An individual is generally held to experience a situation in two basic dimensions. One deals with how adequate or correct the norms, as prescribed by the frame of reference, prove to be when applied in a given situation. In other words, the individual experiences the situation as correctly or wrongly perceived, that is, his or her behaviors prove successful, or they do not. Thus, the dimension of *applicability* of the frame of reference concerns how well behaviors match the situation or match the individual's environment.

The other dimension concerns the degree of faith a person has that the behaviors applied are appropriate in the situation, that is, how much he or she trusts them regardless of their correctness. Thus the *clarity* of the frame of reference is about how strongly a behavior is supported or recommended by cognitive elements in the frame of reference. The two dimensions are illustrated in Figure 2-2.

At a given moment, the two dimensions are assumed to be independent of each other. Regardless of how much behaviors are trusted to be right, they may or may not prove to be so. Over time, however, a dependency between the two dimensions probably emerges. Experienced clarity will dete-

Figure 2-2
Personal Adjustment – Basic Psychological Model

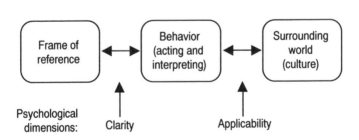

Clarity: Degree of faith in the adequacy of one's acts and interpretations
Applicability: Degree of "success" or experienced adequacy of acts and interpretations

riorate if the used behaviors prove to be wrong. Conversely, clarity will increase if behaviors prove adequate or successful.

How satisfying the situation is perceived to be, that is, how well adjusted a person is, should depend on whether individual needs for clarity and applicability are met. Thus, a person using high standards for what is regarded as adequate in either or both of these respects, can be said to use a *high level of mere adequacy.* This person will find a given situation less satisfying than a person using low standards. This also implies that two persons of the same cultural background could find a situation in a common host culture as differently satisfying. Even if they were equally well adjusted, they might react differently to it. This suggests that the symptoms or strains of cross-cultural adjustment are not the same for everyone.

Moving to an Unfamiliar Culture. A person who is about to move into an unfamiliar culture is likely to be well adapted to the home culture before going abroad. The individual's needs for applicability and clarity relative to the home environment are likely to be satisfied in most respects. Figure 2-3a illustrates what happens upon entering the new culture. Since the frame of reference itself is not changed by the move, it should promote the "old" behaviors or interpretations (A) that are not appropriate in the new culture, which is more likely to reward behaviors according to B. Although applicability of behaviors is thus low upon the arrival, faith in them, or clarity of the frame of reference, is high (IA-BI). This means that behaviors and interpretations are to some extent ethnocentric. Various misperceptions are tolerated because local conditions appear "exotic" compared with the individual's firm conviction about how things should be.

As time passes, however, old views are increasingly questioned because they are not confirmed in the new environment. As the person learns more about local conditions, faith in the old ways decreases, although faith in the new ways is not yet strong. Thus, clarity gradually goes down to reach a low at the time when the propensity to use old and new norms is equally strong. This state is characterized by uncertainty and could be described as "normless," since behaviors get no unequivocal support from the frame of reference. The state corresponds to what is usually termed *culture shock* with regard to reactions and symptoms.

Although after this point in the process the frame of reference is dominated by the adequate, local norms (B), faith in what is normal or appropriate remains weak. The individual's relation to host culture conditions could be described as *conformist.* As recently acquired views are confirmed through applied behaviors, clarity increases, the frame of reference gets more firmly tied to norms of the host culture, and the individual should soon feel well *adapted.*

Applicability and clarity development are illustrated separately in Figure 2-3b. The figure also shows a fictitious level of mere adequacy regarding clarity and applicability. The level of mere adequacy, as it intersects with changes in applicability and clarity, demarcates four *stages* of the adjustment process. The stages are psychologically different and appear in a given sequence. According to the italicized descriptions above, behaviors of a generalized individual should be characterized by:

- Ethnocentric phase (adequate faith - inadequate success)
- Culture shock (inadequate faith - inadequate success)
- Conformist (inadequate faith - adequate success)
- Adapted (adequate faith - adequate success).

Also, since people in every situation or environment will feel better off if they have faith in what they do and if they find it adequately successful or rewarded, the *process of subjective adjustment* could be schematically depicted as the sum of clarity and applicability at each point in time. Figure 2-3c thus displays a U-pattern as derived from figure 3b, that is, from the basic psychological processes of restructuring the frame of reference.

These processes could also explain the U-curve relative to attitudes toward host-culture conditions and the time pattern of an inverted U reflecting attitudes to the old home culture. Both can be understood in terms of normal psychological defense reactions.

As long as the old views dominate the frame of reference, they are being questioned by not being confirmed in the host environment. Thus, they need to be psychologically supported through the degrading of what "threatens" and the upgrading of what is threatened. Such defenses are normal, although they imply that reality is reinterpreted in accordance with how a person might need it to be rather than as it actually is. These defenses are functional in the process of subjective adjustment, serving as temporary buffers against a reality that is perceived as demanding.

As the frame of reference comes to be dominated by host culture norms, defenses of this kind are needed less. Attitudes to the host culture then become more positive, and homesickness and upgrading of home-culture conditions decrease.

Implications for Adjustment. The U-curve of adjustment and culture shock can thus be explained as normal outcomes of the restructuring of the frame of reference. This reorientation does not imply that a person abandons, loses, or forgets old ways of acting or interpreting, only that he or she comes to regard local conditions as normal and appropriate in the host culture setting. This should be functional for later well-being, although it may imply strains at certain phases. The question of how much strain an individual will experience has no general answer. It can be said that high levels of mere adequacy, or high needs for faith and for success in behaviors, will mean that the adjustment process takes place at a lower level of well-being.

Thus strains and reactions vary across individuals, although the basic psychological processes are the same. The length of the various phases of

Figure 2-3
Subjective Adjustment – Process

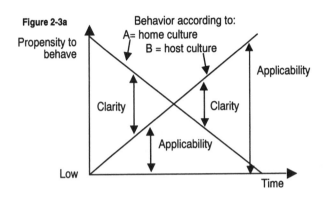

Figure 2-3a

Propensity to behave

Behavior according to:
A = home culture
B = host culture

Applicability

Clarity   Clarity

Applicability

Low

Time

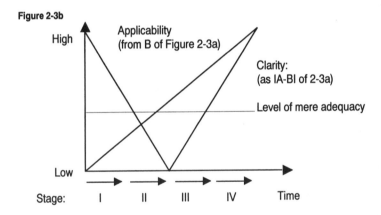

Figure 2-3b

High

Applicability
(from B of Figure 2-3a)

Clarity:
(as IA-BI of 2-3a)

Level of mere adequacy

Low

Stage: I   II   III   IV   Time

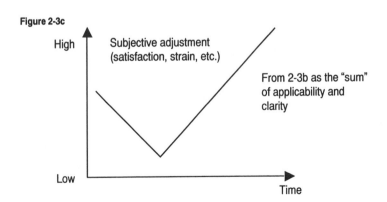

Figure 2-3c

High

Subjective adjustment
(satisfaction, strain, etc.)

From 2-3b as the "sum"
of applicability and
clarity

Low

Time

adjustment will also vary across individuals, due to their varying needs for clarity and applicability and due to different rates of unlearning old views and learning new ones (cf. Grove and Torbiörn 1986).

This view of the adjustment process also implies the following about what may facilitate adaptation:

1. Experience in adjusting to one foreign culture should not "immunize" against strains in adjusting to a second (or third) culture that is unfamiliar to the person, since the frame of reference needs to be restructured again. However, recognizing adjustment patterns and typical reactions in oneself might be of great value.
2. Measures taken to facilitate adjustment should not aim to prevent or avoid reorientation, but to recognize the possible need to mitigate strains associated with it.
3. Preparatory measures that aim to restructure the frame of reference before a person leaves the home culture should have little impact upon adjustment. New material is interpreted in a frame of reference that is necessarily ethnocentric. Thus,the individual will not be amenable to reorientation. Further, the person still at home cannot experience the total immersion that moving to the host culture will bring.
4. Measures that facilitate restructuring should deal with "the grammar" of the host culture. These measures are likely to be most effective if they are administered when a person's reliance upon old views has weakened after a few months stay in the new environment, that is, when clarity is low. The need for measures that can help in the restructuring as well as openness to them should be greater after some time in the new culture.
5. Staying in contact with people and things that support old views (as questioned by host-culture norms) supports subjective adjustment, especially during the culture shock phase.
6. Intellectual awareness of the character and content of the adjustment process is likely to help the individual face possible strains. Information about what is normal, constructive, and temporary about the adjustment process can be acquired before the sojourn.
7. Self-awareness regarding one's own reactions upon facing environments that are poorly structured or defined or are unpredictable can facilitate adjustment. The same applies to cultural self-awareness in the sense of knowing what one represents in the eyes of host-culture members.
8. Self-distance or a detached perspective may facilitate adjustment. The individual can realize that, for some time after arriving in the new culture, his or her own behaviors may not prove efficient. Accepting this outlook would mean that levels of mere adequacy would be lowered and that frustrations could be handled more easily. Assuming this self-distance is easier if the individual possesses some sense of humor.

Measures to Facilitate Adjustment. According to the view adopted here, measures to facilitate adjustment should generally aim to increase clarity and applicability of the frame of reference and lower levels of mere adequacy. More specifically, according to the eight items just listed, measures should deal with three aims:

- Restructuring the frame of reference to bring it into accordance with host culture norms (items 3,4)
- Providing confirmation and support for "questioned" norms of the home culture (item 5)
- Increasing self-awareness (items 6,7,8).

Specific measures are effective only if they are appropriately timed to meet current individual needs and susceptibility.

Predeparture Adjustment Concerns. The content of predeparture training should correspond to what is possible to achieve while in the home culture. Shortcomings in this respect might explain difficulties in demonstrating the usefulness of predeparture training (cf. Black, Mendenhall, and Oddou 1991). Training in the home culture should not primarily emphasize learning behaviors and attitudes that prevail among members of the host culture (items 3 and 4). Thus Triandis (1986), although finding some impact from the use of "culture assimilators," found that the efficiency of this training method was greater among people who had previously visited the host culture and thus were able to relate what was learned to their own experiences. Gregersen and Black (1992) even found a negative correlation between time devoted to host culture-oriented predeparture training and later adjustment.

Training on various aspects of self-awareness (items 6, 7, and 8) is appropriate in the predeparture stage. Weaver (1986) holds that intellectual understanding of the psychological mechanisms underlying the adjustment process is the most effective means of dealing with adjustment strains. Understanding the process demystifies it. Grove (1989) offers a guide for intellectual preparations, especially for youth exchange participants.

Training in the form of simulated cross-cultural encounters can clarify individual reactions. Frequently used simulations include Bafa Bafa (Shirts 1977) and Barnga (Thiagarajan and Steinwachs 1990). Cultural self-awareness can come from culture-contrast methods that highlight and contrast important features of home and host cultures, and from learning about fundamental values and characteristics of one's home culture (cf. Stewart and Bennett 1991; Althen 1988).

A further aspect of self-awareness would be to clarify one's motives for moving to the host culture. Motives preferably should be of the positive, or pull-factor type, implying that the stay, work, or studies are what attracts a person. Push-factors, or negative motives, imply that a person moves abroad primarily to get away from a disliked situation in the home environment. This could mean that the host culture or the stay in it would not be the prime target of adjustment. This also applies to the negative motives of going abroad in order to repair a bad relationship through "starting anew in some other place."

Preparations in the home culture should concentrate on topics of practical relevance for transition and orientation, that is, on the logistical and social aspects of the host society, such as daily life, working conditions, the academic system, and so on. This includes factual information about living, communications, goods, costs, health care, local authorities and institutions, hygiene, and closing times at the place of residence in the host country. Also important is information about where to get more information when it is needed. This "survival material" is specific to each country and place; a general checklist cannot be produced. Americans planning to live or work overseas should, however, be helped by Kohls's (1984) *Survival Kit for Overseas Living*. Generally, information from fellow countrymen who are living or have lived at the sojourner's destination should be of great value. For further readings on cross-cultural preparations and training, see La Brack (1986), Kohls (1984), Pedersen (1988), and Bhawuk (1990).

Adjustment Concerns on Site. The first ten to twelve months in an unfamiliar culture should include the most important development regarding the U-pattern of adjustment. After the initial honeymoon phase comes the stage where faith in the accustomed "old" views has decreased. The sojourner is now prepared to pick up new concepts of normality, and a better understanding and mastery of the host culture is possible. Much of this will inevitably come through "learning by doing," but could be facilitated by measures that provide structures according to which a person could sort out the many experiences and impressions gained so far. Insights into aspects of the host culture such as basic values, traditions, and social conditions should facilitate restructuring the frame of reference. Learning about the host culture should now be more efficient than before, since material on that topic is more relevant to individual needs (stages 2 and 3 of Figure 2-3b). Thus host culture-oriented training should be emphasized on site in the host culture rather than in the predeparture period (cf. Grove 1989; Black, Gregersen, and Mendenhall 1992).

A better understanding of the host culture could be acquired from more experienced compatriots, from acquaintances among the local population, and from readings, including novels dealing with local history, religions, social groupings, systems of government, and power structures. Further, the understanding of indirect or symbolic manifestations of the host culture may be important in everyday life, for example, knowing what is and is not communicated verbally (cf. Hall 1959; Samovar and Porter 1988; Gudykunst and Ting-Toomey 1989; Mead 1990).

To accommodate the host culture, the sojourner might need to take deliberate action or undergo formalized training. The stages marking the trough of the adjustment process are also the most demanding, and the sojourner might be tempted to withdraw from the host environment, to reject or degrade local people and conditions, and to seek support and therefore confirmation of old views and ways that are threatened (cf. Storti 1989). Therefore on-site measures to facilitate adjustment should, on the one hand, promote reorientation towards the host culture, and, on the other hand, support home-culture norms in order to reduce strains of adjustment. These recommendations might well seem contradictory, but they correspond to a conflictual state within the individual. They support subjective adjustment.

Thus, the importance of contact with the home culture or with fellow countrymen on site during this period is well established (cf. Black, Mendenhall, and Oddou 1991; Furnham and Bochner 1989). To the extent that these contacts mean isolation from the host environment, though, they might impede adjustment at a later stage (cf. Weaver 1986; Storti 1989).

Good family relationships are, of course, a major source of social support. On the other hand, since adjustment puts strain on all family members, imbalance within the family regarding the capacity to provide support may create strain on family relationships (cf. Sluzki 1979; Black and Stephens 1989). Affiliation with the home culture can also be maintained through memorabilia, pictures, books, and so on. Contact may be upheld through telephone calls, newspapers, magazines, letters, tapes, and video cassettes. Special attention and support from a mother organization back home might be of special value during the first year abroad.

Measures to increase self-awareness as discussed above should help promote adjustment if attended to on site, although they may be less available to the individual during the demanding stages of adaptation. Discussing experiences with compatriots can be supportive.

Life as Adapted to the Host Culture. After the first period of about seven to twelve months in the new culture (that is, from Stage 4 of Figure 2-3b forward), the restructuring of the frame of reference is essentially over, and so are the strains associated with the initial adjustment. This means that our generalized individual should now find life in the host culture satisfactory. It does not mean that the person has ceased to learn, but that he or she has acquired an adequate basis for more efficient and nuanced learning. Further progress in subjective adjustment now comes from orientation towards the host environment. The individual is well adjusted in the sense of having found a satisfactory way to relate to everyday life. This does not imply mastery of, or being fully committed to, all local norms and values, but rather a spontaneous acceptance of them as normal conditions of daily life. Over time, the individual usually adopts more of the local ways as his or her own. Doing so can be more or less attractive, and take more or less time, depending on what aspect of local ways is at issue and on how strange host-culture conditions appear.

Reentry Adjustment. Readjustment to the home culture is sometimes said to be more demanding than adjustment in an unfamiliar setting abroad. This is quite often interpreted in terms of an extension of the U-pattern into a W, to include the process of readjustment back home. Although this might be an adequate description of symptoms accompanying the adjustment-readjustment processes, such an interpretation implies that the W can be explained in terms of the same psychological mechanisms as is the U. (cf. Gullahorn and Gullahorn 1963)

According to the view of adjustment outlined in this chapter, the psychological mechanisms could be the same only under two conditions, both of which seem unlikely to this author. First, if the restructuring per se, regardless of scope and content, is what produces adjustment strains, then a W should appear and reentry shock would be just as severe as culture shock. Second, if severity of culture shock depends basically on the degree of difference, or the height of the culture barrier, between home and host cultures, then a W-pattern should appear upon reentry only insofar as one or both of the following applies:

- The process of acquiring host-culture norms means that the original home-culture norms were erased from the mind of the individual, that is, "old files are deleted."
- The home culture is changed during the individual's stay abroad, so as to appear "quite unfamiliar" upon the return, that is, "saved files no longer apply."

The position taken here regarding the complete loss of home culture norms is that the restructuring of the frame of reference in accord with host-culture norms does not imply the "losing" of home culture norms, only "not using" them—the " files are saved." Regarding changed "unfamiliar" home culture norms, it seems safe to say that cultures, in the basic meaning of norm systems, change only slowly, so that "saved files still basically apply."

Thus, the transitions in "going out" and "coming home" should differ in character. "Going out" involves both delearning and learning, whereas "coming home" is largely a matter of delearning. Taken together, a W–pattern as it might appear in terms of symptoms is not the result of the same causes in "going out" and "coming home."

This does not deny the strains of reentry, but attributes them to other causes. Thus, during the time that a person has spent abroad, both the person and the home culture have changed in some respects, while not in others. The position taken here is that reentry problems mainly reflect mismatches between person and home culture due to changes or lack of changes on both sides. Reactions upon culture shock and reentry typically differ. While the former are more characterized by confusion, the latter quite often express disappointment. This implies that expectations play an important role in reentry problems. Upon return to the home culture, as opposed to when leaving, the individual expects to find a largely familiar environment.

But changes occur during the absence, often so gradually that the people who remained there do not notice them. To the returnee, the changes appear great and evident. Furthermore the sojourner has changed through acquiring new perspectives that shape expectations for the home environment. The home environment (society, work, school, and so on) has its own expectations for the returnee, often based on the assumption that the returnee will be as he or she was before the stay abroad. The situation is set for mismatches. From a psychological point of view, reentry problems should be of a general social psychological kind, not so much entailing the cognitive restructuring necessary for adaptation abroad.

How much and in what respects the individual and the home culture have changed generally cannot be forecast. The longer the absence, the more both the person and the home situation are likely to have changed, and the more reentry is likely to cause problems. Other things that should affect a person's reentry experiences are the way life was spent abroad and what specifically changed at home—within the family, at the job, at school, among friends. The individual character of conditions upon reentry makes it difficult to attribute possible strains to general psychological processes and also more difficult to devise general recommendations. The basic structure of change versus no change that should account for mismatches of expectations is illustrated in Figure 2-4. The figure does not refer to a typology of individuals or of adaptive styles, but describes schematically the variety of situations that a sojourner might face upon return.

Matched Expectations. Fields A and D of Figure 2-4 denote aspects of the situation upon return where expectations fit together. Here the person has not changed and finds home environment as before, or else new features of the person (such as outlook or capabilities) match new conditions back home (such as study or job opportunities). Thus D could imply a situation where an employer offers new tasks that make use of international experiences, or the employer has a generalist outlook like the one the returnee developed abroad.

The size of Field A in Figure 2-4 is intended to impose proportions on what has changed about the individual and the home environment. Basically, even after a considerable time, the individual is unchanged and so is the home culture. The size of Field A is of reduced, course, the longer an individual has been away. Normally, the individual can, in a great many respects, take up from where he or she left off and quickly refresh or pick up old ways. Preparations for transition could focus on practical matters such

Figure 2-4
Aspects of Returnee vs Home Culture

Individual

	not changed	changed
	A	**B**
Home culture **not changed**	**Match of expectations:** ▼ Person finds old milieu familiar but changing ▼ Old milieu values person ▼ Person picks up where left off ▼ Transition a matter of practical arrangements	**Mismatch between expectations from:** ▼ New person upon old milieu (Person feels grown out of "dull, narrow, provincial" environment ▼ Old milieu upon new person (old milieu cannot value or accommodate new outlook, capabilities, etc. Person "disappointed, underutilized")
	C	**D**
changed	**Mismatch between expectations from:** ▼ Old person upon new milieu (home milieu unfamiliar, old days and ways lost, etc.) ▼ New milieu upon old person (finds views, competence, etc., "outdated")	**Match of expectations:** ▼ New person finds new milieu challenging ▼ New environment "values, accommodates, demands new outlook, capabilities, etc."

as transportation, schools, housing, and job arrangements, that should be planned as much as possible before leaving the host culture.

A somewhat frustrating experience related to transition itself usually appears soon upon return. To the individual, coming home is an important life event. For those who had remained at home, however, the event has less significance. For them, life is "ongoing," and they are preoccupied with their own daily routines. The returnee is expected to pick up where he or she left off, and friends and colleagues seem not curious or "not even interested." Thus, a typical reaction is "Am I expected? Does anybody care? Am I welcome?" Although most returnees soon accept this situation, their frustration can be mitigated by arranging some break in the routine—a ritual, celebration, seminar, or formalized debriefing—that brings attention and respect to the returnee's experience.

Individual Changed. In Field B of Figure 2-4, problems should generally stem from the mismatch between the old home environment and new characteristics of the returnee. Thus, the person may have "outgrown" some conditions back home that are unchanged. The returnee's new characteristics might not be required or be able to be accommodated. A curriculum or job may be designed according to the person's old capabilities and the person is expected to be content with it. Although the person may not expect things at home to have changed, he or she may still expect conditions to match the "new person." Due to age, maturity, or new outlooks this person is able to see things at home in a more comparative perspective than before and is less absolute in ways of thinking. Conditions at home may appear "provincial" or "narrow." A person who has studied or worked abroad may have developed into a "generalist" but is confronted upon return with quite specialized tasks. Thus, Oddou and Mendenhall (1991) found that former expatriate U.S. executives report decreased job independence and responsibilities upon return. According to a study by Adler (1991), about 20 percent of repatriates left their companies within six months after return.

Although a returnee may have some difficulty at first in getting reaccustomed to norms at home (tempo and time schedules, for instance), delearning of former host culture norms should not constitute the main problem of reentry. Rather, changes in the person such as maturity or a relativistic outlook are more likely to be the cause of frustrations. The person may feel discontent or underutilized at work and feel "outside" where one expected to feel at home. Thus, the experience of marginality could describe and explain some strains upon return, and the individual might logically resort to a more or less lasting "out-group" orientation, assuming a "grass grows greener on the other side" attitude.

Measures to facilitate adjustment should generally aim at reducing the mismatch through clarifying expectations in both camps. The individual should, as much as possible, clarify the "new self"—make explicit new capabilities and ambitions, relate them to restrictions in the home setting, and act upon realistic judgments. Upon repatriation, interested parties in the home environment, such as parents, teachers, and employers, may take measures to clarify their view of the "new person," including, for example, new capabilities, international experience, and access to international networks. Furthermore, they should clarify to themselves how the returnee's new characteristics can be valued and used in the home context, and provide tasks or roles that employ the qualifications of the "new person."

Regarding expatriate job assignments, (probably including teaching assignments for faculty who have been abroad), lack of clear repatriation policies can heighten role ambiguity and role conflict upon return to a job in the home company (Gregersen and Black 1992). It is preferable that repatriation policies be made clear to assignees before they go abroad (cf. Oddou 1992).

Home Setting Changed. In Field C of Figure 2-4, the mismatch implies that the returnee might expect things to be the same as before but finds them unfamiliar, and thus feels "lost" or "confused." Also, the home environment might expect the person to know about new conditions, or to stand up to new demands, but finds the person out of touch and out of date. The return alerts the individual to many changes that have occurred. Changes at the societal level concerning laws, regulations, and atmosphere may have taken place. New constellations of roles and job positions may have developed. Patterns of social companionship and relations among friends may have changed, and so may people themselves. Things back home appear unfamiliar. Old roles may not be picked up, and establishing new relations and roles may not come easily.

This is, to some extent, a problem of information, and the individual can promote readjustment by staying updated during the sojourn abroad. He or she should actively seek information about those things that may affect life back home. Companies and institutions to which the individual is to return should recognize the sojourner's need to keep informed, to be briefed upon return, and to be introduced to new people, policies, and roles in the organization. Coming back to a company or a school often means confronting a new climate, new networks, power constellations, and formal and informal communication patterns. Thus, not only individuals, but the organizations to which they return, should benefit from programs aiming to inform and reintroduce the returnee. For further readings on reentry, see Austin (1986), Martin (1986), Grove (1989), Adler (1991), and Chinn (1992).

Culture Barriers

Fundamental to this chapter and indeed this book is the fact that cultures differ. They may, however, differ more or less and in various ways. This variation is reflected in an individual's ways of communicating with, relating to, and reacting to host cultures. In psychological terms, a culture barrier refers to reactions in contexts of cross-cultural contact where cultural differences negatively affect an individual's ability or willingness to understand, adhere to, or adopt norms of a foreign culture. As stated above, a situation of cross-cultural communication does not exclusively denote person-to-person relations, but may also denote person-environment relations in general, for example, attitudes to local foods, climate, and clothing. A culture barrier implies:

1. It refers to reactions of people confronted with cultural conditions that are different from their own.
2. The difference evokes reactions in the direction of negative rather than positive evaluation, dislike rather than like, avoidance rather than approach. This negativity is due not to aversion to the other culture, but simply to the fact that the intercultural exchange is experienced as more

rewarding the more conditions of the other culture are perceived to be similar to those to which a person is accustomed (cf. Gergen, Morse, and Gergen 1980). Le Vine and Campbell (1972, 14) term this a "naive phenomenal absolutism."

3. The degree to which reactions occur should be more pronounced the more different the two cultures are (that is, the barrier between the home and host cultures is higher).

4. An individual's reaction will not be uniformly strong across various aspects of the host culture. A small difference in one respect might constitute a high barrier if it touches upon a central aspect of the individual's own culture, such as norms for raising children. Conversely a big difference regarding a matter of less centrality may not constitute a high barrier (cf. Gudykunst and Hammer 1988).

5. A culture barrier may be low at one reactional level, yet high at another. Thus, barriers may be lower regarding attitudes toward host culture norms than when it comes to actually applying these norms in overt behaviors.

6. Culture barriers are non-reciprocal, that is, they apply in only one direction between two specified cultures. Thus, the barrier between cultures A and B will not be as high as that between B and A. The relevant situation may be interpreted or attributed differently, or be more central to members of B than to A.

7. A culture barrier refers to a particular point of time in the intercultural experience, and tends to become "lower" as time passes.

Implications of Culture Barriers. The notion of culture barriers means that expatriate life will generally be at different levels of subjective and objective adjustment in different host cultures, thus displaying different attitudes and behaviors vis-à-vis host culture conditions. Depending upon the degree of difference between home and host culture, the apparent foreignness or "cultural toughness" (Black, Gregersen, and Mendenhall 1992) varies across cultures, from the viewpoint of a person of a certain cultural background.

The relevance of cultural barriers or "cultural distance" (Church 1982) to adjustment has been stated in various ways. Thus, Furnham and Bochner (1989) found that foreign students in the U.K. reported more symptoms of psychological distress, the greater the "cultural distance" between their home cultures and U.K. Few studies, however, deal with the adjustment of persons from a given home culture in various host cultures.

Torbiörn (1988) reports on Swedes assigned abroad by international companies in twenty-six countries or groups of countries. Self-reported behaviors and attitudes pertaining to the respondent's personal situations in the host cultures were analyzed in terms of country average scores. Culture barriers emerged from the analysis as clusters of host cultures at distinct levels of "liking." The levels coincided with cultural distance from the respondents' home culture.

Barriers were identified as regarding:

- Social contact (measured as extent of host-country companionship, proficiency in a local language, knowledge of local news and topical events)
- Assimilation (measured as the extent to which the host culture language was used by children at home, by adults within the family and outside the family off the job, and as self-assessed adoption of local customs)
- General adjustment (rated as satisfaction with life in the host-culture).

In the above respects, culture barriers for the Swedes were higher—that is, contact, assimilation, and satisfaction were gradually lower—the less akin or related to Swedish culture host countries were in terms of religion and language (which could not be separated). Thus, barriers "grew higher" from a-d for:

a. English-speaking and Protestant cultures
b. Germanic language and Christian cultures
c. Romance language and Catholic cultures
d. Non-Indo-European language and non-Christian cultures.

Regarding other host-culture characteristics, the Swedes' attitudes varied along other cultural dimensions, for example, "societal comfort" (as measured by ratings of orderliness and safety in public places, transportation and communication, and culture and entertainment). Barriers varied along the dimension of technological levels (as measured by aggregates such as GNP or electricity consumption per capita). Attitudes regarding local outdoor life and open-air environment were correspondingly less positive the more densely populated the host culture was.

Because any barrier attributed to cultural differences is a function of particular reactions in particular cross-cultural contexts (items 4, 5, and 6 above), results from this study could not be generalized. The phenomenon of culture barriers is, however, universal, and some underlying cultural dimensions might be of more general relevance than others. Research by Lawler (1991) indicates that the religion and language and the technology dimensions may be relevant for the adjustment of U.S. primary school students, and Black, Gregersen, and Mendenhall (1992) use them to determine the degree of "cultural toughness" facing American and Western business people abroad.

Culture barriers, by definition, reflect the role of culture itself in cross-cultural interaction. However, we need more rigorous studies to improve our understanding of them. Barriers in cross-cultural situations may, in fact, also be the result of person- or situation-specific factors and falsely attributed to cultural differences, which are often more conspicuous. Further, more information on how reactions differ across host cultures does not, in itself, constitute or reveal dimensions of culture. Objective correlates to match reactional data are required as well.

Thus what is needed is descriptive information about cultures that permits objective comparisons along uniform dimensions of several cultures. The dimensions should be more specific than broad ones such as religion and language. The impact of culture could then be understood more usefully, and more adequate measures could be taken to facilitate cross-cultural encounters.

Although not studied precisely enough, the general phenomenon of culture barriers is well established. One implication of the idea is that expatriates cannot expect to be fully adapted to every aspect of life in the host culture. Since culture barriers reflect the extent to which a host culture is difficult to adjust to, the basic approach to becoming better adjusted would be to orient towards, and learn more about, the host culture. This implies a deliberate interest and a will to communicate, rather than the actual mastery of every nuance of the local culture.

Although language proficiency is generally important, it is not enough to guarantee good adjustment in the subjective sense. This applies especially to the first seven to eight months in the new culture. From then on, language becomes a more crucial tool for increased understanding and long-term adjustment. Another implication is that after the initial seven or eight months, adjustment becomes less a matter of "self-awareness" and more a matter of learning the local frame of reference and behavioral guidelines.

Overcoming Culture Barriers. In fact, an adult individual can seldom completely overcome culture barriers, even after a prolonged time in a foreign culture. The question of whether culture shock during the early part of a stay in a host culture will be "tougher" in terms of a deeper U-pattern if one moves to a "high-barrier" culture has not been settled. Some researchers (such as Church 1982; Furnham and Bochner 1989) hold this to be the case, whereas others believe that moving to an "easy culture" may produce just as severe a culture shock (cf. Brewster 1992). The latter position would imply that strain is caused by the restructuring of views per se. As we saw above, this issue also relates to the matter of adjustment upon return to the home culture.

Discussion

In a perspective covering the whole cycle of "going out" for an extended stay abroad and coming back, this chapter has discussed processes and possible strains of adaptation as they normally apply to a generalized individual. The cycle, as outlined here, can be seen as a learning experience with some important implications. First, adaptability to new cultural surroundings is not increased as a result of earlier experiences of cognitive reorientation in another culture. Adaptability should, however, gain from increased self-awareness and understanding of the time schedule and characteristics of the adjustment process.

Second, the learning experience adds new ways of thinking and seeing others and oneself, without depriving the individual of old ways. This goes with the position, as taken here, that "old files are saved" while the person learns new things. It also follows that the person, while living abroad, may be well-adapted without adhering to or deeply internalizing all local norms.

Third, and for the above reasons, cultural identity is not threatened by extended cross-cultural sojourns. Rather, cross-cultural learning experiences promote personal growth by adding maturity and relativistic outlooks, while the cultural roots remain the same.

This also means that cross-cultural sojourns do not produce the "transnational" or "supranational" personalities that are sometimes encountered in the literature. Such "personalities" lack any cultural identity and any preferred set of cultural norms. This notion appears fictive and of low psychological credibility to this author. What is more likely to happen, as La Brack (1986, 233) puts it regarding American sojourners, is that they become more American "but not in a nationalistic sense."

Thus, the impact of a sojourn abroad relative to personal growth is much a matter of increased understanding, not necessarily accompanied by changed behavioral and affective patterns of reaction (cf. Saltzman 1986). Insofar as this means that a person turns into a "marginal man" this should, except for temporary feelings during adjustment and readjustment, be a "constructive marginality," implying an increased capacity to see "oneself as a constant creator of one's own reality" (Bennett 1986, 62).

References

Adler, Nancy. 1991. *International Dimensions of Organizational Behavior.* Second ed. Boston: PWS-Kent.

Althen, Gary. 1988. *American Ways: A Guide for Foreigners in the United States.* Yarmouth, ME: Intercultural Press.

Austin, Clyde. Ed. 1986. *Cross-Cultural Reentry: A Book of Readings.* Abilene, KN: Abilene Christian University Press.

Barna, LaRay. 1983. "The Stress Factor in Intercultural Relations." In *Handbook of Intercultural Training.* Ed. Dan Landis and Richard Brislin. New York: Pergamon.

Bennett, Milton. 1986. "Towards Ethnorelativism: A Development Model of Intercultural Sensitivity." In *Cross-Cultural Orientation: New Conceptualizations and Applications.* Ed. R. Michael Paige. Lanham, MD: University Press of America.

Berry, John. 1990. " Psychology of Acculturation: Understanding Individuals Moving between Cultures." In *Applied Cross-Cultural Psychology.* Ed. Richard W. Brislin. Newbury Park, CA: Sage.

Bhawuk, D. P. S. 1990. "Cross-Cultural Orientation Programs." In *Applied Cross-Cultural Psychology.* Ed. Richard W. Brislin. Newbury Park: Sage.

Black, Stewart, Hal Gregersen, and Mark Mendenhall. 1992. *Global Assignments.* San Francisco: Jossey-Bass.

Black, Stewart, Mark Mendenhall, and Gary Oddou. 1991. "Toward a Comprehensive Model of International Adjustment." *Academy of Management Review* 16, 2: 291-317.

Black, Stewart, and Greg Stephens. 1989. "The Influence of the Spouse on American Expatriate Adjustment in Overseas Assignments." *Journal of Management* 15: 529-544.

Brewster, Chris. 1992." Choosing to Adjust: UK and Swedish Expatriates in Sweden and the UK." In *Proceedings of the First International Conference on Expatriate Management.* Hong Kong: School of Business, Hong Kong Baptist College.

Brislin, Richard, W. 1981. *Cross-Cultural Encounters.* New York: Pergamon.

Chinn, Leiton. 1992. *International Student Reentry: A Select, Annotated Bibliography.* Washington, DC: NAFSA.

Church, Austin. 1982. "Sojourner Adjustment." *Psychological Bulletin* 91, 3: 540-577.

Eide, Ingrid. 1970. *Students as Links between Cultures.* Oslo: Universitets-Forlaget.

Furnham, Adrian, and Stephen Bochner. 1989. *Culture Shock.* London: Routledge.

Gergen, Kenneth, Stanley Morse, and Mary Gergen. 1980. "Behavior Exchange in Cross-Cultural Perspective." In *Handbook of Cross-Cultural Psychology*, vol. 5. Ed. Harry Triandis and Richard Brislin. Boston: Allyn and Bacon.

Gregersen, Hal. 1992. "Commitments to a Parent Company and a Local Work Unit during Repatriation." *Personnel Psychology* 45: 29-54.

Gregersen, Hal, and Stewart Black. 1992. "Antecedents to Commitment to a Parent Company and a Foreign Operation." *Academy of Management Review* 35, 1: 65-90.

Grove, Cornelius. 1989. *Orientation Handbook for Youth Exchange Programs.* Yarmouth, ME: Intercultural Press.

Grove, Cornelius, and Ingemar Torbiörn. 1986 ."A New Conceptualization of Intercultural Adjustment and the Goals of Training." In *Cross-Cultural Orientation: New Conceptualizations and Applications.* Ed. R. Michael Paige. Lanham, MD: University Press of America.

Gudykunst, William, and Mitchell Hammer. 1988. "Strangers and Hosts: An Uncertainty Reduction Based Theory of Intercultural Adaptation." In *Cross-Cultural Orientation: New Conceptualizations and Applications.* Ed. Young Yun Kim and William Gudykunst. Newbury Park, CA: Sage.

Gudykunst, William, and Stella Ting-Toomey. 1989. *Culture and Interpersonal Communication.* London: Sage.

Gullahorn, John, and Jeanne Gullahorn. 1963. "An Extension of the U-curve Hypothesis." *Journal of Social Issues* 19, 3: 33-47.

Guthrie, George. 1975. "A Behavioral Analysis of Culture Learning." In *Cross-Cultural Perspectives on Learning.* Ed. Richard Brislin et al. Beverly Hills, CA: Sage.

Hall, Edward T. 1959. *The Silent Language.* Garden City, NY: Doubleday.

La Brack, Bruce. 1986. "Orientation as Process: The Integration of Pre- and Post-Experience Learning." In *Cross-Cultural Orientation: New Conceptualizations and Applications.* Ed. R. Michael Paige. Lanham, MD: University Press of America.

Lawler, Timothy. 1991. "The Relationships among Gender, Length of Stay, Host Country Culture and the Adjustment Experienced by Minor U.S. Sojourners." Ann Arbor, MI: UMI Dissertation Services.

Le Vine, Robert, and Donald Campbell. 1972. *Ethnocentrism: Theories of Conflict, Ethnic Attitudes and Group Behavior.* New York: Wiley.

Lysgaard, Sverre. 1955. "Adjustment in a Foreign Society: Norwegian Fulbright Grantees Visiting the United States." *International Social Science Bulletin* 7: 45-51.

Kohls, Robert. 1984. *Survival Kit for Overseas Living: For Americans Planning to Live and Work Abroad.* Second ed. Yarmouth, ME: Intercultural Press.

Martin, Judith. 1986. "Orientation for the Reentry Experience: Conceptual Overview and Implications for Researchers and Practitioners." In *Cross-Cultural Orientation: New Conceptualizations and Applications.* Ed. R. Michael Paige. Lanham, MD: University Press of America.

Mead, Richard. 1990. *Cross-Cultural Management Communication.* New York: Wiley.

Oberg, Kalervo. 1960. "Cultural Shock: Adjustment to New Cultural Environments." *Practical Anthropology* 7: 177-182.

Oddou, Gary. 1992. "Managing the Expatriates: What the Successful Firms Do." *Human Resource Planning* 14: 4.

Oddou, Gary, and Mark Mendenhall. 1991." Succession Planning for the 21st Century: How Well Are We Grooming Our Future Business Leaders?" *Business Horizons* 34, 1: 26-34.

Park, Robert E. 1926. "Human Migration and the Marginal Man." *American Journal of Sociology* 33: 881-893.

Pedersen, Paul. 1988. *A Handbook for Developing Multicultural Awareness.* Alexandria, VA: American Association for Counseling and Development.

Saltzman, Carol. 1986. "One Hundred and Fifty Percent Persons: Guides to Orienting International Students." In *Cross-Cultural Orientation: New Conceptualizations and Applications.* Ed. R. Michael Paige. Lanham, MD: University Press of America.

Samovar, Larry, and Richard Porter. 1988. *Intercultural Communication: A Reader.* Fifth ed. Belmont, CA: Wadsworth.

Shirts, Gary. 1977. *"Bafa Bafa": A Cross-Cultural Simulation.* Del Mar, CA: Simile II.

Sluzki, Carlos. 1979. "Migration and Family Conflict." *Family Process* 18, 4: 379-390.

Stewart, Edward, and Milton Bennett. 1991. *American Cultural Patterns: A Cross-Cultural Perspective.* Rev. ed. Yarmouth, ME: Intercultural Press.

Storti, Craig. 1989. *The Art of Crossing Cultures.* Yarmouth, ME: Intercultural Press.

Thiagarajan, Sivasailam, and Barbara Steinwachs. 1990. *Barnga: A Simulation Game on Cultural Clashes.* Yarmouth, ME: Intercultural Press.

Torbiörn, Ingemar. 1982. *Living Abroad: Personal Adjustment and Personnel Policy in the Overseas Setting.* New York: Wiley.

_____. 1988. "Culture Barriers as a Social Psychological Construct: An Empirical Validation." In *Cross-Cultural Adaptation: Current Approaches.* Ed. Young Yun Kim and William Gudykunst

Triandis, Harry. 1986. "Approaches to Cross-Cultural Orientation and the Role of the Culture Assimilator Training." In *Cross-Cultural Orientation: New Conceptualizations and Applications.* Ed. R. Michael Paige. Lanham, MD: University Press of America.

Weaver, Gary. 1986. "Understanding and Coping with Cross-Cultural Adjustment Stress." In *Cross-Cultural Orientation.* Ed. R. Michael Paige. Lanham, MD: University Press of America.

3

Cultural Differences on Campus

Gary Althen

By now, foreign students are familiar fixtures on many American campuses. In times past, students from other countries were relative oddities, and they got special attention from other students, from faculty, and from administrative staff. Sometimes that attention was positive and sometimes it was not.

As the foreign-student population grew following World War II, we heard repeated calls for "awareness" of and "sensitivity" to students from other cultures. The general line was that "we have students here from other countries. They have different customs and viewpoints. We need to be aware of that, and sensitive to how we treat them." More recently, we have been told that we should "appreciate" these differences.

By now, calls for awareness, sensitivity, and appreciation have become clichés. Foreign students in significant numbers have inhabited many campuses for a long time. Domestic students, faculty, and staff know there are foreign students on the campus, and they realize that those students often have different cultural backgrounds. People who want to deal constructively with these cultural differences need to know more than what the terms "awareness," "sensitivity," and "appreciation" imply. They need a more detailed understanding of the issues that arise when people from different cultures come together. This chapter is intended to move beyond the clichés and promote a more refined understanding of cultural differences that are manifest on campuses.

Why do this? Richard Brislin (1986, 18) and his colleagues describe well the typical dynamics of intercultural interactions:

> Difficulties inevitably arise whenever there is extensive cross-cultural interaction. People are socialized, in their own culture, to accept as "proper and good" a relatively narrow range of behaviors. Those behaviors not labeled as good are perceived as less desirable, and, in extreme cases, as absolutely wrong. Further, others who engage in those less desirable behaviors are seen as backward, ignorant, or ill-mannered. In everyday words, people become accustomed to doing things (eating, courting,

working, interacting with others) in certain ways, and the behaviors surrounding these activities are seen as proper. But when they interact with people from other cultures, those proper behaviors are not always forthcoming from the others. In addition, behaviors that people consider "improper" are practiced on a routine basis by those from other cultures. Common responses to this confrontation of past learning with present experiences are intense dislike of culturally different others (leading to prejudice), negative labels (stereotypes), and a refusal to interact with the others (discrimination).

Indeed, Milton Bennett (1986), Albert Bernstein and Sydney Rozen (1989), and no doubt many others argue that the call to appreciate cultural differences runs counter to human nature. Human nature seems to lead people to associate with others who resemble themselves (the "in-group") and to denigrate others ("out-groups"). This practice was perhaps less destructive in earlier eras, when intercultural contacts were far less numerous than they are today, and when the consequences of disharmony were less life threatening.

Bennett maintains that the unique human characteristic of consciousness enables people to examine their own feelings and thoughts, and to change their feelings, thoughts, and actions should they decide there is reason to do so. People interested in the field of intercultural communication generally believe there is reason to do so, given the growing incidence of intercultural encounters and the likelihood that such encounters will become even more common in the coming years.

Not only are foreign students no longer oddities, for example, but they are often essential contributors to the teaching and research that take place on American campuses. They are here to stay. We have little choice other than to learn to get along.

How can we learn to get along? Awareness is a starting point. Knowledge, attitudes, and skills, as many authors point out, also have a role. This essay concentrates on the knowledge component, offering information and ideas that might contribute to a more refined understanding of the intercultural interactions that take place on American (and, in concept, other) campuses. It is on college and university campuses, after all, that one is most justified in expecting human consciousness to be constructively employed and developed.

The approach to this refined understanding of intercultural interactions has two aspects. One is a framework for comparing cultures, drawing heavily on some unpublished work of Robert Kohls. The other is an analysis of various campus settings in which intercultural interactions occur. Those settings include public places, residences (both residence halls for single students and housing for families), offices, the health service, extracurricular activities, and social activities. Two other campus settings where intercultural actions occur, the classroom and the counseling center, are discussed in Chapters 4 and 5, respectively.

A Framework for Comparing Cultures

Kohls suggests the metaphor of an iceberg to represent the degree to which cultural differences are matters of conscious awareness. The iceberg looks like this:

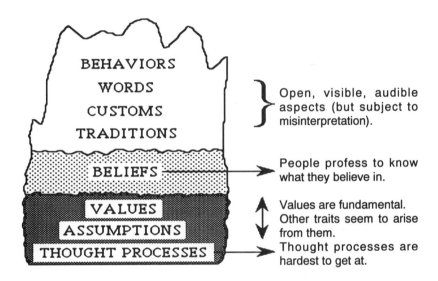

BEHAVIORS
WORDS
CUSTOMS
TRADITIONS

} Open, visible, audible aspects (but subject to misinterpretation).

BELIEFS → People profess to know what they believe in.

VALUES
ASSUMPTIONS ↕ Values are fundamental. Other traits seem to arise from them.
THOUGHT PROCESSES → Thought processes are hardest to get at.

People's words, actions, and customs (which are patterns of actions) are visible, above the waterline. We might misinterpret what other people say and do, Kohls says, but we can hear or see their actual behaviors. Describing customs was long a staple of anthropological study.

A good example of words that are commonly misinterpreted on campuses are those constituting—to Americans—a polite "no." A foreign student might ask a clerk in the bursar's office for a delay in making a tuition payment. The reply might be something like, "I'm sorry, but our policies don't allow that." Or, "I wish we could help you, but we don't have a way to do that." To most Americans either of these replies will mean "No," but to people from many other places they are likely to mean, "We don't usually do that, but I'm open to negotiation." Since Americans are often not so good at negotiating, they feel uncomfortable, and probably annoyed, at the interaction that ensues. Their plain English words have been misinterpreted. For elaboration on the topic this example raises, see Virginia Gross's and my article, "Saying 'No' to Foreign Students" (1984).

Just below the waterline on Kohls's iceberg, perhaps murky but still discernible, are people's values. Kohls asserts that most people know what their values are. They might not often have reason to think about their values and compare them with those of others who are culturally different, but they know, for example, to what degree they are individualists, how much of an action orientation they have, and so on.

Anthropologists Florence Kluckhohn's and Fred Strodtbeck's (1961) framework for comparing value systems was a key building block in the budding field of intercultural communication. Popularized in such publications as Edward Stewart's *American Cultural Patterns: A Cross-Cultural Perspective* (published in 1991 in a second edition written by Edward Stewart and Milton Bennett) and John Condon and Fathi Yousef's *An Introduction to Intercultural Communication* (1975), the Kluckhohn-Strodtbeck framework has found its way into countless books and essays about cultural differences. The framework uses five dimensions for comparing cultures:

- Nature of man
- Form of relations with others
- Form of activity
- Relationship to nature
- Relationship to time.

More recently, the framework Geert Hofstede presents in *Culture's Consequences* (1984) has found much favor among students of intercultural relations. Hofstede's individualism-collectivism dimension has served as the intellectual construct for numerous articles. His other dimensions of cultural difference include uncertainty-avoidance (which some scholars consider comparable to Edward Hall's often-cited high-context, low-context dimension), masculinity-femininity, and power distance.

Further below the waterline on Kohls's iceberg, beneath values, are assumptions. Kohls estimates that approximately 1,000 implicit assumptions underlie a national culture, assumptions on such topics as marriage, employment, religion, sex, negotiation, problem-solving, and so on. "Nobody tells you [as you grow up] they are only assumptions," Kohls (1987) says. "They tell you they are the way the world really works. Some people freak out when they learn that they are only assumptions."

Thorough understanding of an intercultural situation probably requires elucidating the assumptions participants bring to it. The bulk of this essay is devoted to making explicit some of the assumptions various participants are likely to bring to each of several campus settings.

Finally, beneath the assumptions on the iceberg, are thought processes. These are the most difficult aspects of human behavior to discern and describe, Kohls says. In *American Cultural Patterns*, Stewart and Bennett attempt to describe certain aspects of typical American thought patterns, including the conception of "facts" and the premium on analytical thinking. In both of these areas, and in others Stewart and Bennett discuss, disharmony is likely to arise during intercultural interactions on campuses.

Stewart and Bennett say this about "the American view of facts:"

> First, facts possess perceptual content; they are empirical, observable, and measurable. Second, facts are reliable so that different observers will agree about them. Third, facts are objective and therefore valid. They are impersonal and exist separately from perceptual processes and from observers. In American thinking, facts exist in the external world and not inside the mind. Fourth, both the reliability and validity of facts are associated with measurements using coordinates of time and space, leading Americans to speak of "historical" but not "future" facts. (1991, 31-32)

And, of course, it is the facts that truly matter. People's feelings and personal opinions are considered separate from "facts" and are supposed to be "kept out" of the business-oriented conversations that take place in many campus settings. Americans generally become impatient and bewildered when foreign students "bring in all this irrelevant stuff" while talking, not confining themselves to the "facts."

Americans, perhaps especially on campuses and certainly in most classrooms, prize "analytical" thought. "Analysis," Stewart and Bennett explain,

> dissects events and concepts into the pieces which can be linked in causal chains and categorized into universal criteria. This kind of thinking stands in contrast to a more integrated approach, sometimes called "holistic" or "synthetic" . . . . In comparison to American thought, many other cultures such as Japanese, Chinese, and Brazilian are more synthetic than analytical in thinking style. (1991, 41)

Indeed, one very frequently hears American faculty members complain that foreign students "just don't know how to analyze." They might even say that foreign students "don't think straight." What is at issue is not some inferiority on the foreign students' part, but deeply ingrained assumptions about how one is supposed to think. Learning to think analytically when one has been taught to think holistically is a slow process.

These differences in thought processes will manifest themselves in each of the campus settings discussed below, when foreign students and Americans come together in them. So intercultural interactions in these settings are likely to be complicated not just by the assumptions people bring to the settings, but by the way they think in general. That should be kept in mind as we consider the varying assumptions people from different cultures bring to various campus settings.

Campus Settings for Intercultural Contact

The following sections describe some of the assumptions that people from different cultures bring to common campus settings. American assumptions are described and then placed in the context of a foreign student's campus experiences.

Public Places. Americans generally consider it appropriate to make eye contact with, smile at, say "Hi" to, and even trade small talk with perfect strangers they encounter on a sidewalk, in line at the bookstore or registrar's office, or waiting for a lecture to begin. The stranger's age, gender, and apparent social standing do not require or preclude any particular behavior.

Not so in many other countries. As Kurumi Yamazaki learned in her unpublished study of interactions among family housing residents at the University of Iowa, there are differing cultural assumptions on all these points. Koreans, Japanese, and Chinese will generally not make eye contact with people they do not already know, Yamazaki found. Indeed, "gazing" at others is deemed rude. People from Moslem cultures might make eye contact with strangers of the same sex, and might even enter conversation with them, but they would not do so with members of the opposite sex.

Americans generally make some additional assumptions about proper behavior in public places that are not universally shared. Among them:

- People should be able to walk or stand in public places without having physical contact with strangers. Americans walk on the right side, allow departing passengers (from an elevator or bus, for example) to get off before boarding themselves, stand in orderly lines, and otherwise try to make sure physical contact with strangers is avoided. In a crowded place, where contact is inevitable, they will stand erectly, trying to confine the contact to the outer parts of their arms.

- When they settle themselves in a public place, such as a bench outside the student union or a study table in the library, Americans assume they have staked out a territory that others should enter only by invitation. In a campus bus, entering passengers are not expected to share an already occupied seat unless no empty seats are available.

- People in public places should keep the level of noise they make (by talking and playing music, mainly) below a certain level. (That level seems higher for many black Americans than for white ones.)

As Brislin and his colleagues pointed out in the lengthy passage quoted earlier, differences of these kinds are likely to result in prejudice, stereotypes, and discrimination.

Residences. Foreign students on American campuses may find themselves in the role of roommate or neighbor with Americans. Common American assumptions concerning roommates would probably include these:

- There is an imaginary line down the middle of the room, separating one person's territory from the other's.
- Roommates should respect each other's privacy, meaning they should not read each other's mail, listen in on each other's telephone conversations, or ask (unless invited to do so) about "personal" topics such as family history; current relationships; personal finances; ideas or behavior regarding religion, politics, or sex; and personal or family psychological problems.
- One person is not supposed to use the other's possessions without permission.
- Required burdens such as cleaning and paying bills should be shared evenly.
- One person should be quiet and dim the lights when the other wishes to sleep.
- Roommates should be sure to convey messages about telephone calls or visitors that come in the other person's absence.
- At least some attention should be paid to each other's standards of cleanliness and personal modesty.
- A wide range of idiosyncratic behavior should be tolerated.
- No conversation beyond polite greetings is required.
- Complaints or personal preferences should be expressed directly and openly.

Some common American assumptions about neighbors are already stated or implied in the earlier discussion about public places. This is a complicated topic, though, because of the striking regional variations surrounding the concept of "neighbor." People from New York City, Savannah (Georgia), and Boseman (Montana) are likely to have noticeably different assumptions on this topic. So, rather than trying to generalize about those assumptions, we will simply list specific questions that assumptions about proper neighbor behavior will address:

- Should neighbors expect to interact with each other simply because they are neighbors?
- If so, who should initiate the interaction—the new neighbor, the old neighbor, or a third party?
- How much consideration (in terms of such matters as noise levels, odors, and cleanliness) is owed to neighbors?
- How much help can neighbors legitimately expect from each other, simply because they are neighbors (for example, loaning a grocery item or a tool, helping move some heavy furniture, or "keeping an eye on the place" while a neighbor is away)?

- What role, if any, do neighbors have in safeguarding or disciplining each other's children?

Offices. When a college or university hosts foreign students or scholars, many intercultural interactions will take place in administrative offices—the registrar's office, the bursar's office, the housing office, the payroll and personnel offices, the offices of academic departments, and so on. Americans who work in such offices are likely to make a number of assumptions their foreign clients may not share. Among them:

- The institution's rules, procedures, and requirements are reasonably related to the achievement of its purposes (which themselves are clearly legitimate), and are generally fair, logical, and reasonable.
- The people who work in campus offices are generally hired because they have the qualifications required to do the job, and they are promoted because they have demonstrated their competence. Ability, not age, gender, or personal contacts, is the key factor in getting and keeping a job. Relatively young people, and people of either gender, might hold positions of considerable responsibility and authority.
- A staff member's essential purposes in having a job are (1) to carry out the tasks in the job description (so the institution can carry out its larger responsibilities), and (2) to earn an income.
- Clients can expect fair and reasonable treatment as long as they (1) behave politely (by local standards), (2) follow standard procedures (which may involve filling out certain forms), and (3) tell the truth. (There *is* a truth.) Furthermore, clients should speak for themselves, and not allow husbands, older siblings, or friends to speak for them.
- Clients should realize that important information and instructions—deadlines, rules, policies, procedures—are written down in appropriate institutional publications or on appropriate forms, and clients should be familiar with that printed material.
- In making their decisions, staff members will match the facts of the client's situation with the appropriate written guidelines or standards, and will reach a fair, objective decision (that is, one not contaminated by considerations of "personality," "emotions," or "personal preference").

Again, any or all of these assumptions may differ from the assumptions the foreign client brings to the situation. Negative feelings and judgments are likely to arise when, for example, a foreign student does not take a female staff member seriously, or seems to be "playing with the truth" by telling varying versions of his story, or persists in making a request that has been denied after normal procedures have been followed. See my article about assumptions administrators make for additional thoughts on this topic (1992).

Workplaces. Foreign students have jobs in many places on campuses. They work in the food service, the library, the physical plant, and so on. Or, as graduate students, they are members of a "team" or "group" in a scientific laboratory. Wherever they work, they encounter behavior based on certain assumptions they may not share. And, again, the natives may not be aware of their own assumptions related to work and the workplace. Violations of the unspoken and unrecognized assumptions create dissatisfaction on both sides.

The situation is even more complex when several different cultures are represented at the workplace. Supervisors in multicultural workplaces, whether they are Ph.D. scientists or heads of groundskeeping crews, will want to become mindful of their own assumptions about work and the workplace, and, probably, seek to teach them to their supervisees. At the same time, in the interest of harmony, they may want to learn about their supervisee's assumptions, if not to adopt them, at least to understand what underlies the supervisees' perceptions and behavior.

American supervisors assume that a "good" employee is one who does the following things:

- Arrives at work on time, or, if lateness is unavoidable, gives a timely notice about the anticipated lateness
- Follows instructions, and asks for clarification whenever instructions are unclear
- Considers it more important to "get the job done" than to develop and maintain social relationships with co-workers or clients
- Takes the initiative to do related work that clearly needs to be done, and to make suggestions that might lead to improvement in the operation
- Treats co-workers and clients respectfully, whatever their social status and gender
- Behaves rather informally, "chatting" in a "friendly" way with colleagues, and perhaps (depending on the situation) with the clients too.
- Works at least as hard as the other workers do

For further thoughts on this topic, see my *Manual for Foreign Scholars* (1993).

Health Service. A visit to a student health center, like a visit to nearly any doctor's office in the United States, results in a set of experiences based on typical American assumptions about the definition, causes, and cures of sickness, and about the delivery of health care. Here are some of those assumptions:

- Except for maladies caused by genetic factors, accidents, or aging, people can be free of sickness. Sicknesses can usually be cured. If they cannot be cured, it is because scientists have not yet isolated a cause and developed a cure. (They will inevitably do so, though, given enough time and resources.)
- Nearly all sicknesses have physical, material causes that, at least in principle, can be detected through proper testing and measurements.
- The human body is a collection of physical parts and systems, any of which can, at least in principle, be repaired through proper medication or physical rearranging (as through surgery, exercise, or limitations on mobility). Treatment properly focuses on the affected body part, not on the entire physical organism, and not on the spiritual or psychological aspects of a patient's life.
- Diagnosing a medical problem is largely a matter of getting measurements of various factors, including body temperature, blood pressure, composition of the blood, composition of the urine, rates at which various bodily functions are occurring, and the duration and severity of symptoms.
- Patients are expected to provide doctors with detailed information about their medical problems—location and nature of symptoms, patterns in the manifestation of symptoms ("Does it hurt more at night or during the day?"), and remedies that have been attempted. Furthermore, patients are expected to participate in at least some decisions about their treatment. ("This medicine would probably help, but it can cause dizziness and shortness of breath. Do you want to try it?")
- Doctors of either gender may care for patients of either gender.
- Nurses can take notes of routine information, carry out basic diagnostic procedures such as measuring body temperature and collecting blood samples, and give routine vaccinations, but only doctors can give authoritative advice on diagnosis and treatment.
- Should students be hospitalized, they will find themselves in the care of doctors, nurses, and various aides. Their families and friends will be allowed to visit, often only during specified hours, but are not expected to participate in the patient's care.

Beneath these fairly specific assumptions about the workings of the human body and the role of health-care professionals in treating patients lie general assumptions about the health care system. Charles Leslie (1980, 191) writes that most Western-educated health-care professionals conceive of the medical system as

based on a single, historically recent system: a bureaucratically ordered set of schools, hospitals, clinics, professional associations, companies and regulatory agencies that train practitioners and maintain facilities to conduct biomedical research, to prevent or cure illness and to care for or rehabilitate the chronically ill. From this perspective, other forms of health care are outside the medical system and they are usually ignored. When they are not ignored they are derogated as curiosities, or as fringe medicine, quackery and superstition.

Thus, student health centers are not likely to offer care based on the assumptions and methods of homeopathic medicine, massage, chiropractic, reflexology, osteopathy, shamanism, or faith healing. (See Andrew Weil's [1988] *Health and Healing* for introductions to each of these alternatives to traditional Western medicine.) Nor are they likely to give credence to the notion of *qi*, the "energy" that traditional Chinese medicine (and related approaches) assumes to be responsible for much of human health and illness, and that is manipulated through methods such as acupuncture, acupressure, herbal remedies, and diet. Since a large portion of the foreign students and scholars on American and other Western campuses come from parts of the world where medical beliefs incompatible with those of Western medicine are salient if not prevalent, intercultural difficulties in the student health service seem unavoidable.

Extracurricular Activities. American campuses afford a wide range of "student activities" or "extracurricular activities" for their students. Student activities are usually discussed in terms of clubs or organizations or of campus-wide "events" such as homecoming.

Foreign-student participation in student activities is often at a lower level than campus officials would like it to be. While there are no doubt many explanations for this—including unrealistic expectations on the officials' parts—one explanation is likely to be, once again, divergent assumptions about the desirable format and goals for student organizations and activities.

A student organization is usually conceived of as a group of people organized around a common interest, and having a constitution, by-laws, elected leaders, and a non-political, non-religious purpose. Indeed, achieving official institutional "recognition," and thus access to funding and institutional facilities, usually requires these things.

A "good" student organization is one that plans and executes a reasonable number of "activities" or "events" that are carefully planned, well-publicized, well-executed, well-attended, and then evaluated. The good organization has an appropriate number of well-run meetings, meaning that there is an agenda for the meeting, discussion—always temperate—is conducted according to Robert's Rules of Order, decisions are made by voting ("the majority rules"), and minutes are kept and distributed promptly afterwards. A well-run meeting begins at the scheduled starting time and is not "too long."

My article, "The Intercultural Meeting," catalogues cultural variations on many of these points, and seeks to explain why a meeting composed of people from different cultures is likely to be long and fruitless(1981).

A student organization is deemed to provide students with "leadership opportunities" they can list in their resumes. "Leadership skills" including commanding members' attention and respect, organizing tasks, delegating work, following up on delegated assignments, keeping good records, and conducting "good meetings." A "good student leader" is attractive (according to contemporary, local standards), self-confident, articulate in front of a group, fair, relatively unemotional, and well organized (in the sense of being able to keep track of things and to approach topics or tasks in a systematic manner). Student-activities offices are responsible for fostering good student leaders, good student organizations, and good events.

As my colleague Tim McMahon and I discovered in our informal study of "Leadership Styles in Foreign and Minority Student Organizations" on our campus, many of these assumptions do not suit organizations whose members are not exclusively or mainly Caucasian Americans. Here are some statements from foreign and non-white American student leaders we interviewed:

- "We [in our organization] never vote. We talk until we reach consensus. If we don't reach consensus, we don't decide."
- "Feelings are much more important than doing any one thing."
- "If a topic is controversial and people are likely to turn away if we address it, we just ignore it."
- "Starting a meeting on time is not at all important to us."
- "The discussions [in student-government meetings] seem so insincere and lifeless."
- "It is important that our leaders be able to bridge the gap between our members and people in the majority community."
- "Our president could not be a woman. Our religion does not allow it."
- "Our leaders take their jobs out of a sense of duty. They usually don't want to do it. They are not trying to 'build a resume.'"
- "[As the organization's president,] I've been asked to help couples who were having marital problems, students in financial difficulty, and people needing a place to live."
- "Our organization owns a set of tools for working on cars. The tools are kept at my apartment."
- "Our meetings are at someone's apartment, never in the student union."
- "We meet once a week. The main thing we do is discuss and analyze the news from home, so members can talk about it intelli-

gently with Americans. We want Americans to understand our point of view."

- "The most important qualification of a leader is having good interpersonal relationships with a lot of people."
- "The most important qualification of a leader is to be able to get along with people of all the races from our country."
- "The most important qualification of a leader is having the proper orientation about the political situation in our country."

These statements make clear that the assumptions Americans typically make about student activities do not always fit foreign- or minority-student organizations. The latter often have purposes, leadership requirements and responsibilities, and means of operating that are quite different from the ones Americans consider effective or "natural."

Social Activities. A Russian student, talking about her first party with American students, said, "They sat on the floor, and ate potato chips. The music was so loud I could hardly hear anyone talk." This may sound perfectly normal to anyone familiar with American undergraduate social gatherings, but it clearly seemed odd to the Russian. Like virtually everything else people do, social activities are rooted in certain assumptions. Behavior at American receptions and parties will differ noticeably, depending on the setting and the age and social standing of those present, but, in general, the following assumptions underlie what takes place:

- The purposes of a reception are to meet new people, chat with current acquaintances, "be seen" at an appropriate place, and/or share in recognizing or honoring a particular person or group. The principal purpose of a party is to have "fun." Fun is likely to entail some loosening of normal inhibitions, relatively informal conversation with friends or acquaintances, listening to music, eating something desirable, drinking something likely to contain alcohol, perhaps flirting with potential romantic partners, and getting one's daily responsibilities out of one's mind.
- Members of both genders can attend the same social gathering, and can interact with each other.
- People of various social standings can attend the same social gathering and can interact with each other.
- People can approach and initiate conversations with strangers of either gender or any social standing.
- The host or hostess is expected to provide the venue for the gathering and at least a minimal quantity and variety of food and beverage. A host or hostess is not expected to provide a lavish setting or lavish food and drink, although doing so is quite acceptable. Guests may be expected to furnish part of the food and drink.

- Attendees have a fairly wide latitude of behaviors open to them. One can expect to see variety in dress, formality of behavior, consumption of foods and alcohol (and, in some settings, drugs), conversation topics and degree of participation in conversations, and responses to the music, if music is being played.

My article, "Teaching Foreign Students How to Party" (1990), elaborates on these and related ideas, and indicates that students who do not share these assumptions are not likely to have the skills (such as initiating a conversation with a stranger of the opposite sex) that are needed to avoid seeming "shy" or "out of it" in an American social situation.

Conclusion

Understanding the fact that people bring unspoken, culturally-based assumptions into every situation they enter, and being aware of what those assumptions are, can help people interact more constructively with others who are culturally different. This chapter has sought to portray assumptions that underlie interactions in several campus settings. Observant readers will be able to infer additional assumptions in these situations, and make their own lists of assumptions that seem to underlie situations not discussed here.

References

Althen, Gary. 1988. *American Ways.* Yarmouth, ME: Intercultural Press.

_____. 1992. "The American Educational Administrator: Examining Some Assumptions." *NAFSA Newsletter* 43, 4: 1.

_____. 1981. "The Intercultural Meeting," *NAFSA Newsletter* 33, 2: 34ff. Reprinted in *The Handbook of Foreign Student Advising.* Yarmouth, ME: Intercultural Press, 1983.

_____. 1993. *Manual for Foreign Scholars.* Iowa City: Office of International Education and Services, University of Iowa.

_____. 1989. "Teaching Foreign Students How to Party." *NAFSA Newsletter* 40, 7: 11ff.

Althen, Gary, and Virginia Gross. 1984."Saying 'No' to Foreign Students." *NAFSA Newsletter* 36, 1: 1.

Barnlund, Dean C. 1975. *Public and Private Self in Japan and the United States.* Tokyo: Simul Press.

_____ 1989. *Communicative Styles of Japanese and Americans.* Belmont, CA: Wadsworth.

Bennett, Milton J. 1986. "Towards Ethnorelativism: A Developmental Model of Intercultural Sensitivity." In *Cross-Cultural Orientational: New Conceptualizations and Applications.* Ed. R. Michael Paige, 27-69. Lanham, MD: University Press of America.

Bernstein, Albert J., and Sydney Croft Rozen. 1989. *Dinosaur Brains.* New York: Ballantine Books.

Brislin, Richard. Ed. 1990. *Applied Cross-Cultural Psychology*. Newbury Park, CA: Sage.

Brislin, Richard, et al. 1986. *Intercultural Interactions: A Practical Guide*. Beverly Hills: Sage.

Condon, John C., and Yousef Fathi. 1975. *An Introduction to Intercultural Communication*. Indianapolis: Bobbs-Merrill.

Hall, Edward T. 1959. *The Silent Language*. Garden City, NY: Doubleday.

Hofstede, Geert. 1984. *Culture's Consequences*. Beverly Hills: Sage.

_____.1991 *Cultures and Organizations: Software of the Mind*. London: McGraw-Hill.

Ilola, Lisa Marie. 1990. "Culture and Health." In *Applied Cross-Cultural Psychology*. Ed. Richard Brislin, 278-301. Newbury Park, CA: Sage.

Kluckhohn, Florence, and Fred L. Strodtbeck. 1961. *Variations in Value Orientation*. New York: Row, Peterson.

Kohls, L. Robert. 1987. "Understanding Americans." Paper presented at NAFSA's 39th Annual National Conference, Long Beach, CA.

Leslie, Charles. 1980. "Medical Pluralism in World Perspective." In *Social Science and Medicine* 14B: 191-195.

Stewart, Edward C., and Milton J. Bennett. 1991. *American Cultural Patterns: A Cross-Cultural Perspective*. Rev. ed. Yarmouth, ME: Intercultural Press.

Tripp-Reimer, Toni. 1984. "Reconceptualizing the Construct of Health: Integrating Emic and Etic Perspectives." In *Research in Nursing and Health* 7: 101-109.

Yamazaki, Kurumi. n.d. "How to Communicate in Hawkeye Court: Wives of International Students." University of Iowa, Unpublished manuscript.

4

Managing a Multicultural Classroom

Carol Archer

Successful ESL teachers should themselves develop an intercultural perspective by taking care to learn as much about other cultures as possible. They should free themselves from ethnocentrism, prejudice and the tendency to stereotype, develop sensitivity to the culturemes of other cultures and learn to accept them as equal though different. They should believe in the fundamental anthropological truth that no culture is necessarily superior, eschew any kind of cultural value judgement, and evolve teaching strategies, methods and techniques that presume, ensure and reinforce equal status contact. The ESL teachers should envision their roles as mediators and ambassadors of culture and not as purveyors or disseminators, and never as imposers. (Nayar 1986, 13)

Introduction

This rather daunting description of a successful ESL (English as a second language) teacher presents the requirements for an idealized international educator. And, although Nayar is speaking to the ESL professional, his description could pertain to any teacher who has students from more than one culture or even to non-teaching professionals working with international students. While most of the men and women who are drawn to work with international students would agree wholeheartedly with Nayar's description and are more than willing to try to meet the guidelines he sets out, the process of achieving the state he describes is both complex and ill defined.

However, if we break down his requirements, we find that they fall into several categories and become easier to understand and perhaps to implement. The first requirement is simply for the teacher to learn about other cultures. Nayar's other requirements are more subtle and, perhaps, unattainable as stated. However, freeing oneself "from ethnocentrism, prejudice and the tendency to stereotype and developing sensitivity to the culturemes of other cultures" is a realistic, continuing goal for the international educator. Implicit within this goal are several processes that provide the foundation for developing the attitudes and skills Nayar calls for. Before dealing with each of these areas in more detail, it would be beneficial to examine the type of individual who enters this field.

The International Educator Personality

Most international education practitioners share certain characteristics, including a love of their own language and a fascination with other languages. Most are bilingual or polyglots and possess both a deep interest in culture—especially of cultural differences—and a curiosity that drives them to learn as much about these subjects as possible. But above all, international educators are people-oriented. They genuinely like being with people and have a deep appreciation for people different from themselves. In fact, many hope to facilitate better communication and understanding among the different peoples of the world. Therefore, it can be surmised that they enter the field with high and positive aspirations about their students and about themselves. In short, we encounter in the practitioner an individual who is not only willing to make the effort required to meet Nayar's guidelines, but who also most likely possesses certain natural abilities in these areas.

Yet, after a period of time in the field, one of the less positive characteristics of these same individuals is to " 'burn out,' when class after class becomes a battle of wills. Stereotypes may be maintained or strengthened by personal contact, rather than modified. New stereotypes and negative expectations for the future may become crippling self-fulfilling prophecies." (Fitch 1986, 52) To explain the discrepancy between these two sets of characteristics, positive and negative, we need to look no farther than the classroom itself, with its numerous cultural differences. The interesting cultural differences may become clichés as the semesters roll by. For the same cultural differences that attracted international educators to their profession may erode the development of their intercultural perspective. On the surface, managing a multicultural classroom can be somewhat like a marriage between individuals of opposite temperaments: the very characteristics that first attract one become, in time, the most irritating. This chapter examines some specific characteristics of cultural differences and presents some thoughts on dealing with them. The aim is not to alleviate the differences but to build on them in order to enhance the educational possibilities inherent in a multicultural classroom.

Two Approaches to Cultural Differences

Maximizing the opportunities inherent in a multicultural classroom requires the teacher to approach students' cultural differences in two ways—from a content-based perspective and from a process orientation. The content-based approach necessitates learning as much as possible about the students' cultures, as well as about American culture, and becoming familiar with the sojourner adjustment cycle. While the first approach focuses on knowledge acquisition, the second approach requires that teachers develop ways of consistently improving their own skills in intercultural communication. This approach is process-oriented, with an emphasis on developing conscious strategies for interpreting cultural differences. These two approaches to cultural differences are essential in developing teaching methodologies that maximize the potential good of the multicultural classroom. Furthermore, they provide professional educators with a structured approach to cultural differences that builds on their initial enthusiasm and natural abilities. Together, they allow these individuals to amplify their interest in and deepen their commitment to international education. Needless to say, their consistent use also greatly lessens the likelihood of burnout.

Content-Based Approaches

One approach to cultural differences encourages the teacher or international educator to study various cultures. This content-based approach actually includes three subject areas. The most familiar and obvious area is that of learning about the cultures of the various students in the class. Less obvious is the need for teachers to become cognizant of their own culture. Thirdly, teachers should become familiar with the cultural adjustment process of foreign students.

Cultural Adjustment Cycle. Teachers seeking to sensitize themselves to the cultural adjustment cycle find a great deal of information available on this subject, including Peter Adler's "Culture Shock and the Cross-Cultural Learning Experience," Furnham and Bochner's *Culture Shock*, Cornelius Grove and Ingemar Torbiörn's "A New Conceptualization of the Intercultural Adjustment Process and the Goals of Training," Young Y. Kim's *Communication and Cross-Cultural Adaptation: An Integrative Theory*, Mara B. Adelman's "Cross-Cultural Adjustment: A Theoretical Perspective on Social Support," Wendy Searle and Colleen Ward's "The Prediction of Psychological and Sociocultural Adjustment During Cross-Cultural Transitions," and Tom Lewis and Robert Jungman's collection of short stories, *On Being Foreign: Culture Shock in Short Fiction—An International Anthology*. Chapters 1 and 5 in this book elaborate on the cultural adjustment cycle.

While there are different opinions on the distinctions among the various stages in the cultural adjustment cycle, there is general agreement that foreign students experience emotional and physical "peaks and valleys" over an extended period of time. Some students experience few adjustment difficulties, whereas others may become "hostile and resistant and/or catatonic." (Nayar 1986) Naturally, these stressful periods inhibit learning. For example, many students experience a lack of energy or an inability to concentrate, especially in the afternoon. Teachers need to adjust their materials and methods to accommodate this temporary reduction in the students' academic capacity (Reitzel, 1986).

In addition to helping teachers plan their classes, knowledge of the adjustment cycle can help teachers directly assist their international students. Most are not consciously aware of their own adjustment process and experience great relief at understanding their own reactions. Two books that have specific units on teaching the cultural adjustment cycle to international students are *Beyond Language*, by Deena Levine and Mara Adelman, and my own *Living with Strangers in the USA*. Robert Kohls's *Survival Kit for Overseas Living* offers comparable insights for Americans going overseas.

By being aware of the adjustment process, teachers can not only help their students "overcome the debilitating effects of culture shock" (Nayar 1986), but can actually use the information to teach language skills, foster better relationships among members of the class, and sensitize themselves to the difficulties their students may be encountering. This awareness, along with information about the cultures of the various students in their classes, will enable teachers to better take the role of cultural mediator and ambassador.

Culture-Specific Information. Teachers can draw upon a wealth of reference material on the individual cultures of their students, as well as on general and specific aspects of American culture.

Other Cultures. To learn about the cultures of the various students in their classes, teachers can choose from books that focus on specific cultural values and behaviors or from books of fiction or history and politics. Some works combine information from all of these areas. Examples include Gary Althen's *Students from the Arab World and Iran*; Abdulaziz Kamal and Geoffrey Maruyama's "Cross-Cultural Contact and Attitudes of Qatari Students in the United States"; Diane Hoffman's "Beyond Conflict: Culture, Self, and Intercultural Learning Among Iranians in the U.S."; and the U.S. Government Printing Office's country studies on almost every country in the world. Other books include John Condon's *With Respect to The Japanese: A Guide for Americans*; Barbara Finkelstein, Joseph J. Tobin, and Anne E. Imamura's *Transcending Stereotypes: Discovering Japanese Culture and Education*; and Dean Barnlund's *Communicative Styles of Japanese and Americans: Images and Realities*. Boye De Mente's *Korean Etiquette and Ethics in Business* and

Paul Leppert's *Doing Business with the Koreans: A Handbook for Executives* are both useful for educators because they focus on Korean culture. Hu Wenzhong and Cornelius L. Grove's *Encountering the Chinese: A Guide for Americans*, Francis L.K. Hsu's *Americans and Chinese: Passages to Differences*, and Robert A. Kapp's *Communicating with China* are but three of the many resources on Chinese culture. A different kind of treatment of Chinese culture is found in Mark Salzman's *Iron and Silk. A Common Core: Thais and Americans*, written by John Paul Fieg and revised by Elizabeth Mortlock, examines Thai culture, and Theodore Gochenour's *Considering Filipinos* looks at Filipino culture. Many of the books mentioned here contain lists of additional resources for international educators.

Other useful references focus on specific cultural patterns, as do Robert Kaplan's "Cultural Thought Patterns in Intercultural Education" and Carl Becker's "Reasons for the Lack of Argumentation and Debate in the Far East." Many fictional works from other countries are available in English translation. One such book is Gabriel Garcia Marquez's *One Hundred Years of Solitude*, which can help teachers understand a Latin perspective. Other works of fiction, such as James Clavell's *Shogun*, are written in English but give the reader a unique insight into another cultural mindset.

American Culture. While a wealth of information on American culture exists, an extremely valuable source is Edward Stewart and Milton Bennett's *American Cultural Patterns: A Cross Cultural Perspective*. A less theoretical approach, accessible to advanced ESL students as well as to teachers, is Gary Althen's *American Ways*. James Robertson's *American Myth: American Reality* treats American culture from the perspective of a collective mythology. Edward Hall's *Beyond Culture*, with an analysis of high-context and low-context cultures, and his *The Hidden Dimension*, with a classic comparative work on cultural proxemics, are other sources for American and comparative cultural information.

Various models that contrast American culture with other cultures offer another method for understanding American culture. One of the first such "Contrast/American" models is Hoopes and Ventura's (1979) list of cultural values that focuses on the distinctions between an individualistically oriented society and a group-oriented society. It laid the groundwork for later models that focus exclusively on education. One of the most useful of these educational contrast models is Furey's (1986) comparison of individualism and group orientation and their effects on such classroom behaviors as sharing and privacy. She shows that the American attitude toward the use of time underlies our assumption that a certain amount of work should be accomplished within a certain period of time. She also shows that the American attitude toward education in general is the basis for our preference for practical education and credentials. Her comparative look at student and teacher roles shows how these roles affect the rules of deference and formality between student and teacher as well as student and teacher assumptions about teacher authority. The degree to which a culture conditions people to focus on the individual or on the group also influences whether a student expects a teacher to be a scholar, a counselor, and/or a personal tutor. Furey's comparison of the relative emphasis placed on inductive and deductive learning, discovery and receptive learning, rote learning, problem solving, creative thinking, and critical evaluation are invaluable for the teacher who is attempting to meet the needs of a culturally diverse class. Those who are planning and implementing curricula will appreciate her cross-cultural comparisons of teacher-student interaction patterns, emphasis on group work versus individual work, lectures, note taking, volunteering, peer teaching, presentations, individualized instruction, report making, appropriate topics for discussion, self-disclosure in the classroom, turn taking, proxemic patterns, kinesic patterns, and paralinguistic patterns. Furey shows that American assumptions differ significantly from other cultures' assumptions in all of these areas.

Geert Hofstede (1986) presents a different formulation of these and related ideas. His perspective derives from his large-scale research on cultural differences in multinational organizations.

Once teachers have gathered information about their students' cultures, their own culture, and cultural adjustment theories, they face the task of interpreting this information and applying it in the day-to-day management of their multicultural classrooms. Unfortunately, there is very little in the literature to guide educators in this task. The tools needed for interpretation and application of the knowledge are very limited. Educators are given little instruction in the skills they need to develop and even less in how to develop them. However, we can surmise that this stage of development requires a more process-oriented than content-oriented approach.

Process-oriented Approach

A process-oriented approach to cultural differences allows the teacher to accurately interpret and apply culture-specific knowledge. The goal of the process-oriented approach is to provide a structure for developing an awareness of oneself as a cultural being. A personal intercultural perspective arises from that awareness. One aspect of developing this awareness is learning about American "overt" culture at a cognitive level. A more subtle aspect is developing a cognitive knowledge of American "covert" culture. Part of the process of acquiring cognitive knowledge of "covert" culture entails accepting ourselves—at an affective level—as "a product of our society and realizing that . . . our . . . particular style of communication is a reflection of . . . our . . . cultural background" (Wubbels and Levy 1991, 4). It is not easy to become aware of ourselves at this more subtle, intersubjective level. In fact, Hall (1969, 7) writes of this "covert" culture:

Paradoxically, the only way that we can escape the hidden constraints of covert culture is to involve ourselves actively and consciously in the very parts of life that we take most for granted.

Before looking at a specific method for classroom management, it would be useful to understand more about covert culture and its importance in a multicultural classroom.

Covert Culture and Its Importance. Covert culture is synonymous with the intersubjective world. Our intersubjective world is composed of small subjective, implicit, tacit rules—for example, the rule for making eye contact when attempting to change lanes on a slow freeway—in short, "the very parts of life that we take for granted." Our intersubjective world or our covert culture is composed of the myriad of implicit rules that regulate our everyday lives. Regarding implicit and explicit information, Stoddard (1986, 123) says, "Members of every cultural group share a common knowledge based on the defining characteristics of the community. If a member of a particular group, in speaking or writing which is addressed to fellow members, makes this information explicit, it is redundant. To avoid this redundancy, the information is made implicit or simply taken for granted."

Unfortunately, we frequently cannot distinguish which rules are implicit. Too often, even with a great deal of overt knowledge of other cultures, we take for granted that "everyone" knows essentially the same rules. We know there are cultural differences, but we assume that many things, such as the rules that govern changing lanes on a slow freeway, are universal. Therefore, these mostly unconscious rules are potentially the cause of misunderstandings. The best-intentioned teachers have certain expectations of their students and of themselves. These are not the overt cultural expectations but the covert expectations. For example, we would perhaps expect a devout Muslim woman to cover her hair with a scarf, but we might not expect her husband to accompany her to a teacher-student conference. We assume that "everyone" knows that such conferences are private. These "misunderstandings" foster stereotypes of the other culture, focus attention on the other culture, limit the teacher's flexibility to maximize the possibilities of the multicultural class, and—possibly—contribute to the teacher's disillusionment, not with the student, but with his own ability. Stoddard (1986, 124) underscores the difficulty of teachers and students having different expectations of behavior in classroom situations. She says, " . . . [O]ur students need to understand the importance of what is not stated, as well as what is stated." And Furey (1986, 15, 16) points out that the ESL classroom

is most often a culture contact setting where the students' cultural values and expectations of the learning process may diverge significantly from those of the teacher and curriculum designer. . . . Teachers are so often concerned with teaching the body of material and series of skills explicitly designated in an official curriculum that they forget that students are also learning a hidden curriculum—one which transmits the values, attitudes and norms of behavior of the culture in which their education is set. . . . [V]ery often certain values, attitudes and behavioral patterns of the general culture are directly reflected in and reinforced by the educational setting.

Having knowledge of the other culture, even living experience in another culture, does not prevent these discrepancies in expectations. And because of the difference in expectations, stereotypes are formed. As Fitch (1986, 54) notes,

Many teachers, with perhaps considerable overseas experience and continuous contact with individuals very different from themselves, may feel immune to the blinding limitations of stereotypes. ESL teachers should assume that they will always have stereotypes present in their belief structure, try as they may to view each student as an individual. If continuously modified by ongoing experience, stereotypes will at least be complex clusters of cultural characteristics informed by a multitude of exceptions, rather than unidimensional, rigid expectations . . . . [S]uch expectations will be modified by experience . . . . [H]owever it is unrealistic to assume that they ever completely disappear.

Thus, we can see that "to escape the hidden constraints of covert culture" requires becoming conscious of our intersubjective world. Let us look at an example of a specific intersubjective rule that frequently comes into play in multicultural classrooms.

Example of Intersubjective Rules. Intersubjective rules are manifested in specific cultural differences—in simple acts such as "taking turns." Robinson's (1992) examination of turn-taking in the classroom is an example of an intersubjective rule in operation. He studied turn-taking in the classroom and concluded that there is a marked difference in intersubjective rules between American and Asian students. He points out that American students have been molded throughout grade school and high school to recognize a variation of interactional patterns with their teachers. By the time that they enter the university, they are unconscious partners with the professor in choosing a particular interactional pattern. There are specific rules governing which questions to ask, when to ask them, and how to ask them. Of course, the same process occurs in Asian classrooms, where students have been molded into the use of a less verbal pattern. The Asian has learned to make eye contact as a means of "bidding" for a turn. Americans tend to speak more quickly than Asians. This small variation leads to stereotypes—Americans think that the Asians are "reserved, withdrawn, without opinions of their own, unsure, or perhaps even hostile," and the Asians tend to think that Americans are "arrogant, egocentric, pushy, domineering, or impatient." A few seconds difference in the perceived proper timing of an action can cause miscommunication at the cognitive and the affective levels. (Scollon and Scollon, 1983) And Robinson points out that not only are these stereotypes a hindrance to relationships, they are inaccurate. The Asian is not necessarily shy. He is merely manifesting his Confucian cultural value of blending into the group. And Robinson's conclusion that ignorance of the intersubjective rules governing turn-taking is a barrier to effective teaching and learning underscores the importance of understanding one's own intersubjective world.

Yet turn-taking is only one of thousands of minute differences between cultures. Other examples of these intersubjective differences include incidents such as:

- A student walks up to a teacher who is in a conversation, says "Excuse me," and immediately begins to speak rather than waiting for the teacher to complete the conversation.
- A student knocks on an office door, then rattles the handle, and enters, saying, "excuse me."
- A student asks for a letter of recommendation before the semester is ended or without having performed particularly well.

Examples are legion. And Robinson rightly points out that our ESL curricula do not deal with these issues. Nor are they dealt with in related fields. Perhaps the reason that we do not deal with these intersubjective issues is not that we are unwilling to do so, but that, by their very nature, these issues are difficult to define and investigate. Furthermore, since the rules are unconscious, becoming aware of them requires a structure outside of one's self. One such structure that can facilitate identification and analysis of specific intersubjective behaviors relies on the different incidents encountered in a multicultural classroom.

Culture Bump. One approach to understanding cultural differences relies on the concept of the "culture bump" (Archer 1986). The concept blends theories and methodologies from the fields of cross cultural communication and ESL to offer the international education practitioner a structured approach with which to identify, analyze, and learn from specific cultural differences. Having identified a culture bump, the teacher and students can analyze it. The first step is to *identify*, as Robinson did, *the cultural assumptions and values* that underlie the behavior in question. While identifying the underlying assumptions and values has traditionally been thought to be sufficient, the culture bump approach calls for further analysis. Teachers next examine the culture bump, not with the goal of understanding the other culture, but as a means of understanding their own cultural patterns at a deeper level. This process requires that they *define the context for the* *culture bump and their expectations concerning appropriate behavior from members of their own culture* within the context where the behavior arose. Once they have identified their own cultural expectations, they *determine the "human" quality that those behaviors represent for them*. Some examples of human qualities are consideration, cleverness, caring, kindness or inconsideration, stupidity, indifference, or meanness.

Having gone this far, teachers are now in a position to try to understand the other culture from a different perspective. Rather than examining the causes of the behavior of members of the other culture, they now *search for the way that the other culture manifests the "human quality" previously identified in their own culture*. When analyzed in this way, a culture bump is the key with which an international education practitioner answers two important questions: *Why do they do what they do?* and *How do they do what we do?* In other words, why are we different and finally, how are we similar?

Using Robinson's examination of turn—taking as an example, we can analyze one specific culture bump as follows:

> When an American teacher asks a group of Asian students a question, rather than raising their hands or even answering spontaneously, they maintain silence with direct eye contact.

Robinson has already used this culture bump as the impetus for his research into the question of why Asians behave as they do. Now, however, teachers continue with their analysis of the culture bump by contextualizing the situation as:

> The response that a student makes when he knows the answer to a teacher's question.

Teachers now focus on their own expectations of American students in that particular situation as:

> An American student might raise his hand, or perhaps nod his head, maintain direct eye contact, or even answer the question spontaneously.

They now examine the meaning of that behavior in American culture as:

> When an American student behaves in this way, it expresses her interest in the class or the subject, her competence as a student, or even her liking the teacher.

The next question shifts their focus back to Asian culture:

> How do Asian teachers know when their students are genuinely interested in the class or are competent or like them?

Having completed this process, the instructors have gained a number of insights. At a conscious level, they have become aware of their own expectations and the implicit assumptions that underlie them, and they have identified an area for further investigation within the other culture. They have also changed the focus of their investigation from cultural differences to similar, human characteristics. And they have become conscious of the process of stereotyping.

The culture bump approach is just as valuable for the practitioner with years of intercultural experience as it is for the individual who has just entered the field. In addition to providing the impetus for traditional research, this approach also offers a structured way "to involve ourselves actively and consciously in the very parts of life that we take most for granted." (Hall 1969, 7) And it facilitates the "continuous modification" of stereotypes springing from "a few seconds of miscommunication." (Scollon and Scollon 1983, 161) Furthermore, because it is process-oriented, it has no limit. As long as we encounter individuals from another culture, we have fodder for further development of our own "intercultural perspective."

Applying the Two Approaches

Well-prepared instructors enter their multicultural classrooms with a knowledge of their students' cultures and their own culture, and with an awareness of the cultural adjustment of each of their students. In addition, they have an ever-ready structure for processing and interpreting the information they learn—both cognitively and experientially—through interactions with their students. They are now prepared not only to manage a multicultural classroom but to maximize its potential. Having mastered the process themselves, these teachers can introduce it to their students. Specifically, they can make their own expectations explicit, both at the beginning of the semester and as they become aware of them during the semester. Students can use the culture bump approach to help resolve their own culture bumps with Americans and with one another. Moreover, the approach is ideal for language learning based on a notional functional approach. When culture bumps become cultural conflicts in the classroom, teachers can use the culture bump approach to "defuse/avoid the problem, confront and express the problem, and increase students' awareness through learning." (Fitch 1986, 58)

In addition to dealing with culture bumps, teachers in a multicultural class face the possibility of wide variation in preferred learning styles. Individuals tend to learn best through one of three sensory channels—visual, auditory, or kinesthetic. Teachers also tend to emphasize one of these methods over the others. Those who learn visually will gravitate toward visual teaching methods, for example. Therefore, teachers need to understand their own preference and include the other modes. While this is true in a monocultural classroom, it becomes even more important in a multicultural classroom, since cultures tend to emphasize one or more of these learning methods. American culture encourages visual learning, while some Middle Eastern cultures encourage auditory learning. Thus, while individuals within a culture certainly vary in their preferred learning styles, the cultural influence increases this variation. Therefore, the international educator should have a variety of methods ready for presenting any material. Students who are less talkative will benefit from having written assignments. Some will learn better with visual stimulation and others need aural presentations. Field work will help some students and some need a combination of methods.

Just as they can acquaint their students with the culture bump approach, teachers can acquaint their students with the learning style idea. Knowing about it promotes their learning not only about the subject matter, but also about one another and about themselves.

Conclusion

Living up to Nayar's description of a successful teacher calls for layer upon layer of preparatory work on the teacher's part. Nayar's call for a teacher to "free himself from ethnocentrism, prejudice, and the tendency to stereotype" may be difficult to achieve. The suggestions given in this chapter will help teachers become more conscious of these damaging tendencies. With the achievement of this consciousness, they can be more responsible for them. The consciousness brings with it not only the option of responsibility but also the opportunity for continuous self-reflection and growth. This is critical because teachers need to understand not just the nature of culture and the dynamics of adjustment to a new culture, but also their own culturally based expectations. If this ongoing self-reflection and growth can be considered a key to maintaining teachers' enthusiasm, we should take heed of Constantinides's (1986, 138) call for cross-cultural training for the faculty and staff of ESL programs. Cross-cultural training provides the skills and tools ESL teachers and other practitioners need to fully realize their natural abilities and aspirations. Indeed, to deny this training to such highly motivated people is to squander valuable human resources—resources possessed by those individuals who love language, who are driven by curiosity, who possess a love for people, and who have high and positive aspirations. We cannot afford to waste any of these individuals who have the stamina and commitment to do the difficult work required not only to manage a multicultural classroom but to create a classroom in which, to paraphrase Ghandi, the winds of all cultures blow through the windows with no one blown away.

References

Adelman, Mara B. 1988. "Cross-Cultural Adjustment: A Theoretical Perspective on Social Support." *International Journal of Intercultural Relations* 12, 3: 183-204.

Adler, Peter. 1979 "Culture Shock and the Cross-Cultural Learning Experience." In *Readings in Intercultural Communication*, vol. 2. Ed. David S. Hoopes. Pittsburgh: Regional Council for International Education.

Althen, Gary. 1988. *American Ways*. Yarmouth, ME: Intercultural Press.

_____. Ed. 1978. *Students from the Arab World and Iran*. Washington, DC: NAFSA.

Archer, Carol M. 1986. "Culture Bump and Beyond." In *Culture Bound: Bridging the Cultural Gap in Language Teaching*. Ed. Joyce M. Valdes. New York: Cambridge University Press.

_____. 1990. *Living with Strangers in the USA*. Englewood Cliffs, NJ: Prentice-Hall.

Barnlund, Dean C. 1989 *Communicative Styles of Japanese and Americans: Images and Realities*. Belmont, CA: Wadsworth.

Becker, Carl. 1986. "Reasons for the Lack of Argumentation and Debate in the Far East." *International Journal of Intercultural Relations* 10: 75-92.

Clavell, James. 1975. *Shogun*. New York: Atheneum.

Condon, John C. 1984. *With Respect to the Japanese: A Guide for Americans*. Yarmouth, ME: Intercultural Press.

Constantinides, Janet C. 1986. "Selected Annotated Bibliography and References." In *Teaching across Cultures in the University ESL Program*. Ed. Patricia Byrd and Janet C. Constantinides, 137-148. Washington, DC: NAFSA.

De Mente, Boye. 1988. *Korean Etiquette and Ethics in Business*. Lincolnwood, IL: NTC.

Fieg, John Paul. 1989. *A Common Core: Thais and Americans*. Rev. Elizabeth Mortlock. Yarmouth, ME: Intercultural Press.

Finkelstein, Barbara, Joseph J. Tobin, and Anne E. Imamura. Eds. 1991. *Transcending Stereotypes: Discovering Japanese Culture and Education*. Yarmouth, ME: Intercultural Press.

Fitch, Kristine. 1986. "Cultural Conflicts in the Classroom: Major Issues and Strategies for Coping." In *Teaching across Cultures in the University ESL Program*. Ed. Patricia Byrd and Janet C. Constantinides, 51-62. Washington, DC: NAFSA.

Furey, Patricia R. 1986. "A Framework for Cross-Cultural Analysis of Teaching Methods." In *Teaching across Cultures in the University ESL Program*. Ed. Patricia Byrd and Janet C. Constantinides, 15-28. Washington, DC: NAFSA.

Furnham, Adrian, and Stephen Bochner. 1986. *Culture Shock*. New York: Routledge, Chapman and Hall.

Gochenour, Theodore. 1990. *Considering Filipinos*. Yarmouth, ME: Intercultural Press.

Grove, Cornelius, and Ingemar Torbiorn. 1985. "A New Conceptualization of Intercultural Adjustment and the Goals of Training." *International Journal of Intercultural Relations.* 9, 2: 205-223.

Hall, Edward T. 1976. *Beyond Culture.* Garden City, NY: Anchor/Doubleday.

_____. 1969. *The Hidden Dimension.* Garden City, NY: Anchor Press/Doubleday.

Hoffman, Diane M. 1990. "Beyond Conflict: Culture, Self, and Intercultural Learning among Iranians in the U.S." *International Journal of Intercultural Relations* 14, 3: 275-299.

Hofstede, Geert. 1986. "Cultural Differences in Teaching and Learning." *International Journal of Intercultural Relations* 10: 301-320.

Hoopes, David S., and Paul Ventura. 1979. *Intercultural Sourcebook.* LaGrange Park, IL: Intercultural Network, 48-51.

Hsu, Francis L. K. 1953. *Americans and Chinese: Passages to Differences.* Honolulu: University Press of Hawaii.

Hu, Wenzhong, and Cornelius L. Grove. 1991. *Encountering the Chinese: A Guide for Americans.* Yarmouth, ME: Intercultural Press.

Kamal, Abdulaziz A., and Geoffrey Maryuama. 1990. "Cross-Cultural Contact and Attitudes of Qatari Students in the United States." *International Journal of Intercultural Relations* 14, 2: 123-134.

Kaplan, Robert. 1966. "Cultural Thought Patterns in Intercultural Education" *Language Learning* 16: 1-20.

Kapp, Robert A. Ed. 1983. *Communicating with China.* Chicago: Intercultural Press.

Kim, Young Yun. 1988. *Communication and Cross-Cultural Adaptation: An Integrative Theory.* Clevedon, England: Multilingual Matters.

Kohls, L. Robert. 1979. *Survival Kit for Overseas Living.* Chicago: Intercultural Network/Systran.

Leppert, Paul. 1991. *Doing Business with the Koreans: A Handbook for Executives.* Sebastopol, CA: Patton Pacific Press.

Levine, Deena, and Mara Adelman. 1982. *Beyond Language.* Englewood Cliffs, NJ: Prentice-Hall, 198-199.

Lewis, Tom, and Robert Jungman. Eds. 1986. *On Being Foreign: Culture Shock in Short Fiction.* Yarmouth, ME: Intercultural Press.

Marquez, Gabriel Garcia. 1970. Trans. Gregory Rabassa. *One Hundred Years of Solitude.* New York: Harper and Row.

Nayar, P. B. 1986. "Acculturation or Enculturation? Foreign Students in the United States." In *Teaching across Cultures in the University ESL Program.* Ed. Patricia Byrd and Janet C. Constantinides, 1-13. Washington, DC: NAFSA.

Reitzel, Armeda. 1986. "The Fear of Speaking: Communication Anxiety in ESL Students." In *Teaching across Cultures in the University ESL Program.* Ed. Patricia Byrd and Janet C. Constantinides, 127-129. Washington, DC: NAFSA.

Robertson, James Oliver. 1980. *American Myth: American Reality.* New York: Hill and Wang.

Robinson, James H. 1992. "Turn Taking in the ESL Classrooms: An Item of Cross-Cultural Dissonance." Paper prepared for the Forty-fourth Annual Kentucky Foreign Language Conference, Lexington, April 25-26.

Salzman, Mark. 1986. *Iron and Silk.* New York: Random House.

Scollon, R., and S. B. K. Scollon. 1983. "Face in Interethnic Communication." In *Language & Communication.* Ed. Jack C. Richards and Richard W. Schmidt. New York: Longman, 156-188.

Searle, Wendy, and Colleen Ward. 1990. "The Prediction of Psychological and Sociocultural Adjustment during Cross-Cultural Transitions." *International Journal of Intercultural Relations* 14, 4: 449-464.

Stewart, Edward C., and Milton J. Bennett. 1991. *American Cultural Patterns: A Cross-Cultural Perspective.* Rev. ed. Yarmouth, ME: Intercultural Press.

Stoddard, Sally. 1986. "Cultural Assumptions, Frames, and the Allowable Economies of English: A Cross-Cultural Problem." In *Teaching across Cultures in the University ESL Program.* Ed. Patricia Byrd and Janet C. Constantinides, 123-125. Washington, DC: NAFSA.

Wubbels, Theo, and Jack Levy. 1990. "A Comparison of Interpersonal Behavior of Dutch and American Teachers." *International Journal of Intercultural Relations* 15, 1: 1-18, 199.

5

Counseling Student Sojourners: Revisiting the U-Curve of Adjustment

Kay Thomas and Teresa Harrell

Much has been written about adjustment theory and its importance in understanding the sojourner experience. Most writings about the sojourn experience either build theory around the process of culture learning that occurs to varying degrees during the sojourn experience, or address definitional issues. Little has been written to help counselors use these theories in counseling foreign or returning students. This chapter discusses two models that approach the sojourner experience from an individual psychological perspective. The first model, the U-Curve of Adjustment, is a useful tool for counseling. The second, Berry and Kim's (1988) Model of Attitudes Towards Acculturation, is useful for counselors in judging what interventions might be appropriate with a client. Case studies using these models in counseling sessions with sojourners prior to departure, during the sojourn, and after returning home illustrate the models' utility for counseling.

For general overviews of cross-cultural counseling, see Sue and Sue's (1990) *Counseling the Culturally Different* and Pedersen, et al. (1989), *Counseling Across Cultures*. For overviews on counseling foreign students, see Thomas and Althen (1989) and Pedersen (1991).

Who Are Student Sojourners?

Student sojourners are generally young and highly motivated. Older students, who have been returning to campuses in growing numbers over the past few years, may also have an interest in being sojourners. Students abroad are called "sojourners" because their stay in the host culture is temporary, and most return to their home countries upon completion of their educational programs. For those who choose to complete a degree overseas, the sojourn experience may last several years. Because student sojourners have a purpose for going abroad, it is important that they quickly become functional in the new environment.

Although all sojourners have their own motivations for studying abroad, their expectations of the experience and of their return home, as well as their individual personality characteristics, play a role in how they respond to the experience. Sojourners are generally motivated to make the accommodations necessary to accomplish their educational objectives, provided they understand what they need to do to feel comfortable in the host culture and to complete their educational programs.

In the last 25 years, there has been a significant increase in the number of students going abroad to further their educational goals. Despite the economic difficulties and assorted crises affecting many countries, this trend towards greater mobility seems to be continuing. Today, there are over 400,000 foreign students studying in the United States (Zikopoulos 1992) and over 70,000 U.S. students studying abroad (Institute of International Education, 1993). Many countries, such as Japan, are actively seeking student sojourners. Study abroad is quickly coming to be recognized as an important component of a student's education and a necessary prerequisite for certain careers.

The subject of temporary transmigration for educational purposes has caught the attention of scholars, who have sought to explain what happens to people during and after the sojourn. We know that sojourners have a different degree of motivation to adjust to the host culture than do immigrants or refugees. Immigrants generally move to a new country by choice, seeking a better life. Immigrants are likely to have a greater desire to adjust to and indeed assimilate into the new culture, by learning its language and by embracing many of its values and attitudes. The expectation is that life will be better in the new land and the more they can blend in the better.

Refugees, on the other hand, may be fleeing political and religious oppression or may even have been exiled. The choice of where they go is limited by which country will take them. The new land may promise greater safety and freedom, but the refugees may not wholeheartedly embrace the new country if the decision to leave their old country was not their own. Therefore, refugees may feel the need to acculturate only to a limited degree, while maintaining the integrity of their own culture. In other words, refugees might assume a bicultural stance. Sojourner adjustment may differ in that it is temporary and therefore has the advantage of being functional and situational, rather than permanent.

What Do We Know About the Sojourn Experience?

One of the greatest learning experiences one can have occurs when one leaves the comfort and familiarity of one's own environment and travels to live and study in an unfamiliar place. Many aspects of life are encountered for what seems like the first time. Not only does one confront a new culture, but one must also squarely confront oneself. The host culture becomes a laboratory for self-exploration, redefinition, and personal development. One's inner resources or lack thereof become more apparent, and one's skills at forming new relationships, observing the behavior of others, and behaving appropriately are all challenged. In the host country, new norms govern, communication styles differ, and relationships have different rules. One must become a learner in almost all aspects of life if one is to function effectively and accomplish one's goals, especially if the goals involve interacting in a substantive manner with the host culture, which may not be very receptive. In addition, one's perceptions must be checked and evaluated against new value frameworks. Many questions arise: "Who am I?" "Can I handle this?" "Can I function in this environment and get my needs met?" "Can I behave appropriately here?" "Will I be accepted?" "Will I be understood?" "Will they like me?" "Will I like them?" There is no doubt that one's self-esteem (image) is challenged when one decides to study abroad.

The study-abroad experience also challenges counselors, foreign student advisers, and study-abroad advisers who try to help sojourners make sense of their overseas experience and accomplish their goals in an environment that may seem strange, unfriendly, unwelcoming, confusing, and perhaps even hostile. And the challenge does not end when the sojourner returns home. Frequently, what becomes more problematic is dealing with the newly acquired information, skills, values, attitudes, communication and relational styles, and the redefinition of self that inevitably occurs upon returning home. The same questions arise again, to a greater or lesser degree: "Who am I?" "Can I handle this?" "Can I function in this environment and get my needs met?" "Can I behave appropriately here?" "Will I be accepted?" "Will I be understood?" "Will they like me?" "Will I now like them?"

A Question of Terms

In the student sojourn literature, there is no one term that authors agree adequately describes the process of change that takes place when one leaves one's culture and enters another. The term used most frequently to describe this process is "adjustment." However, it is not clear what constitutes "adjustment" (Brein and David 1971, Church 1982). Interestingly, the terms adaptation, acculturation, adjustment, and accommodation have all been used interchangeably in describing the sojourn experience. Adjustment takes place over time and, as Searle and Ward (1990) found in their review, many variables have been used as indices of "adjustment": acceptance of the host culture (Noesjirwan 1966); satisfaction, feelings of acceptance, and coping with everyday activities (Brislin 1981); mood states (Feinstein and

Ward 1990); and acquisition of culturally appropriate behavior and skills (Bochner, Lin, and McLeod 1980; Furnham and Bochner 1986).

Many scholars believe the term "adjustment" implies that a sojourner's failures and problems in the host culture are symptoms of a pathology that requires treatment. Furnham and Bochner (1986) prefer the term "cultural accommodation," which does not rely on the concept of adjustment and also eliminates the notion of cultural chauvinism. Berry (1990) uses "acculturation" to describe the culture change that is initiated when two or more autonomous cultures come into contact. Graves (1967) and Berry (1990) used the term "psychological acculturation" to refer to the process by which individuals change their behavior, identity, values, and attitudes, both by being influenced by contact with another culture and by being participants in the general acculturative changes under way in their own society.

For purposes of this chapter, the terms adjustment and acculturation will be used interchangeably and will refer to the psychological process of culture learning and individual change that occurs when someone enters and attempts to function within another culture.

Adjustment as a Meta-Concept in Counseling Student Sojourners

For some time, it was thought that a counselor who understood a client's cultural framework could be a successful counselor to a foreign student. To a great extent this is true. However, we would like to propose that it is of even greater importance in counseling sojourners that one understand the sojourner adjustment process. Although there is no agreement on the components of the adjustment process, we know that all sojourners have unique reactions to and experiences in the host culture, and that the encounter is stressful. All sojourn experiences should first be viewed in light of the process of encountering the host culture. While cultural and value information is useful, the fact is that sojourners embrace their own cultures and their values in idiosyncratic ways, and this has great influence on the way they experience adjustment and "take in" the new culture. It is the personal story and personal culture that are important and that provide the greatest assistance in counseling sojourners. Therefore, understanding the impact of the adjustment process on a person becomes more important than having specific cultural information. The meta-concept of adjustment must be a central consideration when counseling those confronting another culture. That is, a particular sojourner's description of the adjustment experiences and reactions to those experiences must be at the center of counselors' considerations when working with sojourners, since the stress of the sojourn experience is such that it may affect clients' relationships, inner resources, and intellectual thought.

Sojourners choose whether to fully embrace the new culture, making its norms, values, and behavioral expectations their own; whether to reject all or some of the new culture's norms, values, and behavioral expectations; or whether to learn only those features of the new culture that are necessary to accomplish their educational objectives. This is not simply a matter of making a cognitive decision. Instead, as Chapter 2 of this book makes clear, the adjustment process is very complex and involves not only the affective/intrapsychic domain, but the behavioral and the cognitive domains as well (Searle and Ward, 1990).

A Critical Look at the U-Curve of Adjustment

Much has been written about the adjustment process, and several theories have evolved to explain it. The U-Curve of Adjustment is probably the best known of these theories. Lysgaard (1955) was one of the earliest theorists to describe the adjustment process in terms of stages. He studied 200 Norwegian Fulbright scholars and learned that their degree of satisfaction with the sojourn experience generally had three stages: initial adjustment, then crisis, and later a regained adjustment. Lysgaard himself did not specifically refer to this as a U-curve, but did suggest that the initial satisfaction with the sojourn experience will decline, then increase again with time, thus taking a U-shaped configuration.

Oberg (1960) contributed to the U-curve theory by describing the adjustment process associated with visiting a new culture as having four stages of "culture shock." Culture shock was described as the negative emotional state that results from the loss of familiar signs and symbols of social discourse. Oberg described these stages as follows:

1. Honeymoon Stage—a period of enchantment with the new culture and superficial relationships with hosts

2. Crisis Stage—when differences in language and communication styles lead to feelings of inadequacy, frustration, and anger

3. Recovery Stage—when the sojourner learns more about how to function in the culture and the crisis begins to resolve

4. Adjustment stage—the time when the sojourner begins to function well in and even enjoy the new culture.

Adler (1975), Jacobson (1963), and others have also used stages to describe an adjustment process with a curvilinear shape.

Gullahorn and Gullahorn (1963) extended the U-curve to a W-curve when they found that sojourners seemed to go through a U-shaped adjustment curve again upon returning to their home country. Rhinesmith (1985) suggested a wave pattern in the sojourner's level of adjustment, with high points associated with arrival, "surface adjustment," acceptance and integration, and reintegration at home, and low points associated with pre-departure issues, culture shock, "mental isolation," and anxiety about returning home.

From his review of the literature, Church (1982) found that empirical support for the U-curve hypothesis was weak, inconclusive, and overgeneralized. Furnham and Bochner (1986) conclude that, at the present stage of development, the U-curve hypothesis is too vague and too generalized to be of much use in predicting or understanding sojourner adjustment. It is more of a post hoc description that has focused on a single outcome variable, that of being adjusted, rather than focusing on the dynamics or process of adjustment. Despite the fact that it often "makes sense" to sojourners in discussions of their adjustment process, the U-curve as a theoretical construct fails to take into account the multiple aspects of personality and environment that interact to give a complete explanation of the process. Likewise, the construct offers no explanation of what one looks, feels, and acts like when one is truly adjusting to another culture.

Many believe that Oberg's term "culture shock," and his implication that this state represented the bottom of the U-curve, placed the focus on the individual and the intrapsychic aspects of adjustment to the exclusion of situational factors in the sojourner's environment. Others were quick to jump on the band wagon and to designate other "shocks" inherent in the adjustment process. Thus, "language shock" (Smalley, 1963) referred to the loss of language cues in social relations, and "role shock" to feelings of ambiguity and loss of personal status (Byrnes 1966, Higbee 1969). This "disease-like" aspect of culture shock appears to be the occupational hazard of being a sojourner. As Bennett (1977) suggested, the negative connotation of "culture shock" failed to recognize the sojourn experience as being similar to other life transitions, the resolution of which, whether positive or negative, can lead to learning and personal growth.

Most agree that the U/W-Curve of Adjustment as an explanation of adjustment is unidimensional and incomplete. Because of the limitations of the curve hypotheses, Bochner, Lin, and McLeod (1980) developed a social psychological model in which adjustment was construed as the acquisition, over time, of behaviors, skills, and norms that are appropriate to the social roles sojourners must play, rather than construing it solely as an intrapsychic phenomenon. The social skills approach involves entering into new relationships with significant people in the host country and resuming relationships with significant people in the home country after returning home. Bochner, Lin, and McLeod found that returning students anticipate that they will be subjected to contradictory expectations, particularly from their professional, peer, and family groups. The authors expect that the sojourn experience will cause sojourners to be viewed differently, and that the resulting role conflicts will need to be resolved.

The advantage of a social psychological model of adjustment is that it has some predictive possibilities (Furnham and Bochner 1986). For example, one can say that a successful culture learner should exhibit a normal U-curve in the host country, and after reentry, a W-curve. Experienced culture learners, those individuals who can move comfortably back and forth between cultures, should show a relatively flat curve with few peaks and valleys. Unsuccessful culture learners should show a declining curve during the sojourn and a rising one after returning home, thus suggesting that satisfaction in the host culture steadily declined and did not start to go up until the sojourner returned home. Furnham and Bochner (1986) assert that this model applies to all life events and changes and has the advantage of being able to predict adjustment level based on earlier behavior. In addition, it has implications for remedial action and, therefore, is of interest to counselors who work with sojourners. So, perhaps, does the model Torbiörn sets forth in Chapter 2.

The U/W-Curves of Adjustment provide interesting but incomplete theoretical models for what happens to sojourners adapting to a new environment. From the literature and from clinical work with sojourners, the U/W-Curve of Adjustment is, at best, a unidimensional explanation of a sojourner's adjustment process. The model makes several assumptions that need to be challenged. The first is that it is possible to devise a single global measure of adjustment that covers all facets of one's life. For example, it is possible that someone can feel very much at the bottom of the U-curve academically because she is having a difficult time getting the expected assistance from her adviser. She is afraid to proceed with the research without this approval. On the other hand, the social portion of her life may be quite satisfactory. Conversely, a student may be making outstanding academic progress and yet feel lonely and isolated. In both of these cases, a single measure of adjustment would fail to recognize the multifaceted nature of any person's life and would inaccurately portray the person's overall degree of adjustment.

A second assumption of the U/W-Curve model is that once one has gained a reasonable level of satisfaction with the host culture, one remains adjusted until returning home. This fails to take into account the many possible events that can occur in a sojourner's life to challenge the feeling of satisfaction in the host culture. Such events could include losing a close friend or relative, being the victim of a crime, being discriminated against, failing academically, or making a decision about marrying or securing employment in the host country, to name a few. Any life event can change the level of satisfaction one feels in the host culture and threaten one's sense of adjustment. The U/W construct obscures such developments. In like manner, return to the home country could continue to be an experience of nonadjustment rather than following the pattern predicted by the second part of the W curve.

A third assumption underlying the U/W model is that conditions in the host culture remain relatively stable, so that, over time, there is a cumulative learning of salient cultural rules and social skills appropriate to the new culture. Such stability might not always prevail. It is unlikely that foreign students studying in the Soviet Union when it was dismantled into independent states, or in Los Angeles in 1992 when unrest broke out, or Middle Eastern students studying in the United States during the Persian Gulf War, were unshaken by the events around them. Situations change. Individual responses to these changes are different, and lasting effects cannot be predicted. Changing circumstances can precipitate a crisis in an otherwise "adjusted" sojourner and cause a backslide in the direction of dissatisfaction, anxiety, or even fear.

Developing a New Model of Cultural Adjustment

The U/W-Curve of Adjustment model is also limited in that it does not account for individual personality characteristics such as flexibility, tolerance for ambiguity, locus of control, and level of self-esteem. Nor does it consider the attitudes, values, and expectations that affect an individual's stance vis-à-vis the host culture. It also fails to take into consideration environmental characteristics as they relate to the host culture's stability, inclusiveness, religious tolerance, or sociopolitical climate.

After a review of the literature, Searle and Ward (1990) concluded that the construct of adjustment implicitly incorporates both a psychological dimension—referring to feelings of well-being and satisfaction—as well as a sociocultural dimension—referring to the ability to "fit in" and negotiate interactive aspects of the new culture. The U-Curve of Adjustment suggests that psychological adjustment and well-being may follow a curvilinear path, while the sociocultural aspects of adjustment, such as the acquisition of social skills, including communication abilities, should reflect a more linear improvement over time (Kim 1988).

Three frameworks that focus on various aspects of the sojourn experience have been identified by Searle and Ward (1990) as prominent in studies of cross-cultural transitions. These frameworks can be useful to counselors and advisers who want to help sojourners conceptualize the adjustment process. The first is the *clinical perspective*, which draws attention to the role of personality, changes, losses, and social supports that facilitate or inhibit the adjustment process. Personality variables affect the individual's adaptation to a foreign milieu, and social support acts as a buffer against the psychological effects of stress.

The second framework is the *social learning model*, which emphasizes the acquisition of skills and behaviors appropriate to the host culture through contact with hosts, cross-cultural experience, and training. This model acknowledges the importance of interpersonal relationships, deeming them crucial for learning the skills needed in the new culture. Because of the importance of social learning to cultural adjustment, interventions targeted at overcoming fears and resistance to active engagement with hosts would be useful.

The third framework is the *social cognition model*, which shifts the emphasis away from skills and highlights the importance of expectations, values, attitudes, and perceptions in the cross-cultural adjustment process.

Torbiörn's model in Chapter 2, with its concepts of applicability of behavior and clarity of the mental frame of reference, seeks to incorporate both the social learning and the social cognition dimensions.

Instead of a single measure of adjustment over time, we are suggesting that there are multiple curves over time, each representing one aspect of the sojourner's life. For example, at any given point in time, an individual may be well-adjusted to the academic environment of the host country and function successfully in it, but have a very low level of adjustment to social relationships. At the same time, the individual may also be experiencing a moderate level of adjustment in his ability to handle his living needs, and a low level of adjustment with respect to religious belief and practice. From our counseling work with sojourners, we would say that a model of adjustment that allows for multiple curves at any point in time, reflecting different aspects of their lives, more precisely fits the realities of most sojourners' experiences. It also takes into account the individual aspects of each sojourner's personality, social skills, and cognition (values, attitudes, and expectations).

While the validity of the U/W/Wave Curve of Adjustment has yet to be empirically substantiated, it continues to seem valid when explained to sojourners and therefore can be useful in counseling as a framework for processing foreign and returning students' personal stories.

There are dangers with all models because of people's tendency to use them both to predict and explain. The U-Curve of Adjustment has not been very useful as a predictor of behavior, but has been useful to explain the process. A multiple wave curve can be even more useful. By using the U/W/Wave/Multi Curve diagram in counseling student sojourners, many of the complexities of the adjustment process can be discussed in the interview.

Using the U-Curve of Adjustment as a Counseling Tool

Sojourners often inappropriately blame other people when some things do not turn out as they had hoped. Sojourners may blame themselves and fail to see the impact of the environmental factors on them. Or they may blame the host culture, failing to see any role they themselves play in the situation. In these cases of misattributed responsibility, the counselor can draw the U-Curve of Adjustment and use it as a starting point for discussing the impact of the cultural adjustment or readjustment process. Diagramming and explaining the adjustment process can open new and therapeutic directions for discussion, and make connections between clients' present feelings and thoughts, and their participation in sojourn experiences.

It is important for counselors not to lead clients to believe that adjustment always occurs in a curvilinear fashion. If particular sojourners do not share this experience, but they come to believe that "normal" people do, sojourners may experience stress or depression.

It is also important to explain the adjustment process. One way to explain it is: Sojourners frequently experience a sense of satisfaction and even false mastery over the new culture when they first arrive. This is because they may initially see many of the things they had read about or been told about and therefore may have an unrealistic sense of understanding the new culture. However, when sojourners have to interact substantively with local people to accomplish daily tasks such as finding housing or a job, getting registered, seeking medical assistance, or making friends, it is not unusual for them to experience frustration and confusion when the familiar ways of communicating fail to yield the expected results. At this point, sojourners may evaluate the host culture negatively and view their home culture in an unrealistically positive manner.

Over time, most sojourners will begin to acquire, through observation and cultural information from informants, the knowledge and skills necessary to accomplish what they need to do. In time, sojourners begin to feel more capable of functioning in a manner that allows them to accomplish their goals in an increasingly comfortable manner. There may continue to be ups and downs, depending on the areas of life in question at the time. And certainly not all areas of life are equally affected at the same time or in the same way. But many sojourners recognize the curve depicting initial expectations followed by disillusionment and frustration and then a balance at a higher level of satisfaction.

After discussing the curve models, the counselor can ask the sojourner two questions: (1) Does the model make sense to you, that is, can you relate it to your experience in any way? If so, how? If not, why not?, and (2) Where would you place yourself right now as you think about this adjustment diagram? In our experience, clients are virtually always able to relate the adjustment model to their personal experience and to place themselves on the curve in relation to different aspects of their lives—academics, friendships, family, relationships, work, and so on. Thus, the model seems to have what researchers call "face validity," even if it lacks consistent support from empirical studies.

What Can Counselors Discuss with or Suggest to Clients to Assist in Their Adjustment at Different Points on the "Curve?"

Prior to departure, the U-Curve of Adjustment can be useful in helping sojourners anticipate the ups and downs they will experience in the new culture. It also helps them plan consciously for finding social support, and consider how they will go about learning the host-culture norms and rules. In general, the model helps sojourners establish appropriately moderate expectations for the sojourn. It also can be used to point out that every sojourner has unique responses and behaviors.

A discussion of a sojourner's hopes, fears, and expectations, in the light of the model, can be very productive.

Case Example: During a discussion of the U-curve with some students preparing to go abroad, a male American consciously realized that he could find himself in situations where he would want to drink alcohol. He had been off alcohol for over two years, but talking about the adjustment process brought up his fear of not being able to continue abstaining. We discussed what he might do, how he could find support for himself, and what he would say to others when he was tempted to drink. We rehearsed responses to situations that were likely to arise, and the student made plans for taking care of himself in those situations.

This counseling provided support, behavioral rehearsal, anxiety reduction, and skill building.

Many adjustment problems can arise during the sojourn experience (Paige 1986, Wanga 1989; Thomas and Althen 1989, Pedersen 1991). Some are intrapsychic and some are environmental, and the two types may overlap. Sometimes students bring problems from home that become overwhelming in the host country. Sojourners seek counseling for a variety of reasons. They may be referred to counseling by friends or other institutional staff because they are feeling lonely, angry, homesick, or depressed. Some may have experienced failure, or been sick and received no help from medical personnel. Using the U-curve as an aid to discussing the stresses of adjustment is an excellent way to determine how much of the sojourner's difficulty is related to adjustment and how much may be due to other factors, possibly exacerbated by the sojourn experience. Discussing the U-curve provides a way for sojourners to tell their own stories and to take the discussion beyond the presenting problem. It also provides an opening for sojourners to say what is on their minds and gives them a context for non-threatening discussions of feelings.

Case Example: A foreign student came to a counseling center for help with anger with host-country nationals. He labeled them rude, noisy, unfriendly, and inconsiderate. Most of his interactions with host nationals had been unsatisfying and frustrating. He felt they were impatient with his language limitations and failed to take him seriously. He was tired of being angry. He wanted help in understanding the host nationals and in learning how he could be less angry. While his academic work had been going well, he was in classes that required him to work in small groups with other students, all of whom would receive the same grade. He did not want to have his grade average ruined by having to work with others. He was frustrated and depressed. After discussing the U-curve, this sojourner placed himself as fairly satisfied and adjusted in the academic realm, but at the bottom of the U-curve with regard to his relationships with host nationals.

While discussing the adjustment model, the counselor learned that this student had never before worked cooperatively in a small group with peers. Being from a more hierarchical culture, he had difficulty accepting the notion that all group members had an equal voice, despite the fact that they were from different levels within the university. Also, the counselor learned that the sojourner did not have an accurate picture of the host country's educational system. So the counselor provided some information about that system and the values that underlie it, and offered possible explanations for the group members' behavior. The counselor also worked with this client on some small-group skills so that he could feel on a more equal footing in the group.

This counseling provided information, culture learning, skill building, and support that enabled the student to feel more comfortable in his situation and less powerless in his interactions with peers.

Returning sojourners are often surprised by the readjustment issues they encounter. Things back home make no sense to them; other people do not understand or appreciate the experience they have had. Counselors need to recognize the potential effects of an overseas experience and to realize that coming home may be more stressful than going abroad.

Case Example: A student came to the counseling center because she was not doing well in school. Although she had been a popular, bright, active student in high school, in college she was alone most of the time, did not relate to her classmates or to the material being presented in her classes, and she stayed home most of the time. She complained that her friends and family did not understand her, and she was having a hard time understanding why she had changed so much. Asked about her high school experience and why it was different, she explained that she had been in an international school from seventh grade though her senior year, while her father was on an international assignment. She knew four languages and had friends around the world. She complained that no one seemed interested in her experiences and that her former friends were more interested in boys than in the things that interested her. After hearing the adjustment curve idea, she immediately became excited. The U-curve provided a framework for her experience. We spent only two meetings discussing the stress of being in a familiar, yet unfamiliar, environment. The focus of the counseling was to normalize and validate her experience as a reentering student. We discussed ways she could meet foreign students and perhaps hold onto some of the experiences she valued from her days at the international school. We also brainstormed about ways she could catch up on some of the popular culture she had missed, and we practiced ways she could seek assistance from her friends. By the end she felt more in control, not deficient but rather aware that she had something special to offer others.

Sojourners often feel they lack power in the host environment because they don't have the skills and information necessary to function effectively. This feeling of powerlessness can recur on the return home, especially after a long sojourn during which the sojourner's behaviors and attitudes have changed. One of the goals of counseling in these situations is to help returnees regain a sense of well-being so they can learn and grow from their experience. Using the U-Curve of Adjustment in counseling sojourners has several benefits in this regard:

- It can normalize one's experience and by so doing release some of the anxiety that goes along with feeling that something is wrong within oneself. The U-curve approach focuses on environmental factors and the stress involved in learning to function in a new culture.
- It provides a visual picture indicating that things can get better. It also allows one to talk about actions that can be taken to get to an improved level of comfort.
- It provides a non-threatening way for the client to disclose some of the more personal aspects of life that are rarely discussed openly because they are intrapsychic, and not readily visible to others.
- It introduces some of the issues surrounding the reentry experience and provides a forum for them to be discussed and rehearsed in a deliberate, anticipatory manner.
- It provides an opportunity for information to be exchanged and planning to take place, and, by so doing, makes clients aware of the choices open to them.

A Model of Sojourner Attitudes Towards Acculturation

Not all sojourners have the same motivation to acculturate. Some may want to leave the home culture behind and become as much a part of the host culture as possible. Some may wish to hold on to their home culture and accommodate only to the degree required to accomplish their goals in the new setting. It is crucial for counselors to recognize that not all sojourners approach studying abroad with the same degree of enthusiasm to "fit in." Knowing where a client stands on this issue is essential for appropriate counseling.

Berry and Kim's (1988) model of attitudes towards acculturation provides a conceptual framework counselors can use in determining a sojourner's attitude towards acculturation. Counselors can also use this model to guide their thinking about how to best help the sojourner.

The Berry-Kim model suggests that two fundamental questions can be answered with either a "yes" or "no." The first question is whether the sojourner believes there is value in maintaining one's cultural identity and characteristics. The second is whether the sojourner considers it of value to maintain relationships with the other cultural groups. Sojourners' responses to these questions identify their acculturation attitude and allow them to be placed in one of the model's four quadrants. Each quadrant represents a different prevailing attitude towards acculturation, as shown in the accompanying figure, and suggests different goals for the adjustment process and therefore different counselor tasks.

Berry and Kim use the term *integration* to refer to the stance of sojourners who find value in maintaining both their own cultural characteristics and sense of identity, and their relationships with other cultural groups. Integrated sojourners want to maintain cultural integrity while actively participating in the host culture in some integral way. An example of an integrated sojourner is one who becomes involved in the student government with host-country counterparts, while at the same time being active in her nationality club.

Four Varieties of Acculturation Attitudes

Is it considered to be of value to maintain one's cultural identity and characteristics?

		YES	NO
Is it considered to be of value to maintain relationships with other groups?	YES	Integration	Assimilation
	NO	Separation	Marginalization

Berry and Kim (1988) in Berry (1990)

Unlike sojourners with an integration attitude, sojourners who place a high value on their relationships with the host culture, but see limited value in maintaining their own cultural identity and characteristics, exhibit an attitude of *assimilation*. Assimilators are individuals who "go native," in the broadest sense of the term, and seek active daily contact with the host culture. They will try anything the local people do and, in most cases, find it difficult to return to their home country because they have so completely embraced the host culture. Host cultures sometimes try to force assimilation, often frustrating and angering sojourners in the process.

An attitude of *separation* exists when sojourners wish to maintain their cultural identity and characteristics, while at the same time avoiding any unnecessary interaction with the host culture. Separation in the form of segregation exists when the dominant culture keeps sojourners at a distance. An example of a sojourner with a separation attitude is one who seeks out social activities and living arrangements with those who speak the same language and are from the same country, and makes no attempt to socialize with host nationals.

The remaining quadrant in the Berry-Kim model is labeled *marginalization*. Marginalized sojourners have little interest in either maintaining their own culture or in building relationships with other groups. Perhaps their efforts to build relationships with the host culture were unsuccessful, and they fear making other attempts. Meanwhile, they may have lost contact with or interest in people of their own culture, and they are left feeling isolated. In attempting to learn the language of the host culture they may have disassociated themselves from their fellow nationals, especially those who have not adjusted to the host culture. However, their language skill level is such that they cannot comfortably communicate with host nationals. Therefore, they are marginalized in both cultures.

In using this model with clients, it is important to diagram it and explain what it suggests. Counselors can ask sojourners to place themselves in a quadrant by answering the two questions. However, it may be difficult for sojourners to give honest answers. A social desirability factor may be in operation, leading people to place themselves in the "integration" quadrant. Therefore, counselors should consider the information clients provide but also make their own assessment to use in conjunction with the client's assessment.

Counselors can use the Berry-Kim model to assist clients with issues at various stages of the sojourn experience. For example, counselors who determine that clients are interested in an integrative relationship with the host culture can help clients plan, before departure, various ways to become actively involved in the host culture while maintaining contacts with their own culture. While sojourners are abroad, counselors can help them devise ways to be involved in both the host culture and their own community. In addition, counselors will need to help clients deal with the attitudes, frustrations, and feelings they experience during the time abroad. Clients may lack the skills needed to function effectively in the host culture, so an aspect of the counselor role may be to help clients develop those skills.

Upon returning home, sojourners who have had an integrative attitude may need to deal with the loss of opportunities to be in two cultures to the same extent, and counselors can help them find ways to continue having multicultural experiences, perhaps through contact with host country nationals, teaching the foreign language to others, or acting as a resource person for others going abroad.

Counselors will need different strategies with clients who have an acculturation attitude towards assimilation. Prior to departure, counselors can discuss the sojourners' adjustment goals, and explore ways of assimilating and the feelings that normally accompany the decision to assimilate. It is also important to explore the possibility that the sojourners may not be able to assimilate completely, either because the host culture will not allow it or because the sojourner finds it too difficult.

Counselors working with assimilationist sojourners during the sojourn may find themselves dealing with disappointment and frustration about the inability to assimilate, about the lack of skills, or about issues of loss of their familiar cultural background. Counselors may also need to start helping these sojourners deal with the realities of the return home, including feelings of loss and estrangement and the negative reactions of family and friends. Another way counselors might try to help assimilationist sojourners during the sojourn is to explore ways that the overseas stay might be extended, perhaps by seeking employment in the host country or marrying a host national. Returning assimilationist sojourners may need considerable psychological support, insight into personal changes resulting from the sojourn, and help in understanding the reactions of family and friends. Counselors can also help clients find ways to maintain contact with the host culture after returning home or ways to explain their overseas experiences to others.

Sojourners with an attitude of separation from the host culture face a different set of issues. By choosing to remain as separate as possible from the host culture so as not to loose their own, they limit their own learning. Counselors can be helpful at all stages with such clients. Prior to departure, counselors can help them explore their fears about the sojourn experience, as well as the aspects of the experience they will miss by remaining apart from the host culture. Also, counselors need to explore ways separatists can accomplish their goals while remaining with their own nationals. During the sojourn experience, counselors will have to continue to deal with the sojourners' fears and to help them find ways to accomplish their educational goals. During the experience, the sojourners will undoubtedly experience stress related to goal accomplishment, and helping them ease into contact with the host culture can be beneficial. After returning home, those who remained separate are likely to experience less stress than those who involved themselves more in the host culture. However, they may not return home with the expected level of language ability, or with as much knowledge of the host culture as others expect of them. This can be stressful, and may become a focus of counseling.

Marginalized sojourners have different counseling needs from the others. Such people feel out of step at home and abroad, and, therefore, may feel disappointed or unsuccessful in both places. Prior to departure, it is again useful to deal with hopes, fears, and expectations, so that the clients have information, ideas, or skills on which to rely when things do not work out exactly as hoped. Discussing ways in which these clients can become involved in the host culture may be useful. During the sojourn experience, marginalized sojourners may feel a sense of failure at not being accepted in either culture. Helping them deal with feelings of isolation can be helpful, as can helping them develop social skills and realistic expectations. Upon returning home, marginalized sojourners need social support and perhaps some help in making sense of their experience. They feel alone, and the opportunity to tell their story and reestablish connections at home can be most helpful.

Conclusion

Models relating to sojourner adjustment are limited in the ways they can predict and explain an individual sojourner's behavior and experience. Nevertheless, they can be useful for the counselor in helping sojourners at all stages of their experience. This chapter has shown ways counselors can use the U/W/Wave-Curve of Adjustment model at each stage of the sojourn to help individual clients who have one of four different possible attitudes toward acculturation.

References

Adler, Peter S. 1975. "The Transitional Experience: An Alternative View of Culture Shock." *Journal of Humanistic Psychology* 15: 13-23.

Bennett, Janet. 1977. "Transition Shock: Putting Cultural Shock in Perspective." In *International and Intercultural Communication Annual,* vol. 4. Ed. N. Jain. Falls Church. VA: Speech Communications Association.

Berry, John W., and U. Kim. 1988. "Acculturation and Mental Health." In *Health and Cross-Cultural Psychology.* Ed. P. Dasen, J. W. Berry, and Norman Sartorius. London: Sage.

Berry, John W. 1990. "Psychology of Acculturation: Understanding Individuals Moving between Cultures." In *Applied Cross-Cultural Psychology.* Ed. Richard W. Brislin. Newbury Park, CA: Sage.

Bochner, Stephen, Anli Lin, and Beverly M. McLeod. 1980. "Anticipated Role Conflict of Returning Overseas Students." *Journal of Social Psychology,* 110: 265-272.

Brein, Michael, and Kenneth H. David. 1971. "Intercultural Communication and the Adjustment of the Sojourner." *Psychological Bulletin* 70: 215-230.

Brislin, Richard. W. 1981. *Cross-Cultural Encounters.* New York: Pergamon.

Byrnes, Francis C. 1966. "Role Shock: An Occupational Hazard of American Technical Assistants Abroad." *Annals* 368: 95-108.

Church, Austin T. 1982. "Sojourner Adjustment." *Psychological Bulletin* 91: 540-572.

Feinstein, B. E. S., and C. Ward. 1990. "Loneliness and Psychological Adjustment of Sojourners: New Perspectives on Culture Shock." In *Heterogeneity in Cross-Cultural Psychology.* Ed. Daphne M. Keats, Donald Munro, and Leon Mann. Lisse, The Netherlands: Swets and Zeitlinger.

Furnham, Adrian, and Stephen Bochner. 1986. *Culture Shock: Psychological Reactions to Unfamiliar Environments.* London: Methuen.

Graves, Theodore D. 1967. "Psychological Acculturation in a Tri-Ethnic Community." *Southwestern Journal of Anthropology* 23: 337-350.

Gullahorn, John T., and Jeanne E. Gullahorn. 1963. "An Extension of the U-curve Hypothesis." *Journal of Social Issues* 19, 3: 33-47.

Higbee, Homer. 1969. "Role Shock—A New Concept." *International Educational and Cultural Exchange* 4, 4: 71-81.

Institute of International Education. 1993. *1993–94 Academic Year Abroad: The Most Complete Guide to Planning Academic Year Study Abroad.* New York: IIE.

Jacobson, Eugene H. 1963. "Sojourn Research: A Definition of the Field." *Journal of Social Issues* 19, 3: 123-129.

Kim, U. 1988. "Acculturation of Korean Immigrants to Canada: Psychological, Demographic and Behavioral Profiles of Emigrating Koreans, Non-Emigrating Koreans, and Korean-Canadians." Ph.D. diss. Queen's University, Kingston, Canada.

Lysgaard, Sverre. 1955. "Adjustment in Foreign Society: Norwegian Fulbright Grantees Visiting the United States." *International Social Science Bulletin* 7: 45-51.

Noesjirwan, J. A. 1966. "A Study of the Adjustment of Some Indonesian Students Studying in Australia." Master's thesis. Victoria University, Wellington, New Zealand.

Oberg, Kalervo. 1960. "Cultural Shock: Adjustment to New Cultural Environments." *Practical Anthropology* 7: 177-182.

Paige, R. Michael. Ed. 1986. *Cross-Cultural Orientation: New Conceptualizations and Applications*. Lanham, MD: University Press of America.

Pedersen, Paul, Juris G. Draguns, Walter J. Lonner, and Joseph E. Trimble. Eds. 1989. *Counseling across Cultures*. Third ed. Honolulu: University of Hawaii Press.

_____. 1991. "Counseling International Students." *Counseling Psychologist* 19:1.

Rhinesmith, Stephen H. 1985. *Bring Home the World*. Washington, DC: United States Information Agency.

Searle, Wendy, and Colleen Ward. 1990. "The Prediction of Psychological and Sociocultural Adjustment during Cross-Cultural Transitions." *International Journal of Intercultural Relations* 14: 449-464.

Smalley, William A. 1963. "Culture Shock, Language Shock, and the Shock of Self-Discovery." *Practical Anthropology* 10: 49-56.

Sue, Derald Wing, and David Sue. 1990. *Counseling the Culturally Different*. Second ed. New York: Wiley.

Thomas, Kay, and Gary Althen. 1989. "Counseling Foreign Students." In *Counseling across Cultures*. Third ed. Ed. Paul B. Pedersen, Juris G. Draguns, William J. Lonner, and Joseph E. Trimble. Honolulu: University of Hawaii Press.

Wanga, Lucas. 1989. "Characteristics and Needs of International Students in the United States." University of Minnesota, Unpublished manuscript.

Zikopoulos, Marianthi. Ed. 1992. *Open Doors 1990–91: Report on International Educational Exchange*. New York: Institute of International Education.

6

Cross-Cultural Training

Margaret D. Pusch

The term "training" may suggest a way to transfer specific skills to accomplish a technical or repetitive task; it does, however, have a broader application. Training is a practical and engrossing departure from dry, static approaches to helping people learn and grow. The emphasis in training programs is on hands-on experience and here-and-now human interactions, as participants develop practical skills relevant to their current or anticipated life experience. These skills are generally used soon after they are acquired so the results of the training become quickly apparent. Training is used in a multitude of situations for a great variety of purposes; cross-cultural training is designed to address those issues that arise when people of different cultural origins must work, study, or play together at more than a superficial level. The concern is that they be able to interact successfully, accomplish what is important to them, and develop meaningful relationships.

Underlying the various programs and practices that come under the rubric "cross-cultural training" are several generally shared assumptions:

- Cross-cultural experience is complex, problematic, and stressful to the individual.
- We are relatively unaware of our cultural identities, and have difficulty understanding the impact of culture on human relations.
- People can change their behavior and attitudes and grow in knowledge and skills.

This last assumption implies that, although some people are better equipped than others to handle the opportunities and demands of intercultural contact, most can be helped to deal with them capably.

Training of the sort discussed here is usually conducted within a limited time frame. Programs may last for a half-day or a semester. Within higher education, shorter programs are more common than longer ones. Cross-cultural training can also be delivered in less formal ways over long periods of time to address issues as they arise, rather than in one discrete program.

However, this requires a skilled interculturalist in constant attendance, which is not easy to arrange.

Cross-cultural training programs, in their purposes and outcomes, are tied to events and processes that individuals are experiencing and may find puzzling or distressing. Some of these processes are transitions such as those involved in preparing to enter a new culture or return to one's own. Other situations, such as that confronting an American professor teaching a diverse student population, may be ongoing or cyclical in nature.

Cross-cultural training is trainee centered. The objective is the development of each participant's own capabilities. Participants have a variety of motives for becoming involved in this process. Some want to acquire skills and information that allow them to accomplish the purpose of their stay, such as completing a degree, without extensive contact with host country people. Others may be interested in a far more radical assimilation into the culture than even the trainer finds comfortable. This array of possible participant motives is often overlooked. Though the trainer provides a structure and agenda, professional ethics demand that the trainee's wishes and ideas be considered and respected.

Training programs may differ in the degree to which they focus on specific target cultures, compare and contrast two or more cultures, or treat intercultural communication as a general process. In any case, the purposes of cross-cultural training are to provide a functional awareness of the cultural dynamic present in intercultural relations and to assist trainees in becoming more effective in cross-cultural situations. Therefore, learning must occur at more than an intellectual level and skills must be practiced so they become a practical resource for the trainees.

Steps in Planning and Conducting a Training Program

Careful planning is necessary to ensure that a cross-cultural training program is effective and that the trainer is able to move into and through the program with confidence. The steps in the planning process, as shown in Figure 6-1, are explained in this section, along with comments about carrying out each step.

Identifying Participants and Selecting the Kind of Training Program.
The first step in planning any training program is to determine who the participants will be and the kind of training they need. Participants in cross-cultural training have ranged from Peace Corps volunteers heading abroad for a two-year assignment, to U.S. business executives negotiating contracts in Japan, to volunteers working on a Navajo reservation. In this chapter, we are primarily interested in two kinds of participants, both of whom are involved in international education: students and faculty members who are in

Figure 6-1
Steps in Planning a Cross-Cultural Training Program

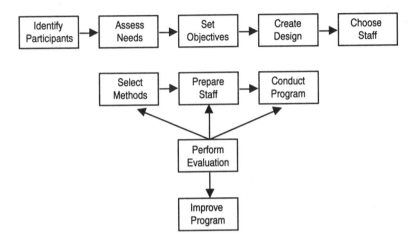

transition from one culture to another, and the variety of individuals with whom they come in contact.

Identifying the potential participants and understanding their circumstances, frustrations, and aspirations is especially important in cross-cultural training. Armed with this information, the trainer can choose the most appropriate kind of training program, conduct a needs assessment, formulate objectives for the program, create a program design, choose an appropriate staff, select the most promising training methods, and then conduct a stimulating and useful program.

First, let us consider students and faculty who are in transition from one culture to another. They leave their home cultures, go through the process of adapting to a new culture, and then return home, where they must readjust to their own cultures. (This complex process of adaptation and readjustment is discussed in more detail in Chapter 2.) Four different kinds of training programs are appropriate at different points in the transition process:

- Predeparture programs—The purpose of predeparture programs is to provide participants with specific information on living, working, and studying in the new country, and with guidelines on what to expect, what to take with them, and how to respond to unfamiliar behavior.

- Orientation programs—The purpose of orientation programs is to help participants clarify their personal and professional objectives and learn ways to achieve those objectives. This includes recognizing their own abilities and how they can be applied in a new cultural environment, learning how to find and use the resources they need, planning specific actions to take upon arrival in their host country (entry strategies), and learning how to develop satisfying relationships with people in the host community.

- In-country development programs—Offered at one or several points during the adaptation process, in-country development programs assist participants in taking full advantage of the opportunities available in the host country. New arrivals can assess the effectiveness of the entry strategies they developed during the orientation program. They can also explore ways to maintain their ability to cope with new experiences over time and to open avenues of culture learning.

- Reentry programs—Having lived in another culture, people in transition have changed; the people at home—family, friends, and associates—also have changed, although the change may not be as radical. Reentry requires readjustment and it can be difficult. A reentry program prepares participants to apply the skills learned in the orientation program and developed in the foreign culture to the process of going home. Expectations are clarified, newly developed capacities are recognized, and applications to the home situation are explored. Finally, a plan for moving back into the home culture can be devised.

While living abroad, sojourners come into contact with many people in the new environment. If sojourners are able to initiate contact with confidence and maintain it with insight and skill, both they and those they encounter will learn more, enjoy more, and pursue still deeper relationships. It is usually assumed that foreign students and American students going abroad will benefit from at least some sort of orientation and cross-cultural training that will assist them through the process of culture learning, adaptation and, ultimately, reentry. It is, however, equally important to develop confidence, insight, and skills in various constituencies of the campus community.

Training for staff and faculty. These programs are designed for people (in international student offices, residence halls, and college or university departments) who are responsible for trying to meet the needs and increase the learning opportunities of a culturally diverse group of international students. This training is intended to increase staff and faculty capacity to provide information, guidance, referral, and a range of services and programs in ways that are useful to students from other countries.

Host training. Host training is designed especially for volunteers, including host families, community program coordinators, fieldwork placement personnel, and students who volunteer to assist new foreign students. Volunteers learn and practice specific ways to enable international students and visitors to become constructively involved in activities, organizations, and families in their community and to themselves respond with greater effectiveness to the people they meet.

Multicultural management skills training. Administrators of universities and colleges today are, in fact, managers of multicultural organizations and designers of multicultural learning environments. Therefore, they are well advised to develop skills in enabling faculty, staff, and students who come from diverse backgrounds to contribute more to the organization. Furthermore, it would be useful for them to develop skills in creating and establishing structures, policies, and procedures that can accommodate the contrasting, and sometimes contradictory, values, priorities, and expectations of the culturally diverse members of their organization.

The kind of training that is appropriate for people who come in contact with foreign students, and the importance of providing each kind of training, depends in part upon the intensity and frequency of contact. The training described above is arranged in descending order: staff training, for example, is designed for those who have the most consistent contact with people who are in transition or are from various ethnic groups. It may be absolutely critical to provide training for those in this category. It must be noted that the divisions among the training programs listed above are arbitrary. There is often considerable overlap among them, with respect to both content and kinds of participants.

Training of Trainers. Training of trainers is designed for those who may have lived in another culture, who are thoroughly familiar with the difficulties and opportunities of people in transition and those with whom they come in contact, and who want to learn how to design, conduct, and evaluate cross-cultural training programs. Developing a cadre of trainers who are available throughout a campus is a wise move. It reduces the pressure on the usually limited resources of those few cross-cultural specialists who exist in the institution and enlarges the pool of knowledge and perspectives for cross-cultural programs. Training skills programs are also very helpful for faculty members and language teachers who wish to integrate intercultural perspectives and intercultural training methods into their courses. Training for trainers can seldom be offered on individual campuses, but advanced training skills are taught at various institutes and through professional associations (see resource list at the close of this chapter).

The Content of Training. Valuable to participants in all training programs, cultural awareness training brings to attention the influence of culture on thinking and behaving. Deeply embedded in each of us is a pervasive and controlling perceptual system heavily conditioned by our cultural experiences and largely out of our awareness. Cultural awareness training is designed to increase the participants' understanding of their own cultural conditioning and of the inherent logic in the ways other culture groups act and reason. Skills that help people respond sensitively to those differences and

113

learn from them may be developed and practiced in cultural awareness training programs. Professors in multicultural classes and teachers of English as a second language, for example, can increase their awareness of the cultural dimensions of their subjects and the cultural diversity of their students. As a result, the teachers can draw upon this diversity, thereby increasing the cultural awareness and the learning of all their students.

There may be a diverse population in the classroom because ethnic groups within the domestic culture are represented. Cultural awareness training is valuable for addressing issues of domestic diversity as well as issues that arise when students are from a foreign country. The basic premises are the same; the manner in which they are approached and the specific dynamic present in relationships between people of different ethnic groups are not.

Specific concepts and information normally covered during training programs are discussed in other chapters of this book. Briefly stated, the dynamics of cross-cultural adaptation, cultural self-awareness, and the theory that applies to intercultural communication tend to form the conceptual core for these sessions. In addition, country- and culture-specific information is often included. The primary aim of cross-cultural training is to move participants beyond acquiring culture-specific data to looking at how their own and other cultures differ, and how those differences affect interactions with culturally different others. Participants are encouraged to reflect on how they judge others, how these judgments are formed, and how they respond even if the cross-cultural contact occurs at some distance or on a relatively superficial level.

Finally, cross-cultural training should provide a conceptual framework for understanding differences among culture groups in general and comprehending how those concepts might be used in face-to-face interactions with people from other cultures. Possibly the most effective and least threatening conceptual sequence to use in designing cross-cultural training programs is perception, non-verbal communication, communicative style, values, culture shock, and cultural adaptation. It is best to address culture-specific information after participants have gained a sense of their own cultural conditioning and the general concepts that are basic to comprehending the effect of culture on one's own behavior. Sometimes it is necessary to deal almost immediately with the anxiety that comes from not knowing what to expect in another culture. Otherwise, the anxiety will interfere with other learning. To help assuage anxiety, one can use techniques that tie together culture-specific information and conceptual frames that engage the learner in recognizing how people perceive selectively, or use different communicative styles. The point is that it is very difficult to approach more threatening topics, such as values that guide behavior, without first laying some groundwork in areas that are less risky, such as perception and non-verbal communication. It is difficult if not impossible to deal with abstract concepts if participants are seriously worried about matters related to their survival.

Assessing Training Needs. The next step in planning a training program is to determine systematically the participants' needs, strengths, and training requirements. This is done using a *needs assessment*, through which the director-trainer tries to discover what knowledge and skills participants already have, what concerns they want addressed in the program, and the extent of their experience with earlier training. More often than not, the trainer must make assumptions about the participants' readiness to function in a new culture or in a multicultural environment because there is little opportunity for extensive pretesting. The trainer may have enough experience to predict the participants' needs and readiness, generalizing from experience with previous groups. Students departing to study abroad, for example, are usually anxious about survival issues and rarely concerned with acquiring intercultural skills. The former concern must be assuaged; the latter introduced in a way that captures their interest. Often this is accomplished by integrating skill-building and cultural awareness training with the acquisition of information the students seek. This model applies, with some modification, to arriving foreign students as well.

Setting Training Objectives. Objectives are nothing more or less than our hopes, dreams, and desires, stated succinctly. They provide the justification for every planning decision, the guiding principles by which we operate, and the foundation for any evaluative process we undertake. It is important, therefore, to learn how to identify or formulate objectives for a training program.

There are several classes of objectives. The broadest and most general is more often called a *goal*, or even a "mission." This is a statement of ultimate aims, such as, "Our aim is to promote world peace," or, "Out of many, one." Although this type of objective tends to be a cliché, it can perform a significant function in the context of a training program, serving as a banner around which to rally the spirit or commitment of those directly affected. It is also geared to the outside audiences' funding sources, administrators, prospective participants, and potential staff members or consultants. The broad goal statement gives the "why" of training.

Next is the more concrete statement of the *desired outcomes* of a particular program for a particular group. There may be several, though one may be paramount. An example might be "to assist foreign students in their adaptation to the American culture, the American educational system, and the University of Kansas campus community." It is important to inform all participants, trainers, trainees, and others of these objectives. Those receiving training should know what they can expect to learn in the program.

From these objectives, we move to more specific and *measurable results*. The first two levels of objectives dealt with purposes or ends. This group of objectives is concrete and operational. In the example of university students, such objectives might include involving a larger number of international students in campus activities or increasing foreign students' ability to find friends. As these objectives are selected, planners can begin to cooperate with those who may be working toward similar goals by other means, such as counselors and academic advisers.

The most specific type of objective is one that indicates a specific skill, behavior, or body of knowledge to be developed in the program. These may include *own-culture awareness*, making conscious the trainee's cultural identity and finding out how others view his or her culture; *other-culture sensitivity*, recognizing how prejudices and stereotypes develop and affect relations between people of different culture groups, or learning specific cultural data, traits, values, and customs of another culture; and *intercultural functioning*, learning about the cultural features of communication between individuals, and learning ways to build constructive and mutually satisfying relationships with people from other cultures, and/or developing coping strategies for living in an unfamiliar cultural environment.

Most training programs require an umbrella goal that provides a central focus. The real guides for constructing the training design, however, are those objectives that indicate what measurable results are expected and what skills are to be learned.

Creating the Program Design. The next step in cross-cultural training is designing a program to achieve the chosen objectives. The design must take into account the situation and concerns of the participants, fit the objectives, serve as an effective vehicle for the content of the program, describe the methods to be used, and provide for program evaluation. Since the design represents the basic pattern that the program will follow, much of the trainer's effort and thought is invested in the design process.

The participants are, of course, the most important part of any training program. Training is designed to accommodate their distinctive cultural backgrounds, learning styles, prior experiences, interests, and, especially, their needs. The diagnosis of their needs influences the formulation of program objectives, and this diagnosis is the foundation for design. Everything revolves around who the participants or trainees are and what they can realistically be expected to learn and do.

Figure 6-2 illustrates the training program design process. Some general principles of learning theory that can be applied to this design process and to selecting training techniques are briefly summarized below:

- Participants must be motivated to learn. They must have an awareness of the need to learn, based on their own concerns or inadequacies, and an understanding of what needs to be learned.

116

Figure 6-2
Aspects of Intercultural Education Activity
Training Program Design

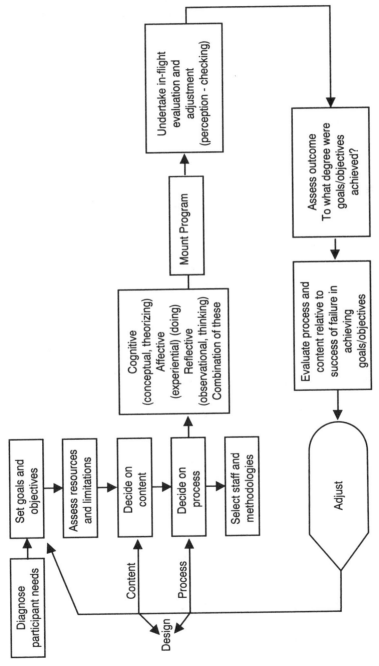

117

- Learning is an active process, so participants learn better when more than one of their senses is engaged in the effort and when they are actively involved in the learning process.
- Most people need guidance to speed and reinforce learning and to prevent them from pursuing unproductive directions. It is the trainers' responsibility to provide this guidance.
- Appropriate materials to aid sequential learning should be provided. These may include case studies, discussion outlines, readings or other materials, some of which are described below in the section on training techniques.
- A variety of learning methods should be used in training. Any method, old or new, can bore some participants if it is overused.
- People need time to assimilate what they have learned, to accept it, to internalize it, and to gain confidence in it.
- Participants must see the usefulness of the learning in relation to their situations.
- Learning must consistently and immediately be reinforced and rewarded, especially if participants' behavior is to change.
- Standards of performance should be set for participants so they can recognize their own accomplishments.
- There are individual differences in the way people learn. These differences can be influenced by culture and must be taken into account in program design.

In assessing the resources available for the program, consideration must be given to the amount of time that will be available for the training, where it can be held, and whether skilled trainers are available. As was stated earlier, training programs can be of varying duration. If it is possible to schedule only a three-hour session, limit the content to one or two topics. It is better to cover these topics thoroughly than to treat a larger number of topics superficially, thereby confusing the participants and producing few measurable results. Even a two- or three-day program has limitations. If it is possible to plan longer programs, careful consideration must be given to building each session upon the preceding one and ensuring that each reinforces what has gone before.

Training programs can take place in virtually any setting, from sophisticated retreat centers to classrooms. Site selection is usually based on such practicalities as accessibility, cost, availability, and size. The characteristics of the training site will influence the design and must be examined to determine the kind of influence they will have. This examination consists of a very critical "walk about" the facilities, and a bit of sitting where participants will be expected to sit. A few things to consider: How is the space organized, how does it channel the movement of people, and how will the general atmosphere enhance or detract from the training? Is there a lounge to which people naturally gravitate? If not, other ways to bring people together will have to be devised. Is a gymnasium the only place available? The "props" will have to be arranged and activities planned to create a sense of some intimacy. Do the chairs have stationary writing arms or are they nailed to the floor? These limitations will form barriers to interaction. It will be necessary to find ways to reduce their effects or to find another location. Are there hard surfaces and glaring lights that will cause fatigue?

No setting is perfect, so be ready to improvise and make your setting work for you. It is helpful, as well, to choose a place that can be viewed as neutral, not belonging to any particular segment of the participant group or to the trainers.

One of the most critical resources for an intercultural training program can be the knowledge and experience individual participants bring to it. Participants can learn from each other, but rarely do so unless this process is deliberately designed into the program. Simply bringing them together is not enough. Activities must be planned and adequate time allowed to encourage this type of learning. Trainers need to realize, though, that, in some cultures, people in the student or participant role will look to the teacher or trainer to provide all substantive ideas or information. Students or participants with such a background will have to be helped to see the value of their own and fellow participants' contributions. Or, at least, they will have to be helped to see that there are cultures in which student and participant contributions are valued.

The content of a program varies with the kind of training being offered. Cultural awareness training will most likely cover perception and communication theory, for example, applying each to the needs of the particular group of trainees. With faculty, an exploration of the assumptions that undergird their subjects and teaching styles can lead to discovering ways in which their assumptions differ from those held by students from different cultures. This can lead to discussion of ways in which faculty members can use this knowledge to assist the students in understanding and using the course material both in the pursuit of a degree and in the work they will undertake when they return home.

The sequencing of training events (process) and the specific methods used will be those best able, in the eyes of the trainer, to provide an effective vehicle for reaching program objectives and covering the content of the program. If, through testing and feedback, it is found that the objectives are not being met, the design can be altered. Opportunities for ongoing feedback should be built into the design so "in-flight" modifications can be made.

Trainers are responsible for checking the group's pulse and, as the program proceeds, adjusting the pace so it does not rush ahead of the participants or lag behind them. Some elasticity should be incorporated into the design so these adjustments can be made easily.

When the design is completed, the training methods (described later in this chapter) are selected. Often trainers are tempted to begin searching for and selecting methods as they design the program. It is best to resist this impulse. The completed design will suggest methods, and starting the search for methods too early greatly complicates the design process.

A post-program evaluation for measuring how well the objectives have been met is developed after the design has been completed. A formal evaluation is useful not only for finding out if the desired results have been achieved, but also for designing future programs. During the design process, notes about the specific purpose of each phase of the training will help in constructing the evaluation instrument.

Training programs generally have four distinct but interlocking phases. *Phase One* provides an introduction to the program, the training staff, and the participants. All group members are new to a training program. They need to be oriented to it and, even if they are already acquainted, to each other. During this time, trainees can express their expectations and find out what the trainer hopes to accomplish. They can also begin to know each other and build rapport among themselves and with the trainers.

When designing this phase, the trainer must decide how to introduce the program's specific objectives, and what kind of information will ease the participants' progress through the program. The trainer must also decide how much interaction should take place among participants and what the interaction is expected to achieve. In orientation programs, for example, participants may be asked to think about and then discuss what they look forward to enjoying in a new culture or how they feel about leaving home. This kind of discussion brings out what is important to each participant. In succeeding phases, as strategies are developed and skills for entering a new culture are learned, this information can provide a reference point.

Since a training program does not have prerequisites or presume prior common educational experience, *Phase Two* of the program provides a conceptual foundation on which the remainder of the program can build. This phase also includes the introduction of the training methods that are going to be used later. In Phase Two, participants should have the opportunity to become accustomed to and experience some success with the chosen methods. A considerable amount of time and material may be needed to accomplish this.

A trainer must decide what basic concepts are appropriate to a particular program and group of trainees, and what approach to these concepts is most likely to engage the group's interest. Ideas about the process of adaptation would be presented in orientation training, for example, but introduced gradually, with appropriate exercises that can make the ideas real rather than abstract, and that allow participants to practice dealing with their own adaptation. These concepts may also be appropriate in other training programs with different participant groups, but would be presented in a different way.

Consideration must be given to the trainees' level of sophistication with regard to the concepts that are being presented. What is common knowledge to one group may be virtually unknown to another. Ways of approaching the concepts vary too. One group might respond best when an activity comes first, followed by discussion. Another group may prefer a brief lecture interspersed with equally brief exercises. (To complicate matters, most groups contain individuals with both of these preferences, as well as others.)

The design, beginning in Phase Two and continuing throughout, should include processes that test and reinforce the learning that takes place. The intercultural communication skills that are introduced must relate to the conceptual material presented. Practicing those skills can demonstrate how well participants understand the concepts and their application to the particular skills. In the event that participants appear not to be learning what they are expected to learn, alternative approaches should be at hand to reinforce the learning.

Phase Three is the heart of the program and consumes most of the time available. It is here that the trainers pursue the program's major aims and participants learn more complex theoretical concepts and acquire more sophisticated intercultural communication and human relations skills. The purpose of this phase is to provide the skill and content learning that is the *raison d'être* of the program.

It is important throughout the program, but especially in Phase Three, that the design allow the trainer opportunities for synthesizing, tying together scattered insights and integrating new learning with old. The design is intended to be a vehicle for this kind of integration and should continually refer to and build on all that has gone before. For example, in Phase Two the trainer might introduce the idea that a nonjudgmental approach to culturally different people is more constructive than a judgmental one. During the discussions and exercises in Phase Three, the trainer might point out instances where a judgmental remark has hindered mutual understanding, or where a nonjudgmental response has led to additional constructive conversation.

Some special requirements must be met in Phase Three. The trainer must decide how the participants can be encouraged to take greater risks, moving from the less difficult intellectual and emotional demands of the first two phases to exploring their own attitudes and behaviors in greater depth. This requires an atmosphere of trust and respect for each individual and for the group as a whole. The trainers can help create this atmosphere by consistently displaying respect for and modeling their trust of each other and of the participants.

Secondly, the design must be flexible, so that when discussion goes in unexpected directions, those directions can be pursued and integrated into the overall plan. It helps to build a little fat into the design, activities that are useful to the learning but can be sacrificed without jeopardizing the overall direction of the program or the accomplishment of its aims. Adequate time for discussing all group experience, planned and unplanned, must be allowed so that the feelings and knowledge that emerge are dealt with fully.

Finally, *Phase Four* brings the program to a definite conclusion, rather than allowing it to simply end or, worse, fade away. A sense of having completed something unified and whole is necessary for both trainers and participants. The program should be brought to an end in a way that is emotionally satisfying, affirms the nature of the experience, and propels participants into the real world. The trainer must determine how to sum up the most significant and useful learning from the training and ensure that participants do not leave with unresolved questions or feelings about the program. In addition, participants should be assisted in devising ways to apply the training to their daily lives, so training experience is not left as an isolated event unrelated to daily life.

The program design, in sum, provides the pattern for the training. A design should be reviewed to ensure that it:

- Fits the participants and program objectives
- Is balanced, so that no one learning style dominates and so that there is harmony between content and process
- Flows smoothly, so that each stage of training yields easily to the next
- Includes periods for reflection, for physical activity, for intense concentration, and pauses now and then for rest and refueling
- Integrates the cognitive, affective, and skill learning in a way that each reinforces and elaborates the others
- Has flexibility, so there can be expansion or contraction in response to the immediate and compelling needs or interests of participants
- Does not demand more than participants can handle in striving for understanding and respect of cultural differences, for example, without expecting participants to accept other ways as valid for themselves.

Selecting and Training the Staff. In selecting a training staff or associate trainer, the abilities of staff members to carry out the intentions of the design and bring complementary capabilities to the program are of paramount importance. The program director-trainer orchestrates the activities of the program, acting as a conductor whose responsibilities begin before the performance. Those responsibilities include starting the action, selecting the hall and time of performance, advertising, deciding who will play, what pieces will be played in what order, and why. The director then selects associate trainers, makes certain they know the score, assigns specific performance responsibilities, and makes sure everything is ready for the players.

Trainers are seen variously as role models, entertainers, teachers, and friends. They have developed a unique combination of knowledge, skills, and personal qualities that the director evaluates when choosing staff members. Professionals in the field of international education often have some of these attributes, and others can be developed through study and participation in training programs.

The director needs trainers who have a working knowledge of communication, perception, culture, cross-cultural adaptation, personal development, the culture-learning process, and learning theory. They must also be familiar with the spectrum of training methodologies, both cognitive and behavioral, and be comfortable and creative in using them to achieve program objectives. In addition, trainers must know their own culture and how it is manifested in their behavior and attitudes.

Trainers must also be able to motivate participants to see, move, think, and feel in new ways, model intercultural effectiveness, and behave like good communicators, actively listening and watching, and giving and receiving feedback. Effective trainers ask provocative questions, are interested, concerned, sensitive to the needs of others, and able to be open and appropriately revealing about themselves.

During the program (and to some extent before and after the program), trainers accept a certain degree of responsibility for the work the participants do to maximize their learning and develop their strengths. They focus on the participants' potential as individuals with varying levels of experience and sensitivity. By identifying strengths, they help each participant make a contribution to the group's learning experience. They build a cohesive group by being sensitive to the levels of trust within the group and anticipating points of conflict. They tolerate ambiguity and confusion well.

Trainers synthesize ideas, taking abstract concepts and making them concrete or vice versa, as participant needs dictate.

With awareness of where participants are going and the problems they may encounter after the program ends, trainers help devise action plans that provide opportunities for continuing growth in intercultural effectiveness.

Trainers must be aware of their personal strengths and limitations for carrying out these tasks; they must be aware of their own needs and expectations and how they affect their role in a program. Each trainer draws on his or her own strengths, attempts to overcome weaknesses, and works synergistically with the rest of the staff, with different capabilities complementing each other to reach program objectives.

The program director-trainer will search for these capabilities as trainers are selected for the staff. Not all these qualities will be present in every prospective trainer. The director may have to suggest ways in which individuals can acquire the needed knowledge and skills to become effective in their roles.

This knowledge can be acquired in many ways—taking courses, reading the books and articles that are seminal works in intercultural communication and related fields, and keeping abreast of new materials that are emerging. Attending training conferences, institutes, and workshops is especially useful. These provide opportunities for testing training techniques, taking a participant role, and establishing contact with others whose interests are similar. People who become trainers often have been "trained" by learning directly from other trainers, almost apprentice-style, observing what they do, taking increasingly prominent roles in training programs, and having their mentors critique their performances.

For each training program, the staff must learn as much as possible about the culture(s) of the participants and about their professional concerns. The director helps staff members locate this information and prepare to conduct the training. The specific methods to be used in this task are selected after the director has acquired a greater sense of the staff's capabilities.

Selecting Methods for Training. As training techniques are discussed, weighed, and evaluated, the ultimate test must be the fitness of each technique for the particular trainees involved and for the purpose of each segment of the design. The phrase "appropriate technology" can be applied to training as well as to tilling soil and generating power. Appropriateness is the criterion that must guide the trainer in choosing among the available training techniques. Trainers ask, "What do we want to accomplish here?" while considering what methods will be used. Trainers must also explore what techniques are appropriate for the participants, given their cultural backgrounds and current responsibilities or situations.

There is a wide array of techniques to draw upon. They range from the highly structured to the very unstructured, with all gradations in between. As Figure 6-3 indicates, when highly structured techniques are used, nearly all the information the participants receive is supplied by the trainer or a

Figure 6-3
Training Methodologies

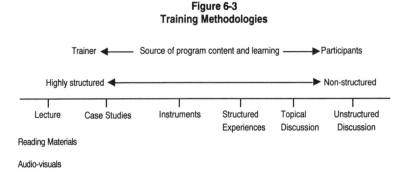

source the trainer selects. As less and less structured methodologies are employed, there is a shift from the trainer as the primary source of information to the participants as that source.

Most trainers agree that all of the methodologies included here can produce learning if they are skillfully integrated into the design. However, like the circus tightrope walker, the trainer must keep both ends of the pole balanced so the program is neither excessively structured nor unstructured.

The methods briefly described below are those most commonly used in training programs. Others exist and more are being developed as trainers test and evaluate new approaches. These are the "tried-and-true." Few require elaborate props or materials. Information about these and other resources can be found at the close of this chapter.

Lecture. The all-too-familiar lecture method has fallen out of favor with many trainers because it is thought to be far too removed from the actual situation of the trainee. However, it has its place and can be especially useful if the lecture is brief, concise, and followed by or interspersed with other methods that actively involve participants and reinforce the lecture's message. The trainer's judgment about using lectures depends on the content, the desired outcome, and the person doing the lecturing, as well as on the attitudes and aptitudes of the participants.

Reading Materials. Reading assigned prior to and during training can start participants thinking about new topics and can provide background for planned discussions. Another approach to readings is to ask participants to look for published information on an assigned subject. (This approach may require scheduled research time, and certainly requires a longer program.) In either case, the readings may be about the nature of culture or communication, or about specific cultures. The latter, of course, is especially appropriate for those in transition training. Handouts are always useful as guides during the training and can also serve as refreshers for participants in the future.

Films, Videotapes, Other Audiovisuals. Audiovisual materials can be used to provide specific information or to provoke reactions and discussion. The content of the materials, the way in which they are used in the program, and the attitudes of the viewers themselves will influence the way audiovisuals can be employed. A film, for example, can be a piece of blatantly manipulative propaganda or a purposefully ambiguous and thought-provoking work that is subject to many different interpretations. Videos that have been developed for specific training purposes require careful review. Often, only a portion of the video may be used, and careful debriefing is always required. A series of slides can be used to fulfill very different purposes by changing the narration or sound-track, order or duration, previewing preparation, or follow-up discussion. Audiovisual materials should be previewed and used with care.

Country-Specific Information. Information about countries is usually in the form of facts about politics, geography, history, and economics, and is most often provided by experts. Some trainers refuse to use it, believing that the experts who provide it detract too much for the flow of the training program. Other trainers rely heavily on area studies information and experts, especially in pre-departure programs.

Culture-Specific Dos and Don'ts. Lists advising trainees how to behave in a new culture are often provided for people who are in, or bound for, another culture. This approach is most appropriate for two areas of social interaction: the obligatory, such as calling your host if unable to attend his dinner party (in the United States), and the taboo, such as stealing (in many cultures).

There are dangers in the dos and don'ts approach. One is its inherent tendency toward oversimplification. Exhaustive (and exhausting) cataloging of dos and don'ts leaves the impression of equivalence between items. (Consider, for example, taboos against incest and shaking hands with one's left hand. Both taboos are absolute, but one is more important than the other.) Finally, the dos and don'ts approach conveys the impression that adjustment to a new culture is merely a matter of learning what is and what is not appropriate conduct in various situations. This approach does not lead to an appreciation of the psychological dynamics of adjustment to a new culture, nor does it encourage participants to engage in critical thinking.

Instruments. Questionnaires, self-assessments, and workbooks are the kinds of instruments usually used in training. While these devices provide considerable structure for participants, they can also provide opportunities for open-ended answers, alternative ways of solving problems, and some wandering contemplation. Questionnaires and self-assessments also allow participants to evaluate where they began and how far they progressed during the training program in acquiring new information or in changing attitudes. If shared with the trainer, completed instruments provide information for evaluating the training program. Although the materials may range over broad territory, the responses called for are verbal or written, rather than active, and are best used for periods of reflection during the program or in preparation for training.

Structured Experiences. The almost endless supply of techniques that can be termed "structured experiences" are categorized and described below. These experiences must follow four basic steps if they are to be effective.

- Introduction—The purposes and procedures of the experience are explained until everyone thoroughly understands what they are expected to do and what they are expected to learn. Some people are unwilling to participate in particular experiences. It should be made clear that participation is voluntary.

- Experience—The action then takes place, facilitated by the trainer(s). The experience is concluded when it has run its course, or enough data has been generated for a productive discussion.
- Debriefing—Participants explain what they did during the experience, inquire about the actions of others, and express how they felt. The emphasis is on what occurred during the experience rather than on why specific things might have occurred. The trainer must carefully guide the debriefing, helping participants maintain a descriptive mode so what was observed and felt is explained thoroughly before interpretations are discussed.
- Discussion (sometimes called processing)—Participants interpret what happened and talk about why they responded as they did. The objective of processing is to relate the experience to the issues that the experience was intended to illustrate, and to extract lessons that might be useful in other situations. The trainer's responsibility for helping participants recognize the cultural dimensions of their reactions and interpretations is critical. Being able to draw general principles from the specifics of the experience helps participants focus on cultural conditioning and to carry what they have learned beyond the training room.

There are a number of structured experiences that can be employed in training:

Simulations. Simulations are probably the most powerful experiential learning tools used in cross-cultural training programs. A good simulation exposes a variety of intercultural issues. In attempting and often succeeding remarkably well to produce a mock reality, simulations are personally involving for participants, producing feelings and thoughts that are very much like those a true intercultural encounter will evoke. These feelings and thoughts constitute a rich resource for discussion and learning. Simulations usually take a long time to play and process, so ample time must be allowed for them.

Role plays. A flexible training method, a role play can be a very brief (one minute or less), "what-if" exercise or a several-hour-long experience in temporarily assuming another persona. Usually, a small number of people interact in a half-structured, half-extemporaneous mini-drama, lasting 5 to 10 minutes. The trainer may prepare a page or two of background or "stage setting" to establish the characters and their reason for interacting. Within that framework, the role players improvise words and action. The heart of the role play, from the trainer's viewpoint, lies in the post-role-play feedback and analysis, which may involve the players, the trainer, other observers, or all three.

Brief exercises intended to illustrate a specific concept or give practice in a particular skill can be called *situational exercises.* The rules of the exercise create a specific and highly structured situation in which the trainees participate. People may be asked to engage in an activity and then discuss their personal reactions to it, or to complete a particular task and offer feedback on how well it was accomplished. Situational exercises provide for an immediate application of a theory or, conversely, provide an experience on which to base a discussion of theoretical questions. These exercises must be fully integrated with the other learning activities that surround them.

Case studies. Using real or fabricated data, a case is offered as a basis for examining certain points or issues. The trainer will often encourage discussion of several alternative solutions, more than one of which may be valid. There should be enough information given in the case so that participants are challenged to pick out the most important factors.

Critical incidents. Close cousins to case studies, critical incidents are brief vignettes or scenarios portraying situations of culture conflict or misunderstanding. They focus on real-life issues (as do case studies) experienced by the participants themselves or by people who are similar to them or who are in comparable situations. Critical incidents involve the participants in problem solving and can generate lively and substantive discussion.

Culture assimilators. Culture assimilators are essentially critical incidents with lists of options from which to select appropriate responses. The participants can then refer to a discussion sheet that indicates whether the selected response is correct (and why) or be directed toward another approach after learning why the one selected would probably not work. Culture assimilators can be used for self-study assignments, but would require an introduction to the concepts being covered and would be greatly enhanced by review and discussion.

Videotaping. Obviously a technique that allows trainees to "see themselves as others see them," videotaping provides immediate feedback on how people interact. Participants can evaluate their own performance and that of others and give and receive suggestions about how they might alter their behavior so that it is more effective and personally satisfying. The trainer must handle this discussion with great concern for personal feelings. Videotapes can be made outside the setting of the training program, of course, in order to show trainees what situations they might encounter and to stimulate discussion about how they might deal with these situations. Using video requires special equipment and a trained operator.

Outside assignments. Not to be confused with reading materials, outside assignments may consist of a trip to a playground to observe interaction among children (or parents and children) or to a shopping area to learn how to purchase needed items, an interview with a university administrator, a search for an item that is symbolic of one's culture or personal identity, and so on. The inventive trainer can choose from a host of possibilities. A little surveying of the surrounding territory may be needed to ensure that the assignment evokes the intended learning.

Brainstorming. Intended to produce as many ideas as possible on a particular topic, brainstorming is a technique in which participants are asked to give immediate reactions to a question or problem, or even an image such as a logo or other symbol. Evaluating ideas is not permitted until everyone has had a chance to respond. Then the list of ideas can be discussed and evaluated and appropriate choices can be made.

Group tasks. The group may be assigned a task that has to be completed within a set period of time. The process is as important as the product—people learn to work cooperatively, assign or assume leadership, and recognize the value of applying the diverse talents available in the group to accomplishing the job. The assigned task should be one the group views as important, and the results of the exercise should be applicable both during and after the training program.

Discussion groups. Discussion groups have a specific topic to consider. Each group member brings a unique point of view to the discussion and shares his or her own readings and experiences to shed light on the subject at hand. These discussions may be oriented towards decision-making or to information- or idea-sharing. Familiar variations on group discussions are "dyads," or conversations between two participants, and "triads," discussion among three participants. In triads, two people may talk while the third observes and then reports on those observations. In any case, participants may eventually be asked to tell the whole group what happened in their small discussion groups.

Unstructured discussion. Unstructured discussion has no assigned topic. Discussion concerns whatever the participants choose to bring up and follow. While the participants provide the information and heavily influence the direction of the discussion, the trainer does not totally relinquish control. The trainer actively participates, listens carefully, facilitates the discussion, and ensures that closure is achieved, so that no one is left hanging. In fact, the trainer's skills will be taxed more in activities that appear to have no structure than in those that have definite guidelines and boundaries.

None of these techniques is inherently noxious or hurtful, and none is always and everywhere wildly successful. The trainer must develop the competence to travel over this landscape or equally commendably to recognize and accommodate his or her own limitations. Some techniques will be modified, others eliminated from consideration. The trainer is responsible for selecting those that best fit his or her own capabilities or those of his or her colleagues, and fit, too, the particular trainees and training program.

Each method has risks for the trainers and for the participants. Each requires that trainers have appropriate skills and an adequate knowledge base. Figure 6-4 shows the span of risk incurred in using the methods discussed here and the skills and conceptual background that the trainer must have to be able to use them.

Figure 6-4
Span of Risk in Using Selected Methodologies

Methodology	Lecture/ette	Critical Incidents/ Case Study	Video	Simulations	Role	
Risk Level	LOW	LOW-MID	LOW-MID	MID- TO HIGH	HIGH-MID	LOW- TO HIGH
Skills and (skill levels) needed by leader	Presentation Theory application (leader can control)	Facilitation (low) Intervention (not too sophisticated) Theory application (relatively low level, unless group is very sophisticated) Group management	Facilitation Theory application Group management (low-to-mid-level depends on video)	Facilitation Intervention Theory application Group management (mid-to-high) Debriefing skills	Facilitation Intervention Theory application Group management (high level)	Facilitation Intervention Theory application Group management (depends on exercise low to high) Most exercises are usually not very trainer dependent
Concepts	Depends on topic selected. Concepts clearly articulated. Leader selects concepts; low risk	Depends on incident Usually: communication, conflict, multicultural group dynamics, culture-specific behaviors, attitudes, investigative skills.	Depends on content *Example:* *Cold Water:* Culture shock, adaptation, American culture, cross-cultural awareness	Adaptation, Intercultural contact, C-C learning, Observation skills Increasingly sophisticated Cultural encounter, Palm Springs, Barnga, BAFA, Star Power	Depends on topic chosen and amount of scripting. Intercultural Interaction. See 2nd column	Generally very pointed. See methodology section of *Multicultural Education* by Pusch, ed.
Audience Readiness (risk for participants)	Ability to sit still for at least 30 min. (low risk)	Ability to work in group. The level of risk the group can tolerate is taken into account when cases/incidents are crafted. (low-to-mid risk)	Willingness to explore helps. (low risk)	Willingness to actively participate and be exposed as "not knowing" (high risk)	Willingness to "perform" in front of a group (high risk)	Depends on exercise (low-to-mid risk)

© Margaret D. Pusch, Intercultural Press, Inc.

The design provides a framework for the training; methodologies are selected to provide substance and carry out the intent of the design. New training techniques are being tested all the time. The foregoing constitute basic approaches that are accessible in most environments.

Evaluation of Intercultural Training Programs

In the previous sections of this chapter we have considered the reasons for doing intercultural training, the formulation of training goals and objectives, and the selection and use of training methods. We come now to a critical question: Having established the objectives and having used these methods, what are the results? Has learning actually occurred? If so, what kind of learning? Is it what was intended? Proof of learning is difficult to obtain. Evidence of the nature and extent of learning that has occurred is usually available, however. Evidence is gathered through evaluation. The person desiring the evaluation must make a number of choices. They are listed here and then elaborated through the remainder of this section.

- Who does the evaluation?
- For whom is it done?
- When is it done?
- What is to be measured?
- How is the measurement to be done?
- How can tabulation be enjoyed?
- What is the appropriate format for the findings?
- How are the findings interpreted and used?

Who Does the Evaluation? The trainer usually does the evaluation, although there is some advantage to having an associate do it because the associate may bring more objectivity and/or expertise to the task. An advantage to having the trainer design the evaluation is that the trainer has the most thorough acquaintance with program goals and content and with the participants' learning styles and aspirations.

For Whom Is the Evaluation Being Done? The choice of audiences for the evaluation significantly influences all subsequent choices. In designing the evaluation, the trainer may choose to give priority to the participants, the trainer, an administrator, or colleagues. The information obtained through the evaluation would then relate most clearly to that particular group's concerns and should be immediately useful in their decisions and plans.

When Is Evaluation Done? Training programs are seldom evaluated at all. When they are, the evaluation is usually looked upon as a means for finding out how things *went*. It is, therefore, tacked on at the end. Evaluation can also be done *during* the program to find out how things are *going*. If evaluation is built into the entire process, it is a means for integrating the program's different phases. In addition, evaluation is a useful means for assessing how things *should* go. It is therefore important to study the findings from previous evaluations before the program, during the planning phase. Finally, the follow-up evaluation, which measures longer term effects, can be conducted one month or more after the program.

What Is To Be Measured? Investigation of certain subjects is inappropriate for people from some cultures. Investigation of other subjects is not only appropriate but expected. Basic cultural characteristics must be kept in mind during the design, the introduction, and the administration of an evaluation, not only out of consideration for the participants, but also out of concern for the accuracy of their responses.

What then is to be measured? There are three alternatives: the trainer, the program, or the consequences or effects of the trainer and program. With regard to the *trainer,* one might want to look at his or her knowledge of the subject, ability to interest and motivate the participants, ability to demonstrate cultural self-awareness, appreciation of the contrasting goals and learning styles of the participants, and ability to act as a cultural interpreter.

If the *program* itself is the focus of the evaluation, one might look at goals, components, sequence (Does one component build upon another?), pace, atmosphere, organization, facilities, and so forth.

There are five major categories of possible *effects* upon the participants: knowledge, perceptions, attitudes, skills, and patterns of behavior. An evaluation of effects seeks to measure changes in one or more of these areas.

How Is the Measurement To Be Done? The trainer must consider carefully the effect of particular evaluation methods upon the participants' learning. The thinking, acting, and interacting required of participants during an evaluation can, if the methods are chosen properly, contribute significantly to the learning process.

Most evaluation methods can be placed into one of two categories, those in which participants do the estimating and recording, and those in which the trainer or other observers do the estimating and recording.

One method used frequently during intercultural training programs is discussion. This can be very open-ended or somewhat structured (through questions from the trainer, for example). A more formal kind of discussion, very appropriate for monitoring and evaluation, is the interview. The trainer can interview each participant or the participants can interview one another.

Pencil and Paper Methods. These measurement techniques require thoughtful preparation but are usually easy to administer. They include checklists, rank ordering, rating scales, analysis of critical incidents, analysis of case studies or films and photographs, completing sentences, answering questions, and keeping a journal. Examples of four of these methods are given here; examples of all the methods can be found in the publications listed at the close of this chapter.

Checklists usually consist of single words, often adjectives, or short descriptive phrases such as:

For me, this course has been (check as many as apply):

_____ informative

_____ boring

_____ motivating

_____ frustrating

_____ enjoyable

_____ tedious

Several kinds of *rating scales* are suitable for evaluating intercultural training programs. The scales that are easiest to respond to and tabulate can be incorporated into questions such as:

To what extent has this program been valuable for you?

(Please circle the appropriate number)

not at all - 0   1   2   3   4   5 - extremely

In *sentence completion*, the first part of each sentence describes a certain situation or identifies particular individuals (often the participant). The participant finishes the sentence in whatever way he or she wishes. This method can be used to estimate the present level of, and subsequent learning in, all five areas: knowledge, perceptions, attitudes, skills, and patterns of behavior. An example of sentence completion is:

When I find I am in strong disagreement with an American student,

I usually _____

Once the trainer has decided specifically what he or she is looking for and has constructed the first part of each sentence, he or she can establish specific criteria against which the responses can be compared.

There are two basic kinds of *questions*, structured and open-ended (or free response). For structured questions, the multiple choice format is standard; it is sometimes the best and (for the student, at least) often the simplest. It is usually used to test specific knowledge only, but it can be used for other areas of evaluation. An example of a multiple choice question is:

When an Anglo-American first meets an African-American, the primary nonverbal difficulty the individual is likely to experience would concern:

a.   personal space

b.   kind of physical contact

c.   eye contact

d.   none of the above would cause difficulty

One variable the trainer should keep in mind as he or she is constructing open-ended questions is the extent to which each question guides and limits the participant's response. More specific questions and longer questions restrict the range of possible answers. For example:

In what specific ways has your own culture influenced your participation in this program?

In addition to discussion and paper and pencil methods of evaluation, the trainer may wish to consider a number of other approaches.

Enactment provides an opportunity for the participants to enact a specific situation, thereby demonstrating what they have learned, reinforcing their learning, and presenting to the trainer or other observers particular behavior that can be evaluated.

Production involves the construction by an individual or small group of a tangible product (photographs, poems, drawings, sculptures, case studies, critical incidents, videotapes, and so forth). Either the product or the process, or both, can be evaluated.

Observation is important to several of the methods described above, especially unstructured discussion, enactment, and production. Observation is usually more penetrating and more useful for evaluation if it is done systematically.

Unobtrusive measures do not interfere with what the participant would normally be doing. The evaluator using unobtrusive measures would look at such things as participation in voluntary activities (multicultural events), enrollment in subsequent programs, and so forth.

How Can Tabulation Be Enjoyed? Seeing the results emerge during the tabulation can be exciting. The sheets on which the tabulation is recorded can be designed in a variety of ways. The evaluators should use the formats which are quickest and simplest for them. Below are examples of formats for tabulating the response to various kinds of evaluative techniques.

NIGERIANS' PERCEPTIONS OF AMERICAN

Number of students: 3

		total responses	% of tota students
sincere	/ / / / /	5	16 %
aggressive	/ /	22	70
etc.			

134

Checklists. The example below illustrates the technique for tabulating checklists:

Question	0	1	2	3	4	5	average rating
1		/	//	/////////	/////		4.1
2	/////	/////////	//				1.7
etc.							

If this kind of question is asked after the program as well as before, the number of Nigerian participants who perceive Americans as being sincere, for example, may have increased considerably.

Scales. The example below shows how responses to scales can be tabulated:

QUESTION 4

		total responses	% of total students
as often as possible	/	1	6 %
frequently	//	2	12
sometimes	///	3	18
seldom	///	3	18
never	////////	8	47

Multiple Choice Questions. In multiple choice questions, the alternatives from which the participants choose are not numbers, so an average rating cannot be derived. Instead, the percentage of students who choose each alternative is determined:

Prose Responses. Prose responses to incomplete sentences and open-ended questions are evaluated in one of two ways, by comparing the participants' responses to one another and then rating each participant accordingly, or by comparing their responses to a general standard or specific set of criteria and then rating the participants or the program depending upon the purpose of the question.

What Is the Appropriate Format for Findings? Sometimes the tabulation sheet itself is the best format for portraying the results. Often, however, it contains more data than are needed. Furthermore, if the findings are to be clear and easily grasped, it is better to use a format that makes a strong visual impression, one that presents the data in lines, bars, graphs, or contrasting locations on the page. Such a simplified, easily assimilated format is especially important when the results are to be presented to someone else (for example, the participants or administrators).

Checklists. The example below illustrates how evaluation results can be displayed graphically:

SAUDI PERCEPTIONS OF AMERICANS

Number of respondents: 32

15. Generally speaking, Americans are (*please check as many as apply*):

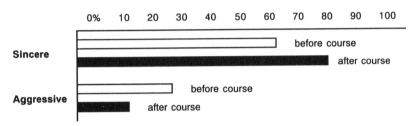

The results of checklists can also be clearly displayed by showing them in rank order, with the number of respondents choosing each alternative reported as a percentage of the total number of respondents:

PARTICIPANTS' DESCRIPTION OF PROGRAM
Number of respondents: 32

17. For me, this course has been (check as many as apply):

82% exciting
80   engaging
76   motivating
68   one of the best

Scales. Scales on which the participant selects a number can yield equally interesting and useful results. One appropriate format is the following:

EVALUATION OF COURSE GOALS
Number of respondents: 33

18.   As a result of this program, to what extent would you say you now recognize more clearly the influence of your own culture upon your particular values, expectations, and ways of relating to other people?

(not at all -   0   1   2   3   4   5   - much more clearly)
Average: 4.1   Range 1-5

When several short items have been rated on a numerical scale, the results can be displayed clearly by rank ordering them. These results, of course, are extremely useful in designing the next training program. An example is shown below:

Evaluation of course components

4.9	exercise on intercultural learning
4.7	film on perceptions
4.7	lecture on communication
4.3	exercise on listening
3.8	case study on conflict

An average of all these figures would give the trainer an overall rating for the program.

Responses. The essence of prose responses (elicited through sentence completion, open-ended question, critical incidents, case studies, films, photographs, or journals) can be clearly presented by summarizing the responses and pointing out those that are most frequent or unique. The summary can be made more engaging by quoting a few representative responses.

How Are the Findings Interpreted and Used? It is the evaluator's obligation (and opportunity) to see that the results of the evaluation are interpreted responsibly. The trainer begins by studying all the results and selecting those that are most important—important in that they are most *unexpected, revealing,* or *useful.* Care must be taken in selecting these results and caution must be exercised in interpreting them. It is with *substantial changes, basic contradictions,* and *consistent patterns* over time that the interpreter is concerned.

Having selected the most significant results, the evaluator tries to account for them, offering the most plausible reasons for the results. Again, caution is appropriate: cause-and-effect relationships are difficult to establish in the social sciences.

The long-term objective is repetition of the evaluation. As the evaluation is conducted and carefully interpreted with different participants during different years, patterns emerge. The adviser's and administrator's knowledge of these patterns then becomes the basis for more accurate, more confident planning and for more effective international education.

One must be cautious, however, about planning the next program based on evaluations from the last. One of the difficulties of planning cross-cultural training programs lies in the diversity among the participant groups. What works for one may fail with another. Thus, what is learned from the evaluation must be applied judiciously, with a practiced eye on each trainee group's distinguishing characteristics.

Finally, it is important to take temperature checks throughout the program and, as mentioned earlier, to adjust the program in response to participants' emerging concerns, pace of learning, and poor or even good response to particular methods. This is, of course, easier to do in longer programs than in brief ones. Three questions asked at regular intervals and responded to in writing can provide an ongoing check for trainers. Those questions are:

- What is the most important thing you have learned today (or during a particular period)?
- What would you like to know more about?
- What do you want to explore that may not have been included in the program?

If the trainer is unable to include new issues or topics or to expand extensively on those already addressed, the participants can at least be provided with references or a brief, private discussion.

Conclusion

Everyone can cite examples of people who manage the most difficult situations with ease and great effectiveness, and of people who seem to have a chronic case of foot-in-mouth disease, even though they apparently mean well. Some scholars have tried, therefore, to identify the components of effectiveness in intercultural relations, and the means by which people can learn to be effective. A final, undisputed compilation of traits, abilities, and/or characteristics that constitute effectiveness has yet to emerge. But certain traits are commonly mentioned in literature about intercultural effectiveness. An effective cross-cultural communicator is often described as a person who has rather vague boundaries of self, who tolerates ambiguity well, and who is adaptable to new stimuli, social conventions, and behavioral demands. This person is skillful at observing and interpreting the cultural features of behavior and displaying respect for people from other cultures. Finally, this person is able to accept his or her own failures, understand his or her own cultural roots and their effect on personal behavior, and has a well-developed sense of humor.

This is a tall order, and we suspect few, if any, individuals can measure up in all these ways. The aim of cross-cultural training is to assist individuals to begin increasing their capacity to incorporate as many of these abilities and attributes as possible into their personal style of behaving and communicating. The process is ongoing, and it is rarely possible for participants to learn all they need to know or to become accomplished intercultural communicators in any one training program. Understanding why people have different patterns of beliefs, values, thinking, behavior, and communicative styles, making tentative adaptations to different cultural environments, and developing respect for those who are unlike oneself are respectable goals for training. Many trainees develop real coping strategies or pick up useful tools that serve them well in cross-cultural situations. All, it is hoped, are challenged to see differences as a resource for living in a multi-cultural world.

Resource List

Most reference lists and bibliographies are composed with a bias, and this one is no exception. The materials listed here are, as much as possible, culture general, although there is a rich literature about specific cultures. This list is composed of those items that the author tends to use repeatedly and that have proven their worth in many situations. This list is also selective rather than exhaustive because it is the author's experience that exhaustive bibliographies are confounding rather than helpful.

Theory

Althen, Gary. 1988. *American Ways: A Guide for Foreigners*. Yarmouth, ME: Intercultural Press. A clear, easy-to-read description of the basic characteristics of American culture (from values to customary behaviors) and how they differ from other cultures.

Barnlund, Dean C. 1989. *Public and Private Self in Japan and the United States*. Yarmouth, ME: Intercultural Press. Barnlund examines the variation in styles of communication between the Japanese and Americans, in particular how verbal and nonverbal self-disclosure is handled. This study is placed in a broad, worldwide context.

Fisher, Glen. 1988. *Mindsets: The Role of Culture and Perception in International Relations*. Yarmouth, ME: Intercultural Press. An examination of how ways of reasoning and thinking, styles of behavior and communication, and fundamental assumptions and values affect international affairs.

Furnham, Adrian, and Stephen Bochner. 1986. *Culture Shock*. New York: Routledge, Chapman and Hall. Explores the psychology of intercultural contact and the long- and short-term adjustment experiences of travelers, refugees, foreign students, business personnel, and others.

Hall, Edward T. 1976. *Beyond Culture*. New York: Anchor Press. Explores the concepts of high- and low-context culture and discusses ways in which cultures manifests itself, for example, in action chains and identification modes.

Hall, Edward T. 1983. *The Dance of Life: The Other Dimensions of Time*. New York: Anchor Press. A study of the differences in perception and the use of time among cultures. Includes a comparison of polychronic and monochronic orientations and their cultural manifestations.

Hofstede, Geert. 1991. *Cultures and Organizations*. New York: McGraw-Hill. Examining attitudes toward work, Hofstede identifies five dimensions along which value systems vary: power distance, uncertainty avoidance, individualism vs. collectivism, masculinity (assertiveness or nurture), and long-term vs. short-term orientation.

Pedersen, Paul. 1988. *A Handbook for Developing Multicultural Awareness*. Alexandria, VA: American Association for Counseling and Development. Pedersen outlines a three-stage process of multicultural development: awareness of culture, knowledge about culture, and skill in dealing with cultural issues. Includes learning activities.

Samovar, Larry A., and Richard E. Porter. Eds. 1991. *Intercultural Communication: A Reader*. Sixth ed. Belmont, CA: Wadsworth A basic text with articles by well-known scholars in the field, this book lays out fundamental concepts in intercultural communication. Focuses on cultures and identity groups, cultural contexts, verbal and nonverbal interaction, and ethical considerations.

Sikkema, Mildred, and Agnes Niyekawa. 1987. *Design for Cross-Cultural Learning*. Yarmouth, ME: Intercultural Press. Defines the nature of cross-cultural learning and offers a carefully constructed design for realizing the potential of study abroad.

Singer, Marshall. 1987. *Intercultural Communication: A Perceptual Approach*. Englewood Cliffs, NJ: Prentice-Hall. Basic perceptual theories covered in this book include the central concept of identity as applied to the communication process and an examination of role of power in the communication process.

Stewart, Edward C., and Milton J. Bennett. 1991. *American Cultural Patterns: A Cross-Cultural Perspective*. Rev. ed. Yarmouth, ME: Intercultural Press. Explores the values and assumptions of mainstream American culture by dividing the patterns of perceptions, thoughts, behaviors, and beliefs that characterize American culture into four major categories: form of activity, form of social relations, perception of the world, and perception of self.

Training

Archer, Carol M. 1991. *Living with Strangers in the U.S.A.* Englewood Cliffs, NJ: Prentice-Hall Regents. An ESL text that examines the ESL classroom from the point of view of international students and their teachers. Extensive use of Archer's "culture bump" approach.

Brislin, Richard, Kenneth Cushner, Craig Cherrie, and Mahealani Yong. 1986. *Intercultural Interactions: A Practical Guide*. Newbury Park, CA: Sage. A cross-cultural orientation and training manual based on the cultural assimilator training technique.

Fowler, Sandra M., and Monica Mumford. *Intercultural Sourcebook*. Yarmouth, ME: Intercultural Press, forthcoming. An in-depth exploration of the major methodologies in cross-cultural training.

Gaston, Jan. 1984. *Cultural Awareness Teaching Techniques*. Brattleboro, VT: Pro Lingua Associates. Twenty techniques that can be used in language classrooms and various orientation and training programs.

Gochenour, Ted. 1993. *Beyond Experience*. Rev. ed. Yarmouth, ME: Intercultural Press. Moving from concepts to practice to assessment, this book contains many of the ideas and experiential techniques used in World Learning (formerly the Experiment in International Living) programs.

Grove, Cornelius. 1989. *Orientation Handbook for Youth Exchange Programs*. Yarmouth, ME: Intercultural Press. Explores the dynamics of the exchange experience and provides a set of carefully selected materials for orientation at each stage of the exchange process.

Kelley, Colleen, and Judith E. Meyers. 1990. *CCAI: Cross-Cultural Adaptability Inventory*. Available from Intercultural Press. A fifty-item, self-scoring instrument designed to explore an individual's potential for cross-cultural effectiveness, based on those factors identified as most useful for interacting with people from other cultures.

Nipporica Associates. 1993. *Ecotonos*. Yarmouth, ME: Intercultural Press. A simulation game that highlights the stumbling blocks operating in a multicultural environment: power issues, cultural assumptions, expectations, and communication styles.

Paige, R. Michael. 1993. *Orientation to the Intercultural Experience*. Yarmouth, ME: Intercultural Press. This book brings together in one volume some of the most insightful writing on intercultural training and education, including descriptions of particular orientation and reentry programs.

Pusch, Margaret D. Ed. *Multicultural Education: A Cross-Cultural Training Approach*. Yarmouth, ME: Intercultural Press. 1979. A practical manual that presents experiential training methods organized by concept. Includes a section on evaluation.

Ogami, Noriko. Producer. 1987. *Cold Water*. Yarmouth, ME: Intercultural Press. A video about cross-cultural adaptation, culture shock, and American cultural values from the perspective—and out of the mouths—of foreign students at Boston University.

Seelye, H. Ned. 1993. *Teaching Culture: Strategies for Intercultural Communication*. Lincolnwood, IL: NTC. A basic handbook that provides practical strategies for combining language and culture study.

Shirts, Gary. N.d. *BAFA BAFA*. Del Mar, CA: Simulation Training Systems. The traditional simulation that examines issues related to crossing cultural boundaries by developing two culture groups that must visit and learn from each other.

_____. N.d. *RAFA RAFA*. Del Mar, CA: Simulation Training Systems. A version of Bafa Bafa for children that has been used successfully with high school students and adults.

_____. 1969. *Star Power*. Del Mar, CA: Simile Training Systems, 1969. How does it feel to be on the short end of an unequal distribution of power (or wealth)? This simulation dramatically brings home the experience. The game leads to the acquisition of wealth and power by one group, which is then given the right to change the rules of the game. This inequality is generally perpetuated by the power group and results in a rebellion by the other players. Whether the focus is majority-minority, mainstream-ethnic, or rich nation–poor nation, here is a way to shed light on the nature of social, political, and economic power and how it is used—and abused.

Summerfield, Ellen. 1993. *Crossing Cultures through Film*. Yarmouth, ME: Intercultural Press. With concrete suggestions for using film as a teaching and learning medium, Summerfield reviews more than 70 classic and current films, many of which are readily available in video shops.

Thiagarajan, Sivasailam, and Barbara Steinwachs. 1990. *Barnga*. Yarmouth, ME: Intercultural Press for SIETAR International. A simulation that explores the effect of cultural differences on human interaction by using a simple card game to demonstrate what occurs when people believe they are playing by the same rules.

Weeks, William W., Paul B. Pedersen, and Richard W. Brislin. Eds. 1977. *A Manual of Structured Experiences for Cross-Cultural Learning*. Yarmouth, ME: Intercultural Press. Fifty-nine exercises designed to stimulate learning in multicultural groups.

Self-Help

Althen, Gary. 1983. *The Handbook of Foreign Student Advising*. Yarmouth, ME: Intercultural Press. A systematic examination of virtually every phase of foreign student advising.

Hansel, Bettina. 1993. *The Exchange Student Survival Kit*. Yarmouth, ME: Intercultural Press. A guide through the process of adapting to a new culture for the exchange student. Functions well as companion to a similar guide for host families.

King, Nancy, and Ken Huff. 1985. *Host Family Survival Kit: A Guide for American Host Families*. Yarmouth, ME: Intercultural Press. A thorough guide to understanding the nature of exchange and adapting to a foreign guest. Explores the stages of the experience.

Storti, Craig. 1990. *The Art of Crossing Cultures*. Yarmouth, ME: Intercultural Press. An analysis of cross-cultural adaptation based not only on psychological and communication theory but also on the vivid perceptions of an assortment of the world's greatest writers and their literature.

Journals and Newsletters

Cultural Diversity at Work. The GilDeane Group, 13751 Lake City Way, NE, Suite 106, Seattle, WA 98125-3615.

Insights on Global Ethics. The Institute for Global Ethics, Box 563, 21 Elm Street, Camden, ME 04843.

International Educator. NAFSA: Association of International Educators (semiannual), NAFSA, 1875 Connecticut Avenue, NW, Suite 1000, Washington, DC 20009-5728.

International Journal of Intercultural Relations. International Society for Intercultural Education, Training and Research, Washington, DC (available from Pergamon Press, Inc., Fairview Park, Elmsford, NY 10523).

Other Resources

Intercultural Communication Institute, 8835 SW Canyon Lane, Suite 238, Portland, OR 97225. Conducts the Summer Institute of Intercultural Communication.

Intercultural Press, Inc., PO Box 700, Yarmouth, ME 04096. Publishers of intercultural materials, books, training strategies, videos.

NAFSA: Association of International Educators, 1875 Connecticut Avenue, NW, Suite 1000, Washington, DC 20009-5728. Professional organization; publications, videos, workshops, conferences.

Pfeiffer and Company, 8517 Production Avenue, San Diego, CA 92121-2280. Training materials and manuals.

Pro Lingua Associates, 15 Elm Street, Brattleboro, VT 05301. Publications, many directed toward language teachers.

Sage Publishing, PO Box 5084, Newbury Park, CA 91359-9924. Academic publications in the field of intercultural communication.

SIETAR International, Suite 200, 808 17th Street, NW, Washington, DC 20006. Professional organization; institutes, conferences, information about resources.

School for International Training, World Learning Inc., Kipling Road, PO Box 676, Brattleboro, VT 05302-0676. Summer professional development program.

Simulation Training Systems, PO Box 910, Del Mar, CA 92014. Simulations and other games on a variety of topics.

7

Multiculturalism and International Education: Domestic and International Differences

Janet Marie Bennett and Milton James Bennett

Long, long ago in a land that seems far, far away, the subject of intercultural relations seldom came up on U.S. campuses. Foreign student advisers and study-abroad administrators would bring it up from time to time, but it was frequently considered a luxury item rather than a necessity.

Enter the nineties—intercultural relations is a daily topic on nearly every campus. Whether the terms used are "valuing diversity," "multiculturalizing the curriculum," "promoting cultural pluralism," "reducing racism," or "internationalizing the campus," institutions of higher learning are facing complex issues concerning intercultural relationships. Now far from a luxury, intercultural relations was recently listed among the top five campus-life "issues of greatest concern" by presidents in the Carnegie Foundation's 1990 study, *Campus Life.*

The impact of this transition on international education professionals is profound; the potential contribution they can make to the dialogue, great. This chapter focuses on the interface between multiculturalism and international education, with an emphasis on the valuable role that international educators can play.

Cultural Diversity on U.S. Campuses

It is not an accident that most of the literature on cultural differences on campuses glosses over precise definitions of the subject. Each of the currently used linguistic conventions carries a certain degree of baggage, the old-fashioned term for political incorrectness. Some writers prefer to describe the current movement in terms of "racism" and "prejudice reduction"

145

(Tatum 1992; Brandt 1986). For these authors, the core issues are the oppression and privilege associated with skin color.

Others, approaching from a different perspective, use the term "multiculturalism," which is related historically to K-12 education. Most recently, "multicultural" has been widely used in higher education to refer to ethnic differences within the United States, and, in particular, to various efforts to transform the curriculum to reflect the cultures and social groups represented in the United States (Auletta and Jones 1990; Banks 1988; C. Bennett 1990; Ferguson 1987; Wurzel 1988). Some writers with similar models have opted for the phrase "cultural pluralism" (Cheatham and Associates 1991; Schmitz 1992a).

By far the largest body of writers, however, have settled on the term "diversity" (Adams 1992; Astone 1990; Border 1992; Katz 1989; Richardson and Skinner 1991; D. Smith 1989; Terrell 1992; Woolbright 1989). The term "diversity" usually carries a connotation of greater inclusivity. It is often construed to subsume the other approaches, with a focus on recognizing and valuing cultural difference and on recruiting and retaining students, staff, and faculty who represent non-dominant groups. While this usage may be viewed by some professionals as de-emphasizing or even neglecting the power differentials that exist between cultures (Brandt 1986), it has, nevertheless, achieved wide acceptance as the term of choice (as of this writing).

These arguments on the precision, inclusivity, and oppressiveness of various linguistic conventions have sometimes created more heat than light in this national dialogue (Aufderheide 1992; Majek 1991). Various models and descriptors are, at one and the same time, defended by the forces of political correctness and denounced by "the killer B's," as one author (Carey 1992, 65) labels Bennett (William), Bloom (Allan), and Bush (George) .

Semantics and philosophies aside, in going to the heart of the matter, most writers agree that the core of diversity is *difference*. To these educators the developmental task of diversity work is to cultivate the affective, cognitive, and behavioral abilities that help people understand differences. The differences most frequently included are national, regional, ethnic, gender, class, race, religion, age, sexual orientation, and physical ability.

In attempting to build a campus sensitive to these constituencies, institutions have responded in many ways (Levine 1991). The earliest of these was to recruit students, staff, and faculty from underrepresented groups, assuming that greater diversity-by-the-numbers would enhance intercultural learning. This was an attempt on the part of the institutions to create an academic community that demographically resembled the ethnic composition of the local region, the state, or the nation (Astone and Wormack 1990; Levine 1989). Despite the success of some campuses in attaining their recruiting goals, there was a growing recognition that mere proximity rarely fulfills its potential as a learning opportunity. The idea that contact always enhances interaction has been repeatedly disproven; simply being in the vicinity of individuals from other cultures does not necessarily improve relationships (Allport 1979; Amir 1969).

Observing the restlessness, disaffections, and frustrations of their new recruits, the institutions developed a second response—special services to meet the needs of these diverse members of the campus community (Green 1989; Ross-Gordon, Martin, and Briscoe 1990; Taylor 1982; Wright 1987). Support units were created. Diversity coordinators were appointed. New interdisciplinary, culture-specific majors, such as ethnic studies and women's studies were constructed.

When services had been established but frustrations continued, it became clear that retaining underrepresented group members was becoming a serious problem. Retention is often connected to student involvement—the amount of time and energy the learner puts into both the academic and the campus social context (Astin 1985). Daryl Smith (1989) contrasts student involvement with student alienation. Referring to Vincent Tinto's model of retention (1987), Smith suggests that alienation results when students do not feel fully integrated into the institution, both socially and academically. "Social integration relates to involvement with peers, campus activities . . . [while] academic integration relates to academic performance, involvement with the curriculum, and contact with faculty and staff." (Smith 1989, 33)

Based on this growing recognition of the need for social integration, the next response to diversity was an emphasis on campus climate (Levine 1991). Co-curricular efforts were designed to create an environment receptive to the population of the nineties. The student affairs unit took a leadership role in programming for diversity. The heavy focus of student personnel administrators on student development made diversity a natural arena in which to respond to students. According to Hardiman and Jackson (1992, 21), ". . . the most significant shift in the evolution of approaches to social diversity on campus can be described as a shift from asking who is on campus to understanding how each group views the world as a function of its experiences with social injustice and the influence of cultural orientation."

Eventually, academic integration became a matter of primary concern, and faculty became deeply involved in "multiculturalizing" the curriculum (Auletta and Jones 1990; Butler 1991; McIntosh 1983, 1990; Minnich 1990; Schmitz 1985, 1992a). The canon was called into question as experts from both the right and the left dramatically—if prematurely—announced the death of education.

Most recently, education professionals have recognized that a changed student body with a changed curriculum requires a changed pedagogy. Faculty members need to adapt teaching methods to our new understanding of culture and its relationship to learning styles, cognitive styles, and collaborative learning (Adams 1992; Border and Van Note Chism 1992; Cones, Noonan, and Janha 1983; Goodsell et al . 1992; Johnson, Johnson, and Smith 1991a; Johnson, Johnson, and Smith 1991b; Lonner and Tyler 1988; Schmitz 1992b). Faculty development programs have been designed to foster the pedagogical transformation deemed necessary to improve the classroom climate.

Lacking a body of theory and models with which to construe the diversity movement on campus, many institutions struggled alone through this process. Campuses experienced with these issues now recognize the systemic approach that diversity demands. The burgeoning literature in this area (referenced throughout this chapter) indicates that diversity efforts are more effective when they include:

- Committed and consistent leadership from the top
- An organization-wide effort including administration, faculty, staff, and students
- Attention to all cultural constituencies
- Creation of an inclusive curriculum
- Efforts to recruit and retain underrepresented groups
- Faculty development for teaching to diverse groups
- Diversity programs in residence halls
- Intercultural communication training for administration, faculty, staff, and students
- Integration of the diversity initiative with the surrounding community
- Preparation of students for future social responsibility in a diverse workforce.

The Nature of the Relationship between International and Domestic Diversity

While campuses across the United States have been rising to the challenge of domestic diversity, international educators have been serving the largest pool of foreign students of any country in the world. In 1990, more than 400,000 sojourners were studying at the post-secondary level in the United States (Pickert 1992, 38).

Meanwhile, in the last decade, a movement to professionalize international education has developed. This movement grew in response to a number of issues, including concern about quality throughout higher education, and the value of international education in particular, as well as recognition of the United States' changing role in the world (Mestenhauser 1988). Moving from a volunteer base to a professional base has created greater credibility and stature for the international education office on campus, and, in turn, a greater need for advanced knowledge and competency on the part of international educators (Willer 1992).

As the diversity movement has become a mainstay of campus life, some international educators have come to regard knowledge and understanding of domestic concerns as necessary components of educating international sojourners. What differences can the educator expect in the challenges of working in the domestic as compared to the international arena? What similarities?

June Noronha's (1992) comparison of international and multicultural practitioners illuminates the difference in their positions in the academic community. She suggests that international education, and its association with international studies, has achieved a degree of credibility in academe that shapes the institutional agenda. Coming from disciplines traditionally integral to the liberal arts, international studies faculty connected to language, humanities, and social science areas are well-funded, have a "safe" political perspective, and have multiple entry points into campus dialogue.

On the other hand, the multiculturalists often need to demand a voice and are then perceived as special interest groups with dangerous agendas that disrupt the tranquillity of learning. As Noronha (1992, 56) states it, "Multiculturalists tend to perceive internationalists as elitist and interested in esoteric agendas; they are perceived in turn as professional victims, exclusionary, and theoretically soft." In sum, the internationalists and the multiculturalists tend to mistrust each other's methods, world views, scholarship, and theoretical bases.

In terms of motivation, the international education field has often attracted professionals with a commitment to global vision, intercultural understanding, and "making the world a better place" (Kaufmann, et al. 1992). This frankly developmental perspective contrasts with the typical multicultural diversity perspective of righting historical wrongs, sharing privilege, and "having a voice" (Smithee 1991).

Despite these contrasts in perspective, the two groups do share some values in common. Each brings a zeal to the subject of culture learning and a willingness to mentor others through that process. Within each community are educators dedicated to facilitating both experiential and structured learning across cultures. And each is working on a fundamentally similar issue— the appreciation of difference as it is manifested in both subjective and objective cultural terms. In addition, in each group, increasing numbers of educators are committed to social justice, shared privilege, and inclusivity. It is on this base of shared concerns that international educators can begin to reach across to multicultural educators and cooperate in fashioning a constructive, campus-wide response to cultural differences and diversity.

Issues for the International Educator

For the professional international educator, these developments have offered both challenge and opportunity. The basic foundation of the daily effort of sending Americans abroad and welcoming foreign students, visitors, and scholars to our shores has been shaken by the needs of the domestic agenda. At the same time, the emergent dialogue has presented educators with the chance to deepen understanding of cultural interaction and to provide students with substantial preparation for intercultural learning.

International education offices may find that they have become the target of scrutiny for their practices related to people of color. The commitment to diversity of office support staff, counselors, advisers, and administrators may be called into question. Concerns will certainly be raised about the inclusivity of study-abroad programs by everyone from regional accrediting agencies to student organizations on campus. It may even be suggested that international program administrators somehow find it easier or "safer" to deal with "exotic" learners from faraway places than to confront the very complex issues of domestic oppression of people of color, gays, lesbians, and women. Gaining the necessary insight and skills into diversity often requires in-service training and a great deal of "cultural humility" (Guskin 1991) on the part of international educators.

Professionals from the international education office may be involved in mediating a new variety of campus conflict. Long-term involvement with issues of culture can lend credibility to these staff members when their skills are needed to resolve problems. For instance, the time-honored concern about foreign teaching assistants' linguistic abilities can sometimes take on a new dimension when it arises in the context of an academic department that is already perceived as ignoring the needs of diverse learners. In short, familiar issues tend to gather additional intensity when viewed through the diversity lens.

As faculty and administration begin efforts to "internationalize," "multiculturalize," or "interculturalize" the campus and the curriculum, the international education office is likely to become a voice in the conversation. With access to speakers, literature, and expertise from all over the globe, international educators are frequently perceived to be a significant resource. Being consulted and recognized as a resource is always a pleasant surprise for prophets in their own land. Actual involvement, of course, may dampen one's enthusiasm as the effort of addressing conflicting agendas becomes stressful.

For the study-abroad staff, a new clientele presents new challenges. More students of color, disabled students, older students, larger students, and gay or lesbian students are enrolling in overseas programs. The campus community and accrediting bodies endorse what they see as progress in terms of access and inclusivity. However, the very nature of intercultural interactions assures that people in the host cultures see these issues quite differently. Recent examples include one exchange organization refusing to host a student heavier than the cultural norm, a medical school refusing female exchangees, and an overseas host family refusing a nonwhite student. What to the U.S. administrator is a clear moral violation appears less clear overseas. Such situations demand intercultural finesse as we begin working on diversity issues with our overseas counterparts, with due respect for all the cultures involved.

For young adults in the United States, these questions about diversity often occur at a developmental stage that is already quite challenging—when they are seeking to establish a sense of ethnic identity within their own country. In the past two decades, many writers have devised developmental models that focus on the psychosocial development of members of different cultural groups. For instance, recent research has focused on African American identity (Cross 1978, 1991; Parham 1989), sexual identity (Cass 1979; Levine and Evans 1991), ethnic identity in general (Banks 1988; Phinney 1991; Smith 1991; Sue and Sue 1990), oppressed peoples' identity (Myers et al. 1991), minority identity (Atkinson, Morten, and Sue 1983), biracial identity (Poston 1990; Root 1992), and white identity (Helms 1984, 1990; Sabnani, Ponterotto, and Borodovsky 1991). Each of these models attempts to describe the development of identity from the perspective of self and group, indicating the shifting degree of identification the person has with the cultural group and the relationship patterns that typically develop with other cultures.

James Banks's (1988) typology of ethnic development is illustrative of these models. His first stage of "ethnic psychological captivity" describes individuals who have rejected their ethnicity and are striving to assimilate into the dominant culture. At stage two, the individuals are "ethnically encapsulated" and prefer to associate only with members of their own group. People next pass through a stage of ethnic identity clarification in which they gain self-acceptance, develop genuine ethnic pride, and reduce intrapsychic conflict. The last three stages consist of a movement toward ever-widening circles of identification—biethnicity, multiethnicity, and globalism.

While there are significant differences in the paths each cultural group is described as pursuing, many of the models describe an identity consolidation period such as the one that Banks calls "ethnic encapsulation." If study-abroad professionals are alert to this stage, they are more likely to have a constructive understanding of the necessary work learners are doing at this point in their development and it may help them to avoid some unnecessary confrontations. Banks classifies certain groups as ethnically encapsulated. These include certain European Americans who have internalized a sense of ethnic superiority and who lead highly ethnocentric lives, and other people who have recently discovered their heretofore oppressed ethnic consciousness. Banks says the following of people at this stage:

. . . [They] tend to have highly ambivalent feelings toward their own ethnic group and try to confirm, for themselves, that they are proud of their ethnic heritage and culture. Consequently, strong and verbal rejection of outgroups usually takes place. Outgroups are regarded as enemies, racists. . . . The individual's sense of ethnic peoplehood is escalated and highly exaggerated. The ethnic individual within this stage of ethnicity tends to reject strongly members of his or her ethnic group who are regarded as assimilationist-oriented and liberal, who do not endorse the rhetoric of separatism, or who openly socialize with members of outside ethnic groups, especially members of a different racial group. (Banks 1988, 195)

These models are useful to the international educator for a number of reasons. First, they familiarize us with the developmental tasks being pursued by participants in our programs. Second, they provide us with tools for audience analysis of our learners. Finally, they can inform our approach in designing pre-departure and reentry programs that address the specific concerns that students at a particular stage will face. For instance, certain sensitive issues arise with young women who are formulating a feminist identity and who sojourn in cultures where feminism is less supported. If the entire sojourn is not to be a major reinforcement of cultural stereotypes, an in-depth pre-departure discussion on gender issues must take place.

The intensity of certain political issues in the United States may inspire some students on study-abroad programs to seek to "export" their perspectives to the host country. Not entirely prepared to become change-agents, they may confront their host families with bewildering questions, failing to take the hosts' perspective into account. For example, the high profile of sexual harassment at home can lead to some ethnocentric interpretations of nonverbal behavior, as in the case of a young man in a Latin American homestay who was concerned that being greeted with kisses on both cheeks represented inappropriate behavior. His interpretation of the warm greeting ritual was "unwanted sexual attention." Once again, such misinterpretations need not arise. Thorough pre-departure training can take into account both the international aspects of the sojourn and the domestic diversity issues. Failure to take both sides of the current cultural context into consideration will likely yield ethnocentric sojourners and negative feedback from everyone involved.

For the international student adviser, the same principle holds true. What used to be a simple task of helping foreign students to succeed in the university environment has become more complex, and now must include a component on domestic diversity. Within the context of the U.S. campus, foreign students suddenly find themselves viewed as "minority students" or "students of color," and they are thrust into diversity issues they probably did not anticipate and cannot readily understand.

Training new foreign students in diversity issues prepares them for the "natural" campus response to change—an increase in *resistance* to diversity. Among professionals in the area of diversity education, there is general agreement that this "pushback" is a sign that efforts to be inclusive are working (D. Smith 1989). However, the resistance may grow to include international sojourners, who may be fearful or uncomprehending of the increased levels of discrimination and prejudice.

The foreign student adviser has a unique responsibility to familiarize the sojourner with potential danger, especially when prejudice and fear can turn to violence. In the tragic killing of a Japanese exchange student in 1992, it was found that one of the contributing factors was the homeowner's very media-based command: "Freeze!" Unfamiliar with this term, the student moved and was fatally shot. Throughout Japan that autumn, students diligently set about memorizing what one learner called "the last word you may ever hear," English words that precede violence. Advisors walk a thin line between under-preparation and overreaction in these situations; the ethical dilemmas are enormous. Nevertheless, the backlash from domestic conflicts is a very real aspect of studying in the United States—one that we ignore at our own peril.

Finally, domestic students of color may invite international students to participate in the diversity agenda, only to experience frustration and perhaps anger when it becomes clear that the sojourners do not identify with persons of the same race, or even the same ethnic origin. To foreign students, status, class, and educational level may be more salient than racial or ethnic identification. They will, in turn, be perceived as elitist and possibly even as members of an oppressor group. If educators assume that a student from Latin America can speak about Hispanic issues, or a student from Africa can represent African American perspectives, there will likely be rejection from the domestic group, which clearly sees a chasm between these different world views. As intercultural educators, we are responsible, in part, for the learning that can emerge from these situations, and we can assume a significant role in facilitating dialogue and understanding.

The Global/Domestic Intercultural Bridge

A bridge between international and domestic diversity can be built on the foundation of intercultural communication. The study of intercultural relations has burgeoned in the last twenty years, based largely on theory and research in international education and business. Until recently, the major domestic application of intercultural communication was in cross-cultural counseling (Atkinson, Morton, and Sue 1983; Pedersen 1984, 1989; Sue and Sue 1990). Now, however, the intercultural perspective is being applied more generally to issues of domestic diversity, as evidenced by some of the new multicultural literature referenced earlier and by current texts in the intercultural field (for example, Brislin 1993; Gudykunst and Kim 1992; Kim 1986; Samovar and Porter 1991). In our consultations with universities and corporations, we see a rapidly growing interest in taking an intercultural approach to dealing with multiculturalism. In the following paragraphs, we will explore how an intercultural approach might link issues now dealt with separately by international and multicultural educators.

Objective and Subjective Culture. Traditional international and multicultural educators have both tended to stress the objective aspects of cultures—their institutions and artifacts, such as economic systems, social customs, political structures, arts, literature, and histories. As a result of this focus on objective culture, many attempts to internationalize or multiculturalize curricula have simply increased the number of topics included in the syllabus. For instance, in addition to the economy of the United States, students now may study the economies of Japan and Nigeria. Or in addition to literature authored by DWMs (Dead White Males), students now delve into more works by women and people of color. These are valuable additions to the body of knowledge we hope educated people will possess, but there are limitations to the benefit.

Some international educators have noticed that teaching sojourners only about the objective culture of their destination does not prepare them very well for relating to the people there. Apparently, it is not sufficient for a North American to know Japanese economics to communicate effectively with a Japanese person (in any language). Multicultural educators are now facing a similar limitation: students' knowledge of the histories, art, and literature of various ethnic groups does not seem to translate into better relationships among the groups.

In contrast to the majority of both international and multicultural educators, interculturalists have emphasized the more subjective side of culture—assumptions, values, and patterns of thinking and behaving (Stewart and Bennett 1991; Hofstede 1991). These patterns are learned, shared, and maintained by groups of interacting people.

With this focus on subjective culture, intercultural training for international sojourners has stressed understanding cultural differences in social ritual, nonverbal behavior, communication style, and value orientation. This kind of sojourner preparation has proved effective in easing cultural adaptation and maximizing culture learning (Brislin 1993). When the intercultural communication approach to culture is applied to domestic diversity, it produces an emphasis on understanding the process of ethnic identification and intergroup relations. This, in turn, seems to provide some avenues for improving strained relationships. International and multicultural educators could find common ground in using subjective culture to improve culture learning.

A Cultural Definition of Diversity. The idea of subjective culture provides a base for viewing "diversity" in a way that includes both international and domestic cultures, but at different levels of abstraction. Discussion of national groups such as Japanese, Mexican, and U.S. American occurs a high level of abstraction—the cultural patterns that characterize most (but not all) members of the group are very general, and many variations of any given pattern exist within the group. At this level of abstraction, we can point to differences such as individualist versus collectivist tendencies and other broad generalizations. While these general differences provide a rich base for analyzing national cultural behavior, there is a lot of room left for individual and group differences within each national culture.

At a lower level of abstraction, more specific cultural distinctions can be made, such as those that characterize ethnic groups. In the United States, some of these groups are African American, Asian American, Native American (American Indian), Mexican/Latino American, and European American. People in these groups may share many of the broad U.S. American cultural patterns while differing significantly in their more specific ethnic cultural patterns.

In subjective cultural terms, ethnicity refers to a cultural rather than a genetic heritage; dark skin and other Negroid features may make one "black," but a given black person has not necessarily experienced African American enculturation. Similarly, "whites" are not necessarily European American, although it is difficult for them to escape being socialized in the patterns that are currently dominant in U.S. American society.

The cultural approach to ethnicity implies that everyone has an ethnic heritage of some kind. Whites are often oblivious to this notion, preferring (perhaps unconsciously) to see themselves as representing the standard from which only deviations are "ethnic." In multicultural contexts, it is particularly important that European Americans claim their own ethnicity, since doing so removes the implicit assumption of superiority embedded in the notion of "standard." Despite such awareness, important social issues surrounding racism and bigotry will remain. An intercultural approach makes some distinction between cultural misunderstanding and racism. In this way, culture learning can be directed at areas of misunderstanding, and other approaches can be used to address pure racism.

Other categories of subjective cultural diversity usually include gender, regionality, socioeconomic class, age, physical ability, sexual orientation, religion, organization, and vocation. While the concept of subjective culture might embrace other long-term groupings such as single parents or avid sports fans, it cannot as easily be applied to temporary groups that do not maintain clear patterns of behavior and thinking. And, by definition, individuals do not have different cultures; the term for patterns of behavior in one individual is "personality."

Whenever a cultural group can be distinguished, culture learning can be applied to improving communication between that group and others. For instance, people with different forms of physical disability may define themselves as cultures (Braithwaite 1991; Emry and Wiseman 1987; Jankowski 1991). Notable among these groups are deaf people who use American

Sign, who share not only the language of Sign but certain patterns of behavior and thought. Hearing people who learn those cultural patterns can better communicate with the deaf.

Gay or lesbian sexual orientation, in addition to its physiological base, is sometimes associated with cultural patterns (not "lifestyles") generated by groups of people who interact more with each other than with heterosexuals (Blumenfeld and Raymond 1988). As is the case with other cultural differences, it is important to distinguish between intercultural misunderstanding that can be alleviated through culture learning and religious or moral bigotry that cannot.

Cultural Generalizations and Stereotypes. Another contribution of intercultural communication to multiculturalism is the distinction between generalization and stereotype. Nearly all forms of behavior and value orientation can be found in every culture, but it is possible to generalize about the "preponderance of belief" represented in any one culture (Hoopes 1979; Stewart and Bennett 1991). Such generalizations are based on research on large populations and are implicit in any description of cultural patterns. In specific situations, generalizations about a culture are useful as hypotheses for approaching communication with members of that culture.

Stereotyping refers to a rigid "picture" that supposedly matches every person in a group. Cultural stereotypes can be generated by applying generalizations (positive or negative, true or false) to every single member of a culture. For instance, the generalization that Japanese people are more group-oriented than North Americans is a useful hypothesis for individual Japanese and Americans to use in approaching cross-cultural conversation. But the assumption that every Japanese person is group-oriented is a stereotype; Japanese culture includes a large (but not the largest) number of relatively individualistic people, something the American in this conversation might discover.

Stereotypes also can be derived from generalizations based on too small a sample, as in the case of a person who assumes knowledge of Mexican culture after meeting one or just a few Mexicans. It is particularly dangerous to generalize about cultural patterns from the first few people one meets from another culture, since those who meet outsiders are often not representative of the mainstream of their cultures. Many international sojourners have discovered this when they are sought out by people on the fringes of the host culture. Also, initial cross-cultural contacts may be with biculturals who have learned to interact constructively in more than one culture. For instance, many of the first women and people of color who establish careers in white male-dominated institutions seem to be bicultural.

In sum, using first contacts as the basis for generalizations is likely to yield a skewed picture of the culture as a whole. (An inaccurate generalization can also result when you see yourself as a typical member of your own culture. If you were truly representative, you probably would not be reading this book.)

Confusion between cultural generalization and stereotype may become political in domestic diversity contexts. For instance, mentioning how the general European-American emphasis on "detachment" contrasts with the general African American commitment to "involvement" (Condon 1986) might lead to an attack by members of both groups—not because it is wrong, but because each group rejects the other's right to express the generalization and labels any attempt to generalize as stereotyping. Additionally, in situations where issues of equality and empowerment are salient, an analysis in terms of cultural difference may appear to the unequal or disempowered to be another ploy to avoid the real issues of oppression.

Under these circumstances, it is tempting to avoid the topic of culture altogether. Yet, in so doing, we fail to distinguish cultural misunderstanding from cultural oppression. Then, rather than addressing our failure to communicate, we argue about which group has more authors in the curriculum. A more constructive approach is to continue to discuss culture, but to accompany that discussion with an overt statement of the distinction between generalizing and stereotyping. With some effort, this approach allows misunderstandings to be recognized and political debate to proceed with more focus and mutual respect.

An Alternative to the Melting Pot. Both international and multicultural educators share an aversion to discovering a melting pot at the end of the multicultural rainbow. They tend to value the differences among cultures more than their similarities. Yet neither group has a particularly well-developed alternative to the assimilationist cast of the melting pot concept. With its stress on cultural adaptation rather than assimilation, intercultural communication may offer a desirable alternative.

As the concept is used in intercultural communication, cultural adaptation is the ability to engage voluntarily in perceptual, behavioral, and valuing activities that are appropriate to a culture different from one's own. Adaptation implies that one's native cultural world view remains intact as one of several viable alternative frames of reference (Saltzman 1986). This approach contrasts with the less voluntary process of assimilation, wherein one is re-acculturated into a new culture, generally with a loss or severe truncation of one's original world view. In the case of assimilation of domestic ethnic groups, a unique ethnic world view may never develop at all. The ideal end product of assimilation is monocultural, where cultural diversity has been absorbed into a single common culture. The ideal end product of adaptation is biculturality or multiculturality, where people have two or more intact cultural frames of reference at their disposal.

Internationalists generally do not urge sojourners to "go native." Similarly, multiculturalists do not advocate assimilation as a healthy solution to

157

pressures from the dominant U.S. American culture. Both groups value the diversity that generates vitality within and between societies. Intercultural communication shares this perspective and contributes techniques for culture learning that are adaptive rather that assimilative.

Intercultural Theory into Practice. Intercultural communication theory and techniques may help bridge the rift that often exists between multicultural and international educators. Noronha (1992) notes that multicultural education is thought to be more accessible by direct experience than by structured learning; it stresses the personal experience of teachers and employs experiential learning strategies. Traditional international education usually is associated with structured learning; it emphasizes abstract knowledge and more didactic methods. In addition to the tensions mentioned earlier that are associated with this difference, multiculturalists often think that internationalists lack relevance, and internationalists often think that multiculturalists lack rigor. Other members of the faculty may think that either kind of diversity demands time and expertise they do not have, and they often wish students of different cultures would stay in their own programs.

Intercultural communication embodies a "theory into practice into theory" methodology that attempts to blend rigor and relevance. The theory tends to rest on one of three social science bases: (1) psychology, such as Brislin's (1981) cross-cultural research on adaptation and other issues; (2) sociology, such as Gudykunst's (1986) work with intergroup relations; and (3) communication, such as Barnlund's (1989) work on verbal and nonverbal style. The practice is guided by the developmental models mentioned earlier and relies, to large degree, on sophisticated training methodology that combines didactic and experiential learning strategies (J. Bennett 1988). This practice, in turn, informs the theory, so that the entire intercultural enterprise is fairly dynamic and responsive to changing conditions, while maintaining a coherent conceptual base.

The blending of theory and practice in intercultural communication offers several possible advantages to both international and multicultural educators. For the internationalist, intercultural techniques can broaden the relevance of sojourning to include domestic applications. By stressing subjective culture-learning, international cross-cultural contact can readily translate into more sensitivity to inter-ethnic relations. For the multiculturalist, intercultural theory provides a rigorous description of how people communicate (or fail to communicate) cross-culturally. This theory can provide more insight into relational behavior than more abstract models of intergroup relations or the thematic analyses that emerge from literature. For both groups, the developmental models used by interculturalists provide an academically acceptable linkage between theory and practice. In other words, intercultural communication may offer a conceptual language that can be spoken by both international and multicultural educators to their own students, to other faculty and staff members, and, most importantly, to one another.

In our experience, the developmental models used by internationalists and multiculturalists are generally perceived as credible by faculty and staff outside either camp. We think the models offer a way for non-specialists to understand how culture learning contributes to overall intellectual development. The models also equip non-specialists to interpret some of the puzzling behavior that accompanies the development of ethnic identity and intercultural sensitivity.

Building on the expertise they have developed in their own field, international educators may need to deepen their mastery of domestic diversity in the following areas:

- Intercultural Sensitivity—Requires familiarity with culture-general and culture-specific identity developmental models
- Culture Shock—Requires familiarity with the "cultural" misfit of the university culture with anyone who isn't a white male
- Communication Styles, Learning Styles, Cognitive Styles—Requires familiarity with the way in which style affects learning, mastery, and social interaction on campus
- Value Differences—Requires a recognition that some domestic diversity issues entail cultural value differences, particularly "individualism" in contrast to "collectivism" (group orientation)
- Privilege, Power, Oppression, and Conflict Mediation:—Requires a familiarity with white privilege, class differences, history and current incidence of oppression, and lack of voice.

This list of issues is formidable, and we know that international educators are already underpaid and overworked. Nevertheless, increasing their ability to address these issues would pay off handsomely in improved relationships with many students and domestic diversity advocates. Luckily, most of the skills necessary are already familiar in some form. In the following paragraphs, we note the topic that is familiar in an international context and show how some minor extensions can make it relevant to the domestic context as well.

Intercultural Sensitivity. As discussed above, the idea of adaptation as opposed to assimilation is a powerful one for multiculturalists (Kim and Gudykunst 1988). The general ability to adapt to different cultures is described by developmental models such as the "Developmental Model of Intercultural Sensitivity" (M. Bennett 1986; 1993). While international educators may be familiar with this or some other model directed at general cross-cultural adaptation, they are less likely to be aware of similar models that describe the development of ethnic identity and interethnic relations, as discussed earlier in this chapter. Understanding these other models would give internationalists insight into some of the behaviors and attitudes encountered in diversity work.

Culture Shock. The symptoms of disorientation that result from encountering an alien culture are familiar to international educators. Discussions of the subject in an international context are readily available (Adler 1975; Barna 1983; Berry and Annis 1974; Furnham and Bochner 1986; Oberg 1960), and some writers have even related the phenomenon to any situation where significant loss and change is experienced (for example, J. Bennett 1977). This latter way of thinking links culture shock to the domestic diversity context. U.S. American students of color, disabled students, and older students routinely experience culture shock when entering the 18-21 year old European American cultural context of most colleges and universities (Jones 1987). Women entering graduate studies are particularly likely to feel disoriented, because the graduate-school culture is typically even more male dominated than the undergraduate culture. In fact, every entering student except able-bodied white males probably experiences a dose of culture shock beyond the stress of normal transition (D. Smith 1989).

International educators can explain culture shock responses to administrators, faculty, and other staff as a way to help them understand new students' reactions and thus decrease negative evaluation of the incoming students. Additionally, international educators could work with multiculturalists to create more effective orientation and counseling sessions for new students. Many of the lessons learned from foreign student adaptation could be modified to help non-dominant students adapt more readily to the institution's culture. At the same time, internationalists could join multiculturalists in helping the campus create a climate of appreciation for cultural diversity—both foreign and domestic.

Cultural and Cognitive Styles. International educators may be familiar with general national cultural differences in styles of thinking, taking action, and communicating (Althen 1988). Contrasts in patterns of thinking encompass the difference, say, between Northern European, abstract, deductive styles and Japanese, concrete, relational styles; and taking action may vary from some South Asian patterns of waiting for fateful intervention to the U.S. American pattern of aggressive problem solving (Stewart and Bennett 1991; S. Smith 1987). Typical cross-cultural examples of communication style include differences in the length and content of greeting rituals, the use of linear or circular approaches to making points in conversation, degree of attentiveness to nonverbal behavior, and the extent to which directness or subtlety is appropriate in asking or answering questions (M. Bennett 1988).

Difference in cultural and cognitive style is also a factor in domestic multicultural relations. In some cases, international differences are carried by immigrants into U.S. society. For instance, the interpersonal indirectness typical of many Asian cultures can be observed to varying degrees in Asian Americans, and the relational style that characterizes many Hispanic cultures is still evident among Mexican Americans. These styles contrast with a typical European American preference for directness and autonomy.

In other cases, a unique style that blends national heritage and ethnic experience in the United States may develop. For example, African American patterns of communication tend to be more involved and experience-based than the European American preference for detached inductive reasoning (Kochman 1981; Weber 1991). And, of course, many native Americans maintain the high-context style that predated the arrival of Anglo low-context style. In other words, the knowledge that international educators have about differences in cultural style may be applicable, with minor modifications, to understanding aspects of domestic diversity. They could join the multiculturalists in explaining how these differences can lead to misunderstanding among both foreign and U.S. domestic cultural groups.

Of particular concern to educators is the influence of cultural and cognitive styles on learning. Here again, this should be familiar ground for international educators (J. Bennett 1988). Some of the same factors that impede learning for foreign students also cause problems for students of non-dominant domestic cultures. For instance, internationalists know that Asian students, in general, do not participate aggressively in class discussions; they are more reflective than active in their learning style (S. Smith 1987). This is often true for American Indian students as well (Condon 1986; Rubin 1986). Similar correlations can be found among many other international and multicultural differences in style. The point here is not to map all these correlations, but to indicate that certain categories of both foreign and non-dominant domestic students may face similar obstacles to learning in U.S. colleges.

On many campuses, international and multicultural educators are being asked separately by other faculty and staff to conduct programs on how cultural differences affect learning and teaching (Border and Van Note Chism 1992; Cones, Noonan, and Janha 1983). If the internationalists and the multiculturalists would combine forces, such programs could address foreign student and domestic student concerns simultaneously. Faculty would appreciate the more coherent frame of reference for adapting their teaching, and both programs would benefit from the higher funding they could command in combination. This same approach could be taken in student orientation, where domestic and foreign students are usually segregated. Jointly-offered programs on learning style differences targeted to both international and non-dominant domestic students could facilitate some useful alliances among the students, and they would help cement relations between the two offices as well.

Value Differences. Beneath cognitive and cultural styles are more basic differences in cultural values. International educators are generally conversant with value differences in one of two forms: cultural differences in orientation toward the nature of self, others, environment, activity, and time

(Kluckhohn and Strodtbeck 1961), or cultural differences in the degree of masculinity, power distance, individualism, and uncertainty avoidance (Hofstede 1984, 1991). The value that often distinguishes U.S. Americans from foreign students is orientation toward relationship to others (individualism versus collectivism). U.S. American students generally are oriented toward individualism, as indicated by their comfort with individual effort on papers and exams, with grading that is competitive, and with the assumption that they should ask the instructor about what they do not understand. Many foreign students prefer to work in groups, dislike or misunderstand competitive grading, and ask questions of each other rather than of the instructor—all indications of an orientation toward collectivism. Most international educators know how this value difference impedes learning by students, fuels disrespect by instructors, and breeds disillusionment on both sides. (Chapter 4 has some ideas for confronting this issue.)

A similar value difference exists between European American ethnic culture and the ethnic cultures of many other U.S. American groups, including African Americans, Mexican/Latino Americans, and American Indians. European-Americans tend to have the more extreme individualistic orientation, while members of the other groups are relatively more collectivist in their orientation. The effects of this difference can be observed in subtle and sometimes rather startling ways. For instance, African Americans and Hispanic Americans tend to walk around, eat, and work in larger groups than do European Americans, who more often operate singly or in pairs. European Americans may be intimidated by the larger groups, avoid contact with them, and thus perpetuate their stereotype of African Americans and Hispanic Americans as "unapproachable" or even threatening and dangerous. In a more overt demonstration of group orientation, many students of color will close ranks when anyone of their ethnic group is criticized. This has been described to us as a natural response to oppression, as well it might be, but it is also a natural expression of collectivism.

The point here is that faculty and staff need not be more puzzled by the collectivist behavior of U.S. American persons of color than they are by the same kind of behavior exhibited by foreign students. If international educators joined the multiculturalists to explain these differences to both faculty and students, the campus climate would be improved for both international and domestic students.

Privilege, Power, Oppression, and Conflict Mediation. The topic of power relationships among domestic groups is probably less familiar to most internationalists than it is to multiculturalists, in whose thoughts and actions it figures prominently. Internationalists need to learn about this area from the multiculturalists to be effective in working with domestic diversity.

Foremost on the list of things internationalists should understand and acknowledge is the notion of "white privilege," a term used by Peggy McIntosh (1992) to indicate a constellation of privileges white people enjoy simply because they are white. Here is a selection from her list:

- I can go shopping alone most of the time, fairly well assured that I will not be followed or harassed by store detectives.
- I can go into a book shop and count on finding the writing of my race represented, into a supermarket and find the staple foods that fit with my cultural traditions, into a hairdresser's shop and find someone who can deal with my hair.
- I can swear, or dress in secondhand clothes, or not answer letters, without having people attribute these choices to the bad morals, poverty, or illiteracy of my race.
- I am never asked to speak for all the people of my racial group.

In her article, McIntosh does not stress white guilt; she explores how these privileges might be shared with others. We would add that, in our experience, successful communication between European Americans and members of various other ethnic groups cannot proceed until European Americans acknowledge their built-in advantages. People of color know that whites have privileges and that the same privileges often are denied to nonwhites. People of color do not expect whites to stop being white, but generally they do expect that whites who say they want equity to recognize that somehow the advantages need to be distributed more evenly.

In a similar vein, people who have experienced oppression by European Americans are wary of members of that ethnic group who deny that oppression exists. It behooves European Americans to school themselves in the ugly reality of racial and cultural oppression, and it behooves males in general to be equally aware of the nature and extent of sexual oppression in U.S. society. This oppression is no secret to women and people of color. When European Americans (especially white males) deny the existence of oppression, they are most charitably viewed as ignorant and more likely judged as defenders of the oppression. It is obvious that continued interaction under these circumstances will become more and more of a power struggle, with each side giving and taking offense at ever escalating levels.

The alternative to an escalating power struggle between dominant and non-dominant group members is conflict mediation. For European Americans, the first step in such negotiation is, again, to acknowledge the existence of white privilege and institutionalized oppression in the white-dominated U.S. American society. Internationalists who happen to be European American, like others from that ethnic group, will probably balk at "taking responsibility" for conditions that they did not individually initiate and that they may actually oppose in principle. This stance emerges from the individualistic value bias of European American culture. From the perspective of more collectivist ethnic groups (which, as noted above, include many non-dominant groups in the United States), to acknowledge a social reality is not to accept individual responsibility for it. In the collectivist view, people cannot separate themselves from their ethnic group, and thus any white person is "associated" with dominant-group oppression. But one particular individual is not held responsible for it unless the person claims the responsibility ("I'm a bigot and proud of it"), denies any responsibility ("Maybe other people are prejudiced, but I'm not at all"), or fails to act against oppression when the occasion arises ("Someone should do something about that racist language"). For European Americans who wish to participate in domestic intercultural conflict mediation, it is best to acknowledge one's association with oppression and then act in good faith.

International educators may be used to mediating conflict during one-on-one interpersonal situations, such as in a counseling session. Members of domestic non-dominant cultures are likely to view this kind of setting as one of unequal power. Interethnic confrontations are more likely to occur in *group* settings, and attempts to resolve conflicts are also more likely to occur in a group. In some cross-cultural circumstances, educators should expect a certain amount of passionate rhetoric to accompany any conflict. For instance, African American communication style generally demands a high level of emotion to indicate real commitment to a position (Kochman 1981). The European American style of using more cold and detached logic under pressure may be perceived by African Americans and some other groups as disingenuous and manipulative (Tatum 1992). When dealing with issues of power and oppression, it is a good idea to care a lot about the issues and to let that caring show.

Conclusion

The preceding discussion of the interface between international and multicultural education is not meant to be exhaustive or final. This subject is one in which there is no "state of the art." Initial blueprints are just being drawn. There are several competing visions of how to proceed in building a viable multicultural society, and how a multicultural college or university will contribute to that effort. This chapter has presented the outline of an intercultural communication approach, which we believe is a promising direction for incorporating both international and domestic cultural diversity into the higher education enterprise. The main strength of the intercultural approach is that it emphasizes respect for all cultures through understanding and appreciating their differences. It assumes that any continuing dialogue on legal, political, and economic issues must be built on this base of mutual respect.

In our view, international educators could—and should—play an important role in developing the base for intercultural dialogue. They have expertise in understanding cultural difference. They have experience in facilitating cultural adaptation in educational settings. And they believe that cultural diversity on campuses is important to accomplishing the goals of higher education in this society. Multiculturalists should recognize the expertise and commitment of internationalists and incorporate them into the campus diversity plan.

To prepare for assuming a role in domestic intercultural relations, international educators can extend their cultural knowledge base to include domestic non-dominant ethnic cultures and other forms of diversity such as gender, sexual orientation, and class. By spending enough time with the ideas of white privilege and oppression, they can become comfortable acknowledging both their own ethnicity and the position of power they occupy. And the internationalists, like the multiculturalists, must really believe that we can make this work.

References

Adams, Maurianne. Ed. 1992. *Promoting Diversity in College Classrooms: Innovative Responses for Curriculum, Faculty, and Institutions.* New Directions for Teaching and Learning 52 (Winter). San Francisco: Jossey-Bass.

Adler, Peter S. 1975. "The Transitional Experience: An Alternative View of Culture Shock." *Journal of Humanistic Psychology* 15, 4 (Fall): 13.

Allport, Gordon. 1979. *The Nature of Prejudice.* Twenty-fifth anniversary ed. Reading, MA: Addison-Wesley.

Althen, Gary. 1988. *American Ways: A Guide for Foreigners in the United States.* Yarmouth, ME: Intercultural Press.

Amir, Yehuda. 1969. "The Contact Hypothesis in Ethnic Relations." *Psychological Bulletin* 71: 319-342.

Astin, Alexander W. 1985. *Achieving Educational Excellence.* San Francisco: Jossey-Bass.

Astone, Barbara, and Elsa Nuñez-Wormack. 1990. *Pursuing Diversity: Recruiting College Minority Students.* ASHE-ERIC Report 7. Washington DC: George Washington University, School of Education and Human Development.

Atkinson, Donald R., George Morten, and Derald Wing Sue. 1983. *Counseling American Minorities: A Cross-Cultural Perspective.* Second ed. Dubuque, IA: Wm. C. Brown.

Aufderheide, Patricia. 1992. *Beyond PC: Towards Politics of Understanding.* Saint Paul, MN: Graywolf Press.

Auletta, Gale S., and Terry Jones. Eds. 1990. "The Inclusive University: Multicultural Perspectives in Higher Education." *American Behavioral Scientist* 34, 2 (November-December).

Banks, James A. 1988. *Multiethnic Education: Theory and Practice.* Second ed. Boston: Allyn and Bacon.

Barna, LaRay M. 1983. "The Stress Factor in Intercultural Relations." In *Handbook of Intercultural Training: Issues in Training Methodology.* Ed. Dan Landis and Richard W. Brislin. New York: Pergamon Press.

Barnlund, Dean C. 1989. *Communicative Styles of Japanese and Americans: Images and Realities.* Belmont, CA: Wadsworth.

Bennett, Christine I. 1990. *Comprehensive Multicultural Education: Theory and Practice.* Second ed. Boston: Allyn and Bacon.

Bennett, Janet M. 1977. "Transition Shock: Putting Culture Shock in Perspective." *International and Intercultural Communication Annual* 4: 45-52.

_____. 1988. "Student Development and Experiential Learning Theory." In *Building the Professional Dimension of Educational Exchange.* Ed. Joy Reid. Yarmouth, ME: Intercultural Press.

Bennett, Milton J. 1986. "A Developmental Approach to Training for Intercultural Sensitivity." *International Journal of Intercultural Relations* 10, 2: 179-196.

_____. 1988. "Intercultural Communication." In *Building the Professional Dimension of Educational Exchange*. Ed. Joy Reid. Yarmouth, ME: Intercultural Press.

_____. 1993. "Towards Ethnorelativism: A Developmental Model of Intercultural Sensitivity." In *Education for the Intercultural Experience*. Ed. R. Michael Paige. Yarmouth, ME: Intercultural Press.

Berry, John W., and Robert C. Annis. 1974. "Acculturative Stress: The Role of Ecology, Culture and Differentiation." *Journal of Cross-Cultural Psychology* 5: 382-406.

Blumenfeld, Warren J., and Diane Raymond. 1988. *Looking at Gay and Lesbian Life*. Boston: Beacon Press.

Border, Laura L. B., and Nancy Van Note Chism. Eds. 1992. *Teaching for Diversity*. New Directions for Teaching and Learning 49. San Francisco: Jossey-Bass.

Braithwaite, Dawn, O. 1991. "Viewing Persons with Disabilities as a Culture." In *Intercultural Communication: A Reader*. Sixth ed. Ed. Larry A. Samovar and Richard E. Porter. Belmont, CA: Wadsworth.

Brandt, Godfrey L. 1986. *The Realization of Anti-Racist Teaching*. London: Falmer Press.

Brislin, Richard W. 1981. *Cross-Cultural Encounters: Face-to-Face Interaction*. New York: Pergamon Press.

_____. 1993. *Understanding Culture's Influence on Behavior*. Fort Worth, TX: Harcourt Brace Jovanovich.

Butler, Johnnella E., and John C. Walter. Eds. 1991. *Transforming the Curriculum: Ethnic Studies and Women's Studies*. Albany, NY: State University of New York Press.

Carey, James W. 1992. "Political Correctness and Cultural Studies." *Journal of Communication* 42: 2 (Spring).

Carnegie Foundation for the Advancement of Teaching. 1990. *Campus Life: In Search of Community*. Lawrenceville, NJ: Princeton University Press.

Cass, V. C. 1979. "Homosexual Identity Formation: A Theoretical Model." *Journal of Homosexuality* 4: 219-235.

Cheatham, Harold E., and Associates. 1991. *Cultural Pluralism on Campus*. Alexandria, VA: American Association for Counseling and Development.

Condon, John C. 1986. "The Ethnocentric Classroom." *Communicating in College Classrooms*. New Directions for Teaching and Learning 26. San Francisco: Jossey-Bass.

Cones, James H., John F. Noonan, and Denise Janha. Eds. 1983. *Teaching Minority Students*. New Directions for Teaching and Learning 16 . San Francisco: Jossey-Bass.

Cross, William E., Jr. 1978. "The Thomas and Cross Models of Psychological Nigrescence: A Review." *Journal of Black Psychology* 5, 1: 13-31.

_____. 1991. *Shades of Black: Diversity in African-American Identity*. Philadelphia: Temple University Press.

Emry, Robert, and Richard L. Wiseman. 1987. "An Intercultural Understanding of Ablebodied and Disabled Persons' Communication." *International Journal of Intercultural Communication* 11: 7-27.

Ferguson, Henry. 1987. *Manual for Multicultural Education.* Second ed. Yarmouth, ME: Intercultural Press.

Furnham, Adrian, and Stephen Bochner. 1986. *Culture Shock: Psychological Reactions to Unfamiliar Environments.* London: Methuen.

Goodsell, Anne S., Michelle R. Maher, Vincent Tinto, Barbara Leigh Smith, and Jean MacGregor. 1992. *Collaborative Learning: A Sourcebook for Higher Education.* University Park, PA: National Center on Postsecondary Teaching, Learning, and Assessment.

Green, Madeleine F. Ed. 1989. *Minorities on Campus: A Handbook for Enhancing Diversity.* Washington, DC: American Council on Education.

Gudykunst, William B. 1986. "Towards a Theory of Intergroup Communication." In *Intergroup Communication.* Ed. William B. Gudykunst. London: Edward Arnold.

Gudykunst, William B., Stella Ting-Toomey, and Elizabeth Chua. 1988. *Culture and Interpersonal Communication.* Newbury Park, CA: Sage.

Gudykunst, William B., and Young Yun Kim. 1992. *Communicating with Strangers: An Approach to Intercultural Communication.* Second ed. New York: McGraw-Hill.

Guskin, Alan E. 1991. "Cultural Humility: A Way of Being in the World." *Antioch Notes* 59, 1 (Fall). Yellow Springs, OH: Antioch College Publications Office.

Hardiman, Rita, and Bailey W. Jackson. 1992. "Racial Identity Development: Understanding Racial Dynamics in College Classrooms and on Campus." *Promoting Diversity in College Classrooms: Innovative Responses for Curriculum, Faculty, and Institutions.* Ed. Maurianne Adams. New Directions for Teaching and Learning 52 (Winter). San Francisco: Jossey-Bass

Helms, Janet E. 1984. "Toward a Theoretical Explanation of the Effects of Race on Counseling: A Black and White Model." *Counseling Psychologist* 12, 4: 153-165.

_____. Ed. 1990. *Black and White Racial Identity: Theory, Research, and Practice.* New York: Greenwood Press.

Hofstede, Geert. 1984. *Culture's Consequences: International Differences in Work-Related Values.* Beverly Hills, CA: Sage.

_____. 1991. *Cultures and Organizations: Software of the Mind.* London: McGraw-Hill.

Hoopes, David S. 1979. "Intercultural Communication Concepts and the Psychology of Intercultural Experience." In *Multicultural Education: A Cross-Cultural Training Approach.* Ed. Margaret Pusch. Yarmouth, ME: Intercultural Press.

Jankowski, Kathy. 1991. "On Communicating with Deaf People." *Intercultural Communication: A Reader.* Sixth ed. Ed. Larry A. Samovar and Richard E. Porter. Belmont, CA: Wadsworth.

Johnson, David W., Roger T. Johnson, and Karl A. Smith. 1991a. *Cooperative Learning: Increasing College Faculty Instructional Productivity.* ASHE-ERIC Higher Education Report 4. Washington, DC: George Washington University, School of Education and Human Development .

_____. 1991b. *Active Learning: Cooperation in the College Classroom.* Edina, MN: Interaction Books.

Jones, W. Terrell. 1987. "Enhancing Minority-White Peer Interactions." *Responding to the Needs of Today's Minority Students.* New Directions for Student Services 38 (Summer). San Francisco: Jossey-Bass.

Katz, Judith H. "1989. The Challenge of Diversity." In *Valuing Diversity on Campus: A Multicultural Approach.* Ed. Cynthia Woolbright. Bloomington, IN: Association of College Unions International.

Kauffmann, Norman L., Judith N. Martin, Henry D. Weaver, and Judy Weaver. 1992. *Students Abroad: Strangers at Home.* Yarmouth, ME: Intercultural Press.

Kim, Young Yun. Ed. 1986. *Interethnic Communication: Current Research.* International and Intercultural Communication Annual 10. Newbury Park, CA: Sage.

Kim, Young Yun, and William B. Gudykunst. Eds. 1987. *Cross-Cultural Adaptation: Current Approaches.* International and Intercultural Communication Annual 11. Newbury Park, CA: Sage, 1988.

Kluckhohn, Florence Rockwood, and Fred L. Strodtbeck. 1961. *Variations in Value Orientations.* New York: Row, Peterson.

Kochman, Thomas. 1981. *Black and White Styles in Conflict.* Chicago: University of Chicago Press.

Levine, Arthur, and Associates. 1989. *Shaping Higher Education's Future: Demographic Realities and Opportunities, 1990–2000.* San Francisco: Jossey-Bass.

Levine, Arthur. 1991. "The Meaning of Diversity." *Change* (September-October).

Levine, Heidi, and Nancy J. Evans. 1991. "The Development of Gay, Lesbian, and Bisexual Identities." *Beyond Tolerance: Gays, Lesbians and Bisexuals on Campus.* Ed. Nancy J. Evans and Vernon A. Wall. Alexandria, VA: American College Personnel Association.

Lonner, Walter J., and Vernon O. Tyler. Eds. 1988. *Cultural and Ethnic Factors in Learning and Motivation: Implications for Education.* Twelfth Western Symposium on Learning. Bellingham, WA: Western Washington University.

McIntosh, Peggy. 1983. *Interactive Phases of Curricular Re-Vision: A Feminist Perspective.* Working Paper 124. Wellesley, MA: Center for Research on Women, Wellesley College.

_____. 1990. *Interactive Phases of Curricular and Personal Re-Vision with Regard to Race.* Working Paper 219. Wellesley, MA: Center for Research on Women, Wellesley College.

_____. 1992. "White Privilege and Male Privilege: A Personal Account of Coming to See Correspondences through Work in Women's Studies." *Race, Class, and Gender: An Anthology.* Ed. M. L. Andersen and P. H. Collins, 70-82. Belmont, CA: Wadsworth.

Majek, Jonathan, A. 1991. "A Critical Assessment of Bloom: *The Closing of an American Mind?*" In *Transforming the Curriculum: Ethnic Studies and Women's Studies.* Ed. Johnnella E. Butler and John C. Walter, 313-324. Albany: State University of New York Press.

Mestenhauser, Josef A. 1988. "Making a World of Difference through Professionalism." In *Building the Professional Dimension of Educational Exchange.* Ed. Joy Reid. Yarmouth, ME: Intercultural Press.

Minnich, Elizabeth K. 1990. *Transforming Knowledge.* Philadelphia: Temple University Press.

Myers, Linda. J., et al. 1991. "Identity Development and Worldview: Toward an Optimal Conceptualization." *Journal of Counseling and Development* 70, 1: 54-63.

Noronha, June. 1992. "International and Multicultural Education: Unrelated Adversaries or Successful Partners?" *Promoting Diversity in College Classrooms: Innovative Responses for Curriculum, Faculty, and Institutions.* Ed. Maurianne Adams. New Directions for Teaching and Learning 52 (Winter). San Francisco: Jossey-Bass.

Oberg, Kalvero. 1960. "Cultural Shock: Adjustment to New Cultural Environments." *Practical Anthropology* 7: 177.

Parham, Thomas A. 1989. "Cycles of Psychological Nigrescence." *Counseling Psychologist* 17, 2: 187-226.

Pedersen, Paul B., Norman Sartorius, and Anthony J. Marsella. 1984. *Mental Health Services: The Cross-Cultural Context.* Beverly Hills, CA: Sage.

Pedersen, Paul B., Juris Draguns, Walter J. Lonner, and Joseph E. Trimble. 1989. *Counseling across Cultures.* Third ed. Honolulu: University of Hawaii Press.

Phinney, Jean S. 1991. "Ethnic Identity and Self-Esteem: A Review and Integration." *Hispanic Journal of Behavioral Sciences* 13, 2: 193-208.

Pickert, Sarah M. 1992. *Preparing for a Global Community: Achieving an International Perspective in Higher Education.* ASHE-ERIC Higher Education Report 2. Washington, DC: George Washington University, School of Education and Human Development.

Poston, W. S. Carlos. 1990. "The Biracial Identity Development Model: A Needed Addition." *Journal of Counseling and Development* 69: 152-155.

Richardson, Richard C., and Elizabeth Fisk Skinner. 1991. *Achieving Quality and Diversity: Universities in a Multicultural Society.* New York: Macmillan.

Root, Maria P. P. Ed. 1992. *Racially Mixed People in America.* Newbury Park, CA: Sage,

Ross-Gordon, Jovita M., Larry G. Martin, and Diane Buck Briscoe. Eds. 1990. *Serving Culturally Diverse Populations.* New Directions for Adult and Continuing Education 48. San Francisco: Jossey-Bass.

Rubin, Donald L. 1986."'Nobody Play by the Rules He Know': Ethnocentric Interference in Classroom Questioning Events." *Interethnic Communication: Current Research.* International and Intercultural Communication Annual 10. Newbury Park, CA: Sage.

Sabnani, Haresh B., Joseph G. Ponterotto, and Lisa G. Borodovsky. 1991. "White Racial Identity Development and Cross-Cultural Counselor Training: A Stage Model." *Counseling Psychologist* 19, 1 (January): 76-102.

Saltzman, Carol. 1986. "One Hundred and Fifty Percent Persons: Guides to Orienting International Students." In *Cross-Cultural Orientation: New*

Conceptualizations and Applications. Ed. R. Michael Paige. Lanham, MD: University Press of America.

Samovar, Larry A., and Richard E. Porter. Eds. 1991. *Intercultural Communication: A Reader.* Sixth ed. Belmont, CA: Wadsworth.

Schmitz, Betty. 1985. *Integrating Women's Studies into the Curriculum: A Guide and Bibliography.* Old Westbury, NY: Feminist Press.

_____. 1992a. *Curriculum and Cultural Pluralism: A Guide for Campus Planners.* Washington, DC: Association of American Colleges.

_____. 1992b. "Cultural Pluralism and Core Curricula." *Promoting Diversity in College Classrooms: Innovative Responses for Curriculum, Faculty, and Institutions.* Ed. Maurianne Adams. New Directions for Teaching and Learning 52 (Winter). San Francisco: Jossey-Bass.

Smith, Daryl G. 1989. *The Challenge of Diversity: Involvement or Alienation in the Academy?* ASHE-ERIC Report 5. Washington DC: George Washington University, School of Education and Human Development .

Smith, Elsie J. 1991. "Ethnic Identity Development: Toward the Development of a Theory within the Context of Majority/Minority Status." *Journal of Counseling and Development* 70 (September-October).

Smith, Shelley L. 1987. "The Cognitive Learning Styles of International Students." Thesis. Portland State University.

Smithee, Michael. 1991. "Internationalism, Diversity, and Multiculturalism: Are They Compatible?" *NAFSA Newsletter* 42, 6: 1ff.

Stewart, Edward C., and Milton J. Bennett. 1991. *American Cultural Patterns: A Cross-Cultural Perspective.* Rev. ed. Yarmouth, ME: Intercultural Press.

Sue, Derald Wing, and David Sue. 1990. *Counseling the Culturally Different: Theory and Practice.* Second ed. New York: Wiley.

Tatum, Beverly Daniel. 1992. "Talking about Race, Learning about Racism: The Application of Racial Identity Development Theory in the Classroom." *Harvard Educational Review* 62: 1 (Spring). Cambridge: President and Fellows of Harvard College.

Taylor, Clark. Ed. 1982. *Diverse Student Preparation: Benefits and Issues.* New Directions for Experiential Learning 17. San Francisco: Jossey-Bass.

Terrell, Melvin C. 1992. *Diversity, Disunity, and Campus Community.* Washington, DC: National Association of Student Personnel Administrators.

Tinto, Vincent. 1987. *Leaving College.* Chicago: University of Chicago Press.

Weber, Shirley N. 1991. "The Need to Be: The Socio-Cultural Significance of Black Language." In *Intercultural Communication: A Reader.* Sixth ed. Ed. Larry A. Samovar and Richard E. Porter. Belmont, CA: Wadsworth.

Willer, Patricia. 1992. "Student Affairs Professionals as International Educators: A Challenge for the Next Century." In *Working with International Students and Scholars on American Campuses.* Ed. David McIntire and Patricia Willer. Washington, DC: National Association of Student Personnel Administrators.

Woolbright, Cynthia. Ed. 1989. *Valuing Diversity on Campus: A Multicultural Approach.* Bloomington, IL: Association of College Unions International.

Wright, Doris J. Ed. 1987. *Responding to the Needs of Today's Minority Students.* New Directions for Student Services 38. San Francisco: Jossey-Bass.

Wurzel, Jaime S. 1988. *Toward Multiculturalism: A Reader in Multicultural Education.* Yarmouth, ME: Intercultural Press.

8

Promoting Culture Learning on Campus: Internationalizing Student Life at Michigan State University

Nancy Mark

Diversity, generally understood and embraced, is not casual liberal tolerance of anything and everything not yourself. It is not polite accommodation. Instead, diversity is, in action, the sometimes painful awareness that other people, other races, other voices, other habits of mind, have as much integrity of being, as much claim on the world as you do . . . . And I urge you, amid all the differences present to the eye and mind, to reach out to create the bond that . . . will protect us all. We are meant to be here together.

—William M. Chase

One of the greatest challenges for U.S. education in the 1990's is to create and provide an environment in which students can learn to accept and respect people of diverse cultures and backgrounds. The demographic shift to a multicultural society is well documented and presents major challenges to higher education. As Ernest Boyer (1990, 4) writes in a Carnegie Foundation report:

Today, men and women students come [to U. S. campuses] from almost every racial and ethnic group in the country and from every other nation in the world. While colleges and universities celebrate this pluralism, the harsh truth is that, thus far, many campuses have not been particularly successful in building larger loyalties within a diverse student body, and there is disturbing evidence that deeply ingrained prejudices persist. Faculty, administrators, and students are now asking whether community can be achieved.

These demographic changes, along with the growing international interdependence about which so many speakers and writers have commented, provide special challenges for international educators who wish to assume leadership in assisting U.S. and international students to develop "cultural competence." According to Cross (1988, 1) cultural competence

> acknowledges and incorporates—at all levels—the importance of culture, the assessment of cross-cultural relations, vigilance toward the dynamics that result from cultural differences, the expansion of cultural knowledge, and the adaptation of services to meet culturally unique needs.

The Development of Internationalizing Student Life

Michigan State University (MSU), long committed to international education through teaching, research, and community service, has embraced the concept of cultural competence at the global level. In elaborating on Michigan State University's mission statement concerning the type of person the university should be graduating, the Council for the Review of Undergraduate Education (CRUE) (1988, 2) asserted that

> education should provide students with an understanding of diverse social, economic, political, scientific, spatial, and historical characteristics and issues. Their daily lives and careers will bring them increasingly into contact with ideas and cultures of peoples and societies far different from their own. The need to understand the complex world and its many interrelated parts has never been greater; that need will undoubtedly grow.

In 1990, responding to the CRUE Report and also to the Michigan State University IDEA (Institutional Diversity: Excellence in Action), the University's mission statement on achieving a successfully diverse community, the Division of Student Affairs and Services created the office of Internationalizing Student Life (ISL).

Though housed in Student Affairs and Services, ISL was the product of a task force that combined the talents of personnel in:

- Student Affairs and Services
- International Studies and Programs (ISP)
- Office for International Students and Scholars (OISS)
- Office of Overseas Studies (OOS)
- Area Studies Centers.

The co-chairs of the task force were the Directors of Residence Life and the OISS. I believe this cross-fertilization at ISL's birth contributed importantly to the collaboration between Student Affairs and Services and ISP that has marked ISL's maturation.

As a programming and consultative unit, ISL's two major goals are to provide:

- Opportunities for students to learn about the variety of cultures that co-exist in the contemporary global environment and the social, political, economic, and cultural forces which affect international relations.
- Experiences that assist students in the further refinement of the interpersonal skills, including cross-cultural communication, deemed essential for them to succeed in their chosen careers.

The former goal emphasizes the need for culture-specific knowledge, while the latter stresses the need for cross-cultural sensitivity. Culture knowledge does not necessarily lead to cross-cultural sensitivity. For example, a student may know something of German culture but know very little about how to communicate with a German. Thus, both culture knowledge and cross-cultural sensitivity are ISL's concerns.

With these goals, ISL hopes to provide students with opportunities to:

- Learn about cultures other than their own through expanded co-curricular interactions with members of the University community.
- Develop interpersonal communication skills for successful cross-cultural exchange in preparation for life in a more culturally heterogeneous, global, and increasingly mobile environment.
- Experience out-of-class interactions among faculty, students, and staff of diverse international backgrounds.
- Learn how international social, political, cultural, and economic forces affect their lives.

ISL tries to provide opportunities for students at all developmental levels in their own internationalizing process, from those who dislike the idea of anything "foreign" to those who would happily study abroad every semester.

Though ISL functions as an administrative unit, it is perhaps more productive to think of it as a sort of Grand Central Station, with trains heading to many parts of the campus. ISL serves as a center through which students can access skills, ideas, people, and motivation to further their internationalizing quests and their cultural competence.

Because of this strong "bridging" function, it has been essential for the ISL office, staffed only by a coordinator and two graduate assistants, to develop and maintain strong liaison and collaborative networks among numerous campus units. Several components of this network deserve mention.

Networks

One of ISL's primary partners in the internationalizing process is the Strategies to Advance the Internationalization of Learning (SAIL) program. SAIL is funded by the Fund for the Improvement of Post-Secondary Education and housed in International Studies and Programs. SAIL's goal is to promote global and cultural awareness through the use of international and internationally experienced U.S. students who serve as "Cultural Consultants." Currently, some 200 students representing over 40 countries volunteer as Cultural Consultants. Of this group, 65 percent are international students, mostly graduate students, representing a wide array of majors, cultures, geographical backgrounds, and areas of expertise.

The U.S. students include former Peace Corps volunteers and undergraduate students who have studied overseas. Information about Cultural Consultants is maintained in a Student Talent Bank. This facilitates matching the skills and experiences of particular Cultural Consultants with the preferences and needs of those who wish to use them. Some examples of programs and activities to which Cultural Consultants might contribute include:

- Serving as experts for discussions or presentations in classes on internationally related topics
- Enhancing the learning of comparative, international, and cross-cultural phenomena during campus activities and programs
- Helping train staff in cross-cultural sensitivity and about issues and concerns of international students
- Commenting on foreign news events and/or writing opinion columns for local media
- Serving as program assistants for presentations, dinners, and other activities with international or cross-cultural emphases.

SAIL Consultants receive continuing training on such topics as the meaning of internationalization, articulating one's cultural knowledge, improving cross-cultural communication skills, facilitating cross-cultural discussion, and responding to conflicting opinions.

The limitless possibilities for programs and strategies in which Consultants can be used include workshops on internationalizing the curriculum, new international-student orientation, speaker's programs, overseas studies departure/reentry orientation, and ISL programs.

In fact, ISL coordinates much of the Consultants' co-curricular programming. Examples include cultural, dinner, or panel forums in residence halls; presentations at student leadership conferences; presentations at new U.S.-student orientation programs; and student forums on world events. SAIL Consultants are bright, articulate, enthusiastic messengers and ambassadors in the internationalizing process!

ISL, housed in Student Affairs and Services, also enjoys strong liaison relationships with many people in ISP, a unit of Academic Affairs. These relationships have helped form significant linkages to faculty, staff, and students who have either requested ISL programming or collaborated with us in some other way. I attend ISP and OISS staff meetings and am a member of the Overseas Study Advisory Committee.

On a monthly basis, ISL staff meet with nationality club leaders, a group that is coordinated out of the OISS. Many nationality clubs have co-sponsored events with ISL when their purpose has been to reach a wider undergraduate student audience. These events range from cultural celebrations to political issue forums.

Coordination with Michigan State University's excellent area studies centers (African, Asian, Canadian, European and Russian, Latin American and Caribbean, and Middle Eastern) includes such activities as joint sponsorship of current event forums. For example, a program on the Middle East peace process might include faculty from the Middle Eastern Studies Center; a talk on Somalia would involve African Studies staff; and a panel discussing U.S.-Japan trade issues would involve Asian Studies staff.

ISL began functioning amidst the Persian Gulf crisis of January-February, 1991. During that time, we collaborated with numerous student groups to coordinate forums and discussions on the crisis, presenting a wide variety of cultural, historical, and political perspectives. It was a point at which many students were ready and anxious to listen to such perspectives. Subsequently, ISL has initiated or supported many other programs intended to provide multiple perspectives on current world issues.

Though outreach to academic units is primarily a goal of the SAIL office, ISL has collaborated in student-oriented programs organized by internationally focused academic units such as the International Business Center and the Center for the Advanced Study of International Development.

In sum, ISL has developed into a consultative, programmatic, and resource office for units all over the campus. Student government at the undergraduate and graduate levels, various student activities offices, student organizations, and many others have sought ISL's help in strengthening their organizations through an international perspective.

In the early stages, ISL consciously nurtured these relationships, seeking to show staff and students how internationalizing could enhance what they were already doing. Our staff made presentations at on-campus conferences, seminars, and numerous other forums to educate faculty, students, and staff about ISL's purpose. These presentations served to educate the campus community as well as to establish a number of connections that have evolved into collaborative relationships.

ISL enjoys a particularly strong partnership with the Department of Residence Life (which currently houses the largest number of on-campus students in the United States). Because the leadership in Residence Life is committed to the internationalizing process—and not merely for those residence halls that house international students—they have placed great emphasis on encouraging both graduate and undergraduate staff (approximately 450 people), as well as their professional staff, to capitalize on the training, resources, and linkages ISL can provide. Training topics have included issues of individualism and collectivism, Milton Bennett's 1986 "Developmental Model of Intercultural Sensitivity," gender roles viewed cross-culturally, and the use of silence in communication across cultures.

ISL Activities

Through a COOP Grant from NAFSA: Association of International Educators, ISL and Residence Life developed a cross-cultural training program for undergraduate residence hall leaders. These student leaders—resident assistants, minority aides, hall government leaders and others—are responsible for a myriad of programs on health, safety, diversity, and academic success. Piloted in 1992 and co-facilitated by trained U.S. and international graduate students, the training provides an interactive, audiovisual, problem-solving approach to increasing global sensitivity and communication skills. The training is now incorporated in each hall's training schedule. Some of the topics addressed are listed below:

- The role of internationalism in the U.S. diversity picture
- The meaning of "culture"
- Language issues for U.S. Americans communicating with international students: colloquial usages, accents, and feedback strategies
- Communicating with international teaching assistants
- Communicative style: topics of conversation, forms of interaction, non-verbal communication, levels of meaning
- Strategies for dealing with those who are culturally different

ISL regularly provides cross-cultural training for upper level (full-time) staff as well. Response to the interactive, lively, and practical training has generally been quite positive. Some ISL activities related to student programs are listed below:

- Use ISL world maps at ethnic dinners
- Use "cultural cassettes" (traditional music from 22 countries) as background music to any special event
- Request international talent for special "coffee house" events
- Use ISL's Culturgrams/World Calendar information for Resident Assistant/Minority Assistant bulletin boards
- Ask SAIL Consultants to give an international perspective in programs such as "Race Relations on Campus"
- During U.S. religious holidays, ask international students to discuss their own religious traditions
- Ask SAIL Consultants to discuss their country's perspective on substance use/abuse.

Some of the initiatives ISL has created for residence hall use have gained recognition throughout the campus. One example is the program and accompanying video entitled "From 'Oh No' to 'Ok': Communicating with your International Teaching Assistant." The "Oh, No" refers to the response of many undergraduate students when an international teaching assistant (ITA) walks into the class on the first day.

"Oh No" was initiated by a SAIL Consultant who is an ITA and also an ISL graduate assistant. His desire to assist U.S. students in understanding ITAs provided much of the impetus for this program. Mary Bresnahan and Min Sun Kim (1991), who have studied the U.S. student-ITA relationship, have found U.S. students' attitudes toward ITAs to be on a continuum ranging from highly negatively disposed to highly positively disposed. Their findings show that students whose attitudes are at the center of the continuum are highly responsive to the message they receive about ITAs—whether positive or negative. We observed a great need on our campus for more positive messages about ITAs. ISL's goal has been to develop a practical, problem-solving approach to assist undergraduates in developing more constructive relationships with their ITAs. The video consists of role plays depicting actual interaction between U.S. students and ITAs. An ITA and a U.S. student facilitate discussion of "Oh, No." Recently, we recently developed an evaluation instrument that accompanies the program.

One of many reasons for this program's success lies in its highly practical nature. For the many U.S. undergraduates who view internationalization as a "far out," abstract concept, improving communication with their teaching assistants—who hand out the grades—brings the concept very close to home. The program also challenges the widely held notion that it is acceptable to blame all problems in the U.S. student-ITA relationship on the ITA's accent or language ability. Though some U.S. students have directed legitimate complaints towards their ITA, many have camouflaged their prejudices through these complaints. Our goal is to help students learn to use the relationship with the ITA as an opportunity to develop and practice communication skills.

"Oh No" was developed with support from MSU's International Teaching Assistant Orientation Program, and Educational and Support Services. At present, ISL staff are giving this program wide visibility among academic units in order to bring it to the faculty's attention.

ISL activities include not just programs and sessions, but acquiring and encouraging the use of audiovisual materials such as videos, maps, simulation games, cassette tapes of traditional music from various countries, recipes for ethnic foods, a small library of culture-specific information such as Culturgrams and books about particular countries, and readings on cross-cultural communication. SAIL Consultants are frequently used, and ISL offers many, many ideas on how to make internationalizing programs as accessible as possible to primarily U.S. audiences.

Obstacles

While ISL has received an excellent reception, obstacles of various sorts have appeared. For example, developing sessions that can address the array of development readiness levels (Bennett, 1986) of the large residence life audiences is quite challenging.

It is also difficult for many students to move beyond such topics as language or nonverbal communication and begin to wrestle with their own values as they contrast and possibly conflict with cultural values that prevail elsewhere.

> It is far more difficult to identify value orientations in another culture than to identify patterns of speech and nonverbal behavior. . . . The best starting point for appreciating differences in cultural values is, of course, some understanding of our own values. . . . We are likely to be far more resistant in altering our values to accommodate those persons from another culture than we are with either language or non-verbal behavior. (Condon and Yousef, 1975, 262-263)

Recently, we were asked to provide some training for a group that had attended one of our more general cross-cultural communication programs. We were asked to deal with some cross-cultural issues at a "deeper" level. We chose to address the issue of value differences. Though some participants responded positively to the session, many reported that the first program was far more fun!

A more general obstacle than the wish for fun has emerged from many quarters. As ISL has developed, it has become clear that not everyone relishes the idea of internationalization. Not everyone shares the view that a global vision requires openness to multiple perceptions. Absorbing that vision would, for some individuals, require an identity shift that seems completely undesirable. Many students and staff have difficulty comprehending the globalization the United States is experiencing. They seem unconcerned with matters they perceive as being "out there" (in another country) when there are so many ethnic and racial issues within the United States.

These factors, among others, have contributed to an often silent, subtle resistance to ISL's philosophy and activities. Though such a response was, to some degree, anticipated, it remains a challenge. In fact, the question of "why are we developing this office?"—a question I heard frequently when I arrived on campus—has impelled me to become even clearer and more articulate about why ISL was developed, what we do, and our role in facilitating the change to a global society.

Overcoming Obstacles

There are a number of responses to those who ask, "Why internationalize student life?" First, we have made vigorous attempts to make ISL's philosophy and activities as visible as possible. This is no small task on a campus of over 35,000 students. Many international educators on campus helped us by speaking on our behalf. Our many consultations and programs have received publicity not only through word of mouth but through an extensive public relations strategy. ISL activities are mentioned in numerous newsletters, e-mail bulletin boards, and student and staff newspapers. This helps all faculty, staff, and students understand what an "internationalizing" office does and demonstrates the wide range of activities in which we are involved.

Secondly, I have made great efforts to actively support those concerned with domestic "diversity" activities on the campus. Participating in multicultural training in residence life as a planner/facilitator, serving as a divisional representative to the Student Affairs and Services Diversity Committee, facilitating the all-university sexual harassment training, and offering assistance to the Lesbian-Bi-Gay Task Force survey, are a few examples. Supporting these endeavors is done not merely to provide some global perspective (when relevant) but to truly join in the advocacy process for all cultural groups. Supporting such endeavors also counteracts any perception that ISL is singularly focused on non-U.S. issues, and, in fact, demonstrates the successful interweaving of domestic and international concerns as discussed in Chapter 7.

Future Directions

Continuing this interweaving of ISL into the academic community is perhaps one of the greatest challenges for the future. In addition to those already mentioned, many further opportunities exist to integrate the efforts of ISL with programs that are already in place. For example, though ISL staff have been involved in planning Internationalizing the Curriculum workshops (through ISP), we have not done enough to educate individual academic units about how our co-curricular activities might support their internationalizing efforts.

Additionally, ISL needs to provide a wider array of programs and approaches, to accommodate the fact that different kinds of activities are appropriate for people at different points on the "ethnorelativism scale" (Bennett, 1986). For example, it has become quite clear to us that nothing is gained by talking about the need for skill in intercultural communication with participants who deny that cultural differences even exist.

ISL has evolved during an era in which Michigan State University, like most other U. S. colleges and universities, faces increasing budgetary concerns and possible staff and program reductions. Pressure mounts to focus on domestic rather than international issues. Simultaneously, students at the university are graduating into a world where cross-cultural competence has never been more essential. Though supportive of ISL, the university is not likely to be able to commit additional dollars for staff or program growth. Thus, we need to seek outside funding, use current resources judiciously, and find other ways to enhance our effectiveness.

With limited staff and endless ideas for program expansion, it becomes increasingly necessary to use our energies efficiently. Strategies for doing so include:

- Using more faculty, staff, student, and community volunteers.
- Increasing use of computerized technology through which students can access culture-specific information.
- Continuing to collaborate with others.

In times of limited resources, it becomes increasingly important for programs such as ISL to join other internationally oriented units on campus in advocating for international programs of all types.

In an essay entitled "What is Culture," former Indian Prime Minister Jawaharlal Nehru (1988) describes his own India, but his words could easily describe the challenge currently facing Internationalizing Student Life at Michigan State University:

My own view of India's history is that we can almost measure the growth and advance of India and the decline of India by relating them to periods when India had her mind open to the outside world and when she wanted to close it up. The more she closed it up, the more static she became. Life, whether of the individual, group, nation, or society, is essentially a dynamic, changing, growing thing. Whatever stops that dynamic growth also injures it and undermines it . . . . When it is claimed that the last word has been said, society becomes static.

References

Bennett, Milton. 1986. "A Developmental Approach to Training for Intercultural Sensitivity." *International Journal of Intercultural Relations* 10: 79-196.

Bresnahan, Mary I., and Kim Min Sun. 1991. "The Effect of Authoritarianism in Bias toward Foreign Teaching Assistants." Paper delivered at the Forty-first Annual Conference of the International Communication Association, Intercultural Division, Chicago, IL, May 23–27.

Boyer, Ernest. 1990. In *Campus Life: In Search of Community—A Special Report*. Carnegie Foundation for the Advancement of Teaching. Princeton, NJ: Princeton University Press.

Condon, John C., and Yousef Fathi. 1975. *An Introduction to Intercultural Communication*. New York: Bobbs-Merrill.

Council for the Review of Undergraduate Education. 1988. "Opportunities for Renewal." East Lansing: Michigan State University.

Cross, Terry L. 1988. "Cultural Competence Continuum." *Focal Point* 3: 79-96.

Nehru, Jawaharlal. 1988. "What Is Culture?" *The Times of India*, October 15, p. 910.

9

Recurring Issues in Intercultural Communication

Gary Althen

Eternal questions about the nature of human nature occur in the field of intercultural communication as they do in many other fields of inquiry or endeavor. Other questions that recur in the intercultural communication field, and that will be discussed in this brief chapter, concern power and politics, the nature of "intercultural learning," cultural relativism, certain issues in intercultural training, ethical guidelines, and the matter of practicing what one preaches. Some implications of these issues for international educators and cross-cultural trainers are also explored here.

Human Nature

Most countries of the world include representatives of more than one linguistic, religious, and/or ethnic group, and in most countries the relationships among those groups are unsettled and sometimes violent. "Ethnic cleansing," a term used to describe intergroup strife in the former Yugoslavia, is a recent example of people's age-old proclivity to divide themselves into in-groups and out-groups, to assume the superiority of the in-group and defend its territory (Bernstein and Rozen, 1989), and to display animosity (at least) toward the out-group.

By nature, then, human beings seem inclined toward *ethnocentrism* (Sumner, 1906; Barna, 1991; Bennett, 1993; and many, many others). Bennett (1993) argues that people who teach or train in the intercultural area must always bear this in mind. While human beings seem uniformly ethnocentric, they have the capacity of consciousness. They can pause and reflect on their visceral responses. They can learn to overcome some of their baser instincts. But, evidently, they cannot always do that, and they can rarely, if ever, do it easily. Teachers and trainers need to be gentle, compassionate, and skillful if they hope to help students or trainees move through what Bennett calls the *stages of ethnorelativism* to the point where they can at least reduce, if never altogether eliminate, their ethnocentric judgments of people who are different.

Another aspect of human nature that confronts teachers and trainers in intercultural communication is differences in *learning style*. In contemporary American social science writings, this idea is often attributed to David Kolb (1976), who posits that different people learn best in different ways. He specifies four different learning styles: reflective observation, abstract conceptualization, concrete experience, and active experimentation. The implication of this idea is that teachers and trainers must approach their students and trainees with a variety of techniques, because, for example, some will learn best from an experiential approach, while others will learn best from readings and lectures. Employing all four learning styles in a class or a training program has another advantage as well: it gives all participants the opportunity to practice with styles they "naturally" avoid, thus helping them become more flexible learners.

Power and Politics

Marshall Singer (1987, 2) argues convincingly that "every communication relationship has a power component attached to it." Communication relationships in educational exchange often involve relationships with obvious power differentials—students and teachers, students and advisers, visiting scholars and their supervising faculty or administrators, foreigners and natives, guests and hosts. Singer says "we might as well deal . . . openly and consciously" with the power component.

But Americans rarely do that. In teaching about intercultural communication, we often leave power out of our frameworks, and discuss only such topics as customs, assumptions, values, and thought patterns. In intercultural training, we are likely to promote "awareness," "sensitivity," "appreciation," and "communication skills" that are presented without regard to power differentials among trainees themselves or between the trainees and the people with whom they are being trained to interact.

Intercultural interactions are affected not just by the power differentials among the individual participants, but by differentials, or perceived differentials, in the power of the countries and institutions the participants represent. A foreign student from a poor country is likely to be perceived differently from a student from a wealthy country, and is less likely to be accorded respect in interpersonal dealings, at least not until the student has had the opportunity to establish a reputation for intelligence, good sense, and perhaps a bit of charm as well.

Americans might be particularly inclined to ignore, overlook, or minimize the influence of power differentials and politics on intercultural interactions, since Americans are so imbued with the notion of "equality." Among Americans, say Stewart and Bennett (1991, 90), "Interpersonal relations are typically horizontal, conducted between presumed equals." Their adherence to the ideal of equality "makes it difficult for Americans to understand hierarchical patterns of organizations abroad; consequently, they tend to ignore political issues." Americans also have difficulty understanding—and indeed even perceiving—power differentials among members of particular nationality groups on their campuses and in their communities. The fact that a 27-year-old Korean student expects obedience from a 26-year-old Korean student, or that a graduate of a Chinese "key university" has more influence than a graduate of a lower-ranking institution, is easily lost on most Americans.

If they are going to be taken seriously by exchange participants from other parts of the world, American intercultural educators and trainers will need to overcome their culturally based inclination to overlook or discount considerations of power and politics in intercultural interactions. In Chapter 1, Judith Martin has some additional observations on this point.

The Nature of "Intercultural Learning"

Educational psychologists do not agree on how human learning takes place. At least, they do not agree beyond certain basic points. What actually happens in the brain when people learn? What promotes learning of different sorts? What inhibits or precludes it?

In the area called "intercultural learning" or sometimes "culture learning," such questions abound. Proponents of culture learning seem to realize that their learning goals fall somewhat outside the goals of most academic enterprises. In a famous 1967 essay, Roger Harrison and Richard Hopkins contrasted the "university model" of learning with the "experiential" model most interculturalists prefer, or at least consider essential for some aspects of what they want to teach.

Roughly speaking, the university model is based on the notion of acquiring new information or more sophisticated ways of thinking about things. These acquisitions are not considered academically respectable unless they can be measured in a widely acceptable way, usually with a paper-and-pencil examination.

The experiential model, though, is said to promote a "broader perspective" on a subject or situation. Educational exchange participants are said to develop "enhanced awareness" and "greater sensitivity," whether or not they acquire more factual information. But this awareness or sensitivity is not readily amenable to measurement by paper-and-pencil methods. So proponents of intercultural learning are often left on the fringes of the academic world. Faced with that, some argue for "more research" in the sense of more quantitative studies that make clear—that is, convey in quantitative terms—the presumably beneficial outcome of educational exchange activity.

Others argue that what is needed is not more quantitative research into outcomes that do not lend themselves to quantitative assessment, but a broader conception on the part of traditional academics of what constitutes learning.

Cultural Relativism

Many interculturalists say they believe in cultural relativism. "Other people's ways are not right or wrong, just different," is their motto.

On the other hand, there is the view Henry Bagish (1981) puts forth in his thought-provoking essay, "Confessions of a Former Cultural Relativist." Bagish points to several behaviors he cannot accept as "just different," including the chopping off of young girls' fingers to placate certain ghosts, as practiced by the Dani of New Guinea; the extermination of Jewish people, as practiced in Nazi Germany; and ritual clitoridectomies, as practiced in a number of African and Arab countries.

Practitioners in international educational exchange are not likely to encounter the extremes of difference Bagish discusses, but they still encounter behavior they have trouble accepting as "just different." These include, for most Americans, certain ways men from male-dominated societies tend to treat females; approaches to child care that may fall under the local definition of "abuse" or "neglect;" "arrogant" behavior on the part of upper class people from more stratified societies; certain religious activities, such as the ritual slaughtering of animals; certain forms of academic behavior that, in the local context, carry the label "cheating;" and the offering of reasons, explanations, and justifications that violate local standards concerning "truth" and "honesty."

Tolerance, then, is not always easy to come by, and indeed might not always seem warranted. Bagish points out that each person has many values, tolerance being but one among them. Sometimes other values rank higher than tolerance. Sometimes we see things we want to try to change because we cannot accept them as "just different."

Bagish offers two conclusions under the heading "Going Beyond Cultural Relativity," and they deserve quoting at length:

> First, I urge that we recognize that it's not only possible, but indeed desirable to compare, evaluate, and judge many cultural practices, not on the basis of a naive ethnocentrism, or on the presumed possession of absolute standards, but rather from an objective, cross-cultural perspective. Such judging can be done in terms of the pragmatic "if. . .then. . ." formula. . . . [An] example. . .: *If* you value your children's lives, and don't want them to die of smallpox, *then* vaccination is better than goat sacrifice.

Second, I urge that as we compare, evaluate, and judge, that we make our values explicit. We need to be aware of what our values are, of course; examine them, think them through, become aware of what order they stand in our own personal hierarchy of values. But then I urge that we not be bashful; let's speak up for our values, each of us; let's express them, even attempt to persuade others to share them with us. I don't fear this process; rather, I welcome it. If it should turn out that our values are actually narrow and parochial and are only self-serving, I'm sure that others will rapidly let us know. . . . If, on the other hand, our values should touch a responsive chord in others, if they should agree, "Yes, that *would* make for a better world," why, then perhaps we'd all be a little bit closer to achieving consensus on the kind of world we *could* all live in, in peace and harmony. (1988)

Mitchell Hammer (1992) agrees. In a short essay called "Ethics and the Impotent Interculturalist," Hammer opines that most cultural relativists take a "say nothing" approach in public life. Ethical values (and values in general, we can add) are not created by "culture" *per se*, but by people talking about them, that is, by communication. "Ethical values created through communication are, by definition, potentially changeable and *subject to communicative discourse*," Hammer writes,

> Because ethical values are created and changed through persuasive communication, the cultural relativist has the same moral responsibility as anyone else to participate in the public dialogue: To assert one's own ethical judgments across cultural boundaries. (1992, 1, 3)

In entering this dialogue, though, cultural relativists must realize that they may be persuaded that their own values are the ones in need of change.

Issues in Cross-Cultural Training

In a 1978 presentation, Robert Kohls listed seven "issues in cross-cultural training" that are still alive today, even if the intervening decades have brought about more sophisticated thinking about them. Kohls's issues form the basis of this section.

1. Different Approaches Appropriate for Different Cultures. While it seems clear that there is considerable variation among individuals concerning preferred learning styles, it also seems clear that cultures affect people's preferences for ways of learning. In the last two decades or so, many American educators and trainers have become supporters of "experiential learning," in which students or trainees take an active part in some structured experience, which is then discussed ("processed") under the trainer's direction. Trainers may assume that the experiential approach, which can be quite effective with typical American audiences, has a universal appeal.

Not necessarily so. Yuichi Kondo studied Japanese students' responses to intercultural communications workshops, experience-and discussion-based programs conducted by facilitators who guided the process but did little in the way of didactic presentations. Generally, American students responded favorably to these workshops, but the Japanese Kondo studied did not. The Japanese operated on some assumptions that differed from those of most of the Americans, and from those on which the workshops were based. Some examples of the Japanese participants' assumptions, according to Kondo:

- Trainees learn concepts and information through didactic methods; learning by doing is more appropriate for acquiring manual skills.
- The group, not the individual, should be the focus of training.
- Assertive verbalization is not at all valued. Training should emphasize listening, observing, and reflecting, not speaking. Expressing a view contrary to that of another participant is particularly unseemly.
- The trainer's role is that of the professor or expert, not that of the facilitator. The trainer-trainee relationship should be formal.
- Hearing about other participants' personal experiences cannot be as helpful as hearing from the teacher.
- Workshop participants are not all equal. There is a status hierarchy within the group, based mainly on age, and that fact cannot be overlooked.

In a thoughtful discussion of "Using a Western Learning Model in Asia: A Case Study," Reginald Smart (1983) lists several "erroneous assumptions underlying our model of management training." One of the erroneous assumptions was that "participants can identify and role-play varied responses to their own real-life situations." Most of the Asian managers in their training program could not, Smart and his colleagues found. In trying to account for that, Smart cites some "deep" factors, including

skepticism about the notion of personal change, lack of commitment to change oneself, no real sharing of the Western concept of the individual, and the potential loss of respect among fellow trainees upon disclosure of "real-life" shortcomings ... (11)

Kohls lists the assumptions underlying contemporary American approaches to training (experiential, trainee-centered, tailored to individual trainee needs, etc.), and states that the approach is "radical and absolutely inappropriate for seven-eighths of the world."

190

Smart makes clear that it is one thing for trainers to *recognize the need* to change their approaches depending on the cultural backgrounds of their trainees, and quite another thing to *make the changes.*

Michael Bond's (1992) article, "The Process of Enhancing Cross-Cultural Competence in Hong Kong Organizations," suggests some ways to accommodate Chinese (or Confucian) and American cultural difference in management training programs. For example, Bond found that training workshops were more effective if, at some point in the program, the Chinese participants had the opportunity to teach non-Chinese participants how to write their names in Chinese characters. This activity, he said, gave the members of the subordinate (Chinese, in this case) group the opportunity to teach something to members of the dominant group. This seemed to reduce the Chinese resistance to the workshop, and to engage their attention and interest. Bond's ideas could be applied to other cultural mixes and other training objectives.

2. The Hidden but Very Obtrusive Cultural Assumptions That Underlie All Our Statements and All Our Actions. Edward Stewart and Milton Bennett (1991) do an excellent job of identifying assumptions most Americans make about the way the world works, and they offer enlightening comparisons with assumptions that prevail elsewhere. One way to convey some of those common American assumptions is to recount a few dictums frequently heard among Americans:

- "One person, one vote." (This reflects the assumption that people are essentially equal to each other, or the value usually labelled "equality.")
- "He who hesitates is lost," and, "Don't just stand there. Do something." (Action)
- "The difficult we do immediately. The impossible takes a little longer." Or, more modestly, "Where there's a will there's a way." (Action; control of the environment; change)
- "Let's get down to brass tacks." (Action; directness)
- "Let's don't stand on ceremony." (Equality; informality)
- "You made your bed. Now lie in it;" "Look out for Number One!" "MYOB" (shorthand for "mind your own business"); and "Question authority!" (Individuality; independence; self-reliance)

Other American assumptions that are not necessarily shared by people from other places, and that arise in training programs, include the value of compromise, the importance of being cordial even in the face of conflicts, and the importance of fair play in disputes or confrontations.

3. The Generic Versus Specific Argument. Kohls says the argument between supporters of culture-general approaches to training and those who support culture-specific agendas has been resolved. The resolution, he says,

191

is that training should begin with an effort to increase trainees' insight into their own culture, then address the general notion of cultural differences, and finally focus on the target culture.

This resolution might exist in the minds of trainers, but trainees do not always see the logic in it. They wonder why they should spend ("waste," they will say) time talking about their own culture when they are gathered to learn about another one. (American trainees, in keeping with their individualist orientations, sometimes deny that they even *have* a culture.) Intercultural educators face the need to get trainees to see the sense in the general-to-specific organization of a training or educational program.

4. The Content Versus Process Argument. Some intercultural trainers get so caught up in conducting "exercises" to make their sessions and workshops personally involving ("fun," some will say) for participants that they overlook the importance of engaging in substantive debriefing or of having substantive information to impart.

On the other hand, traditional educators sometimes overlook the benefits of experiential approaches to culture learning, with their ability to involve participants on the emotional as well as the intellectual level (or, as some would say, to engage both the left and the right sides of the participants' brains). Lessons learned through experience are often better understood and retained.

5. The Debate as to Whether Behavioral Objectives Can or Should Be Imposed onto Cross-Cultural Training. Since Kohls offered his list of issues, preparing "behavioral objectives" has become a generally accepted practice among educators and professional trainers. However, people such as foreign student advisers, ESL teachers, and study-abroad advisers, who do training as only one of their responsibilities, are less likely to impose upon themselves the discipline of developing behavioral objectives for their training. More often they will say their purpose is to help students or trainees develop "awareness," "sensitivity," or "appreciation for cultural differences." Such objectives are much too vague, from the viewpoint of exponents of behavioral objectives.

On the other hand, excessive focus on behavioral objectives can result in inadequate sensitivity to the overall intellectual-and-visceral effect of a program. Behavioral objectives might not make much sense to people from cultures lacking the American proclivity to dissect things into parts and assume that the whole is nothing more than the sum of those parts.

6. Disincentives to Cross-Cultural Learning. Kohls cites two disincentives, the participants' demand for lists of dos and don'ts, and the "all-people-are-basically-alike" copout. To these several others could be added:

- Anxiety (or Even Fear)—LaRay Barna's (1991) often-quoted essay lists six "Stumbling Blocks in Intercultural Communication," one of which is "high anxiety," which she says compounds all the others. People in intercultural situations often fear appearing foolish or incompetent, losing power or influence, or simply not feeling respected by others.
- Arrogance or Ethnocentrism—Students and trainees may assume that the other parties to the intercultural interaction should be the ones to change. Or, if they are unwilling to change, they should go home.
- Not Seeing Any Need or Any Point—Students or trainees sometimes profess to see no reason for undertaking intercultural learning activities, or any point in a particular aspect of a session they are attending. "Prove to me that I need this," they seem to be saying.
- Resistance to Required Educational or Training Programs—American students and trainees often follow the advice of the "question authority" bumper sticker, whether by openly challenging or by passively resisting teachers and trainers in sessions where attendance has been required.

Milton Bennett's (1993) essay, "A Developmental Approach to Training Intercultural Sensitivity," offers a framework that can help teachers and trainers understand some of the underlying causes of the resistance they often encounter, and think constructively about ways to try to overcome it. ("Try to" because overcoming resistance does not always seem possible.)

7. The Need for Materials Development. Since Kohls presented the paper on which this section is based, several books containing cross-cultural educational and training materials have been published. They include Batchelder's and Warner's *Beyond Experience*; Brislin, et al., *Intercultural Interactions: A Practical Guide*; Grove's *Orientation Handbook*; Hoope's and Ventura's *Intercultural Sourcebook*; Pusch's *Multicultural Education*; Kohls's *Survival Kit for Overseas Living*; and Weeks, et al., *A Manual of Structured Experiences for Cross-Cultural Learning*. See the Resource List in Chapter 6 for complete information about these and other publications.

Videos suitable for intercultural training and education are now available through NAFSA: Association of International Educators, Intercultural Press, and elsewhere. Again, the Resource List in Chapter 6 has more information.

Even though all these training materials have become available, most such material remains in fugitive form, passing from hand to hand at conferences and workshops. People continue to develop their own case studies, critical incidents, culture assimilators, simulations, and exercises. With examples such as those listed above to serve as models, developing one's own materials is no doubt easier than it formerly was.

Ethical Guidelines

Somewhat after the first edition of *Learning Across Cultures* was published, ethics became a major concern throughout American society. Many organizations, including NAFSA: Association for International Educators and SIETAR International (the International Society for Intercultural Training, Education, and Research) developed codes of ethics that were intended to guide their members' professional conduct.

While these codes might have made sense to Americans and people who are accustomed to working with them, they encountered difficulties in other cultures. It became clear that the idea of having a code of ethics (that is, a set of written guidelines, complete with detailed procedures for implementation) was itself the product of a society that gives more weight than many other societies do to written, impersonal rules.

Not only is the code of ethics idea itself culture-bound, but, it became clear that some of the provisions typical of such codes seemed to have arisen from a particular cultural tradition. Codes of ethics that stress equal treatment of all clients, for example, seem to overlook the status differences and human relationship elements that play a significant role in many societies.

Typical American ethical provisions related to "truth in advertising" and "full disclosure" assume an absoluteness of truth that people from many other cultures are not likely to assume, and they rank the value of truth higher than some others might.

"The Western Concern with Truth," Hofstede (1991, 171) writes,

> is supported by an axiom in Western logic that a statement excludes its opposite: if A is true, B, which is the opposite of A, must be false. Eastern logic does not have such an axiom. If A is true, its opposite B may also be true, and together they produce a wisdom which is superior to either A or B. This is sometimes called the complementarity of *yin* and *yang*. . . . Human truth in this philosophical approach is always partial.

A final example: The American emphasis on confidentiality attributes more sanctity to the *individual* than people in many other societies normally do.

Thus, NAFSA has had to modify its code of ethics to accommodate different cultural perspectives, and SIETAR, which is making a concerted effort to become a truly international organization, felt compelled to scrap its code of ethics and seek to replace it with a very general statement of principles that members in different cultures could use as the basis for a code that made sense in their own context.

All this produces a conundrum for international education practitioners who want specific guidance in their intercultural dealings, and puts a very high premium on the characteristic of "tolerance for ambiguity" that the practitioners often tell their clients is necessary for success in intercultural interactions.

Practicing What One Preaches

The late Howard Higman, a University of Colorado sociologist, coined what he called "Higman's Law," according to which "hatred is inversely related to difference." The more that people have in common, he was saying, the more intensely they feel about their differences. His examples came mainly from the political realm, where assorted Stalinists, Leninists, and Trotskyites divided into small groups that were hotly devoted to eliminating each other, or at least each other's ideas.

The intercultural communication field provides its own examples of Higman's Law. Educated, white, middle-class American educators who conceive of themselves as open-minded and tolerant frequently show no tolerance whatever for other educated, white, middle-class American educators whom they consider closed-minded and intolerant, and who are not interested in international or intercultural matters. In other words, many people who would call themselves intercultural educators are not at all tolerant of people who are not as tolerant as they consider themselves to be, or of people who resemble them in many other ways but who do not share their values. They are intolerant of intolerance.

Intercultural educators can also find it difficult to live according to their professed values when they are working with culturally different others whose behavior violates key values of their own. These days, American intercultural educators have particular difficulty practicing what they preach when they encounter what they perceive to be sexism, dishonesty, and deviousness among their participants or clients. For example, deftness in working the system might be admired when a native does it but is labelled "abuse" when someone from another country does it.

The first step in practicing what one preaches is probably what William Gudykunst (1991) calls "mindfulness." One must be aware of the values one is employing and the interpretations and imputations one is making in order to operate constructively in intercultural relationships, and one must accept (with some provisos—see the words above about cultural relativism) that other people have their own values, interpretations, and imputations. This is not always easy to do.

Conclusion

We all appreciate clarity and certainty. We like it when some authoritative person tells us, "This is how it is," or, "Here's the best way to do that." It is reassuring when someone can explain to us just why Malay people are so averse to displays of temper, for example, or how best to accommodate a participant group that encompasses a wide range of ages as well as nationalities.

Unfortunately, to work in the field of intercultural communication is to work in a field where clarity and certainty are in short supply, and where complexity and ambiguity abound. Practitioners realize, as their experience mounts, that they can never be certain what is happening in someone else's mind, or even in their own. Unexpected and sometimes inexplicable things happen. Practitioners are likely to develop predictions and generalizations, but they continue to encounter behavior that surprises them. This can lead to a sense of excitement, but it can also be disconcerting. The dictum I have found most helpful in coping with the continuing uncertainty in this field was quoted by Reginald Smart. He was facing a group of frustrated adult participants who wanted specific dos and don'ts concerning some teenage exchange participants who were coming to stay with them. Smart could not give the detailed guidance the participants wanted. "There is no answer," he said to them. "Seek it lovingly."

References

Bagish, Henry. 1981. "Confessions of a Former Cultural Relativist." Santa Barbara: University of California at Santa Barbara.

Barna, LaRay M. 1991. "Stumbling Blocks in Intercultural Communication." Reprinted in *Intercultural Communication: A Reader*. Sixth ed. Ed. Larry Samovar and Richard Porter. Belmont, CA: Wadsworth.

Bennett, Milton J. 1993. "Towards Ethnorelatavism: A Developmental Model of Intercultural Sensitivity." In *Orientation to the Intercultural Experience*. Ed. R. Michael Paige. Yarmouth, ME: Intercultural Press.

Bernstein, Albert J., and Sydney Croft Rozen. 1989. *Dinosaur Brains*. New York: Ballantine Books.

Bond, Michael H. 1992. "The Process of Enhancing Cross-Cultural Competence in Hong Kong Organizations." *International Journal of Intercultural Relations* 16, 3: 395-412.

Gudykunst, William B. 1991. *Bridging Differences: Effective Intergroup Communication*. Newbury Park, CA: Sage.

Hammer, Mitchell R. 1992. "Ethics and the Impotent Interculturalist." *Communiqué* 22, 3: 1, 3.

Harrison, Roger, and Richard Hopkins. 1967. "The Design of Cross-Cultural Training: An Alternative to the University Model." *Journal of Applied Behavioral Sciences* 3, 4: 431-461.

Hofstede, Geert. 1991. *Culture and Organizations: Software of the Mind*. London: McGraw-Hill.

Kohls, Robert. 1978. "Issues in Cross-Cultural Training." Paper presented at the Speech Communication Association Second Summer Conference on Intercultural Communication, Tampa, FL.

Kolb, David. 1976. *Learning Style Inventory: Technical Manual*. Boston: McBer.

Kondo, Yuichi. 1993. *Validating the Intercultural Communication Training Methods on Japanese: The Intercultural Communication Workshop*. College of Education, University of Minnesota.

Singer, Marshall. 1987. *Intercultural Communication: A Perceptual Approach*. Englewood Cliffs, NJ: Prentice-Hall.

Smart, Reginald. 1983. "Using a Western Learning Model in Asia: A Case Study." *Occasional Papers in Intercultural Learning*, no. 4. New York: AFS International/Intercultural Programs.

Stewart, Edward C., and Milton J. Bennett, 1991. *American Cultural Patterns: A Cross-Cultural Perspective*. Rev. ed. Yarmouth, ME: Intercultural Press

Sumner, William G. 1906. *Folkways*. Boston: Ginn.

Contributors

GARY ALTHEN is assistant director for foreign students and scholars in the University of Iowa's Office of International Education and Services. A long-time foreign student adviser, he is author of *The Handbook of Foreign Student Advising* and *American Ways*, and author, co-author, or editor of more than forty other publications related to international educational exchange, including the original edition of *Learning Across Cultures*.

CAROL ARCHER has taught classes in cross-cultural communication in the Language and Culture Center at the University of Houston for over fourteen years and has been adjunct faculty at the Center for Executive Development in the College of Business at the University of Houston for over four years. She has over twelve years' experience in developing cross-cultural training programs for organizations and international corporations. Clients include Americans, Japanese, Indonesians, Saudis, and others. She served as cross-cultural consultant for the PBS series "Images of America," and wrote *Living with Strangers in the USA*.

DR. JANET BENNETT is a co-director of the Intercultural Communication Institute in Portland and conducts intercultural training related to workplace diversity for businesses, educational institutions, and international educational programs. Formerly Chair of the Liberal Arts Division at Marylhurst College, she teaches courses at Portland State University.

DR. MILTON BENNETT is a co-director of the Intercultural Communication Institute in Portland, and does intercultural training for a variety of kinds of organizations. Formerly an associate professor of communications at Portland State University, he is co-author of the revised edition of *American Cultural Patterns: A Cross-Cultural Perspective*.

TERESA HARRELL is program manager and counselor of International Student Funding in the Institute of International Studies and Programs at the University of Minnesota. She has done training in cross-cultural communications and cultural diversity for NAFSA, SIETAR, and independently. She has most recently conducted research in Indonesia concerning alumni of U.S. colleges and universities.

DR. JUDITH MARTIN is an associate professor of intercultural communication at Arizona State University. Trained at the University of Minnesota, she has taught at Pennsylvania State University and the University of New Mexico as well. Her areas of research include sojourner adjustment, intercultural communication competence, and re-entry. She is a co-author of *Students Abroad: Strangers at Home.*

NANCY MARK is assistant director and coordinator of internationalizing student life in the Department of Student Life at Michigan State University. She has served as associate director of the Office of International Student Affairs at the University of Illinois, and as assistant director of the Twin Cities International Program. She has conducted numerous workshops and presentations on aspects of intercultural relations.

MARGARET ("PEGGY") PUSCH is a co-founder and president of Intercultural Press, Inc. Active in both NAFSA and SIETAR, she has done intercultural training and consulting with a variety of educational and community organizations. She is editor of *Multicultural Education: A Cross-Cultural Training Approach*, and co-author of *A Guide for Leaders of Professional Integration and Reentry Workshops.*

DR. KAY THOMAS is the associate director of the Institute of International Studies and Programs at the University of Minnesota, and director of its Counseling and Advising unit. A psychologist, she counsels clients from many countries, teaches cross-cultural counseling, and supervises counseling students. She has done extensive training in cross-cultural counseling and cultural diversity, both through NAFSA and independently.

DR. INGEMAR TORBIÖRN is associate professor of psychology at the University of Stockholm. His principal research area is the psychology of intercultural relations, at both the organizational and the individual levels. He has written *Living Abroad: Personal Adjustment and Personnel Policy in the Overseas Setting*, and numerous articles in academic journals.